MW01602784

Island of Peace
in an Ocean of Unrest:
The Letters of Dorothy von Moltke

Catherine R. Hammond

Island of Peace
in an Ocean of Unrest:
The Letters of Dorothy von Moltke

Catherine R. Hammond

Catherine R. Hammond

Nebbadoon Press

www.NebbadoonPress.com

Island of Peace in an Ocean of Unrest:
The Letters of Dorothy von Moltke

© 2013 Catherine R. Hammond

All rights reserved. No part of this book may be used or reproduced in any manner whatsoever without written permission, except in the case of brief quotations embodied in critical articles and reviews.

Nebbadoon Press
www.NebbadoonPress.com

ISBN 978-1-891331-44-2

Library of Congress Control Number: 2013951723

Printed in U.S.A.

Photos and Graphics

Cover photo: After World War II, *Shloss* Kreisau, now in Poland, was taken over by the Polish Government and then fell into disrepair. Beginning in 1989, it was restored by Poles and Germans working together. The former Moltke estate, including the renovated *Schloss*, as seen, is now owned by the Kreisau Foundation for European Understanding.

Oval inset photo on cover: This photograph was taken when Dorothy was sixteen and still living in her homeland of South Africa, two years before she met her future husband, Helmuth von Moltke, while traveling in Germany with her mother.

Back cover photo: Dorothy and Helmuth von Moltke seated in a carriage in front of the Moltke *Schloss* in Kriesau, 1912.

Back cover inset photo: Wedding photo of Dorothy Rose Innes and Helmuth von Moltke, Pretoria, South Africa, 1905.

All black and white photos were provided by the Moltke family with permission for reproduction except for the photo of the Translation Committee.

Cover color photo provided by the Kreisau Foundation for European Understanding, Krzyżowa, Poland. Photographer: Miroslaw Budzanowski, 2004.

Photo of the "Translation Committee" reproduced by permission and was provided by Longyear Museum, Chestnut Hill, Massachusetts.

Cover design: Gary S. Albright.

Maps: Michael Grivakis.

Text

Dorothy von Moltke's and Helmuth James von Moltke's letters have been provided by the Moltke family. Permission for use granted by Helmuth Caspar von Moltke (Dorothy's grandson and Helmuth James von Moltke's son). Original letters are in the Deutsches Literatur Archiv, Marbach, Germany.

© The Mary Baker Eddy Collection. Used by permission: Notes 182, 183, 184, 188, 194, 196, 198, 199, 216, 219, 220, 232

© The Christian Science Publishing Society. Used by permission: Notes 198, 199, 207

All sources from The Mary Baker Eddy Collection and The First Church of Christ, Scientist, Boston, are used courtesy of The Mary Baker Eddy Collection and The Mary Baker Eddy Library.

Any opinions expressed in this book are those of the author and not necessarily approved or endorsed by The Mary Baker Eddy Collection, The Christian Science Publishing Society, or The Mary Baker Eddy Library.

Documents attributed to Longyear Museum are by permission of Longyear Museum, Chestnut Hill, Massachusetts: Notes 163, 178, 179, 217, 293.

We are all well & cheerful & call our dear little Berghaus an "Island of Peace" in the ocean of unrest & difficulties around us.

Dorothy von Moltke to James and Jessie Rose Innes
Kreisau, September 17, 1931

Note: Dorothy von Moltke usually spelled Kreisau with a C.

In 1930, Germany changed the C at the beginning of the names of many towns and cities to a K, so Creisau became Kreisau.

In 1945, Kreisau was changed to the Polish name, Krzyżowa.

CONTENTS

WHO'S WHO IN THE MOLTKE FAMILY

Keeping the Helmuth von Moltkes straight:

Helmuth Carl Bernhard von Moltke (1800-1891)
Helmuth von Moltke the Elder. Field Marshal under Bismarck and Kaiser Wilhelm I of Germany; masterminded winning of Franco-Prussian War, in 1871. Title: Count. No heirs.

Helmuth Johannes Ludwig von Moltke (1848-1916)
Helmuth von Moltke the Younger. Nephew of Helmuth von Moltke the Elder. Chief of the German General Staff from 1906 to 1914 and beginning of World War I. Title: Count.

Helmuth von Moltke (1876-1939)
Nephew of Helmuth von Moltke the Younger and grandnephew of Helmuth von Moltke the Elder. Title: Count. Christian Scientist and husband of Dorothy Rose Innes von Moltke, who wrote these letters.

He is referred to alternately as "the Count," "Count von Moltke," "Helmuth," or "Helmuth von Moltke." It is hoped that the context of these references will clarify which "Helmuth von Moltke" or "Count von Moltke" is being referred to. (He is also affectionately referred to in his wife's letters as "the Y.T.," for "the Young Teuton.") His wife and author of the letters is referred to alternately as "Countess von Moltke," "the Countess," "Dorothy," or "Dorothy von Moltke." Context here should also clarify which "Countess" is being referred to.

Helmuth James von Moltke (1907-1945)
Eldest son of Helmuth von Moltke (the Christian Scientist) and Dorothy von Moltke. Celebrated hero of the German Resistance and leader of the Kreisau Circle. Hanged by the Nazis on January 23, 1945.

Letters to his wife, Freya von Moltke, published as *Briefe an Freya 1939-1945,* and subsequently in English as *Letters to Freya 1939-1945*. Second volume of letters from Helmuth James to Freya was published by C.H. Beck in 2011 as *Abschiedsbriefe Gefängnis Tegel September 1944-Januar 1945* (*Farewell Letters Tegel Prison September 1944-January 1945*).

Helmuth Caspar von Moltke (1937-   )

Eldest son of Helmuth James and Freya von Moltke, and grandson of Helmuth and Dorothy von Moltke. Retired businessman, living in Montreal, Canada. Active in promoting the Freya von Moltke Stiftung (Foundation) and the Kreisau Foundation for European Understanding, located on the former Moltke estate in Krzyżowa, Poland (formerly Kreisau, Germany).

Hans Adolf von Moltke (1884-1943)

A Moltke cousin. Ambassador to Poland until Germany invaded Poland in 1939. Hitler appointed him Ambassador to Spain in 1943, but he died soon after his arrival in Madrid.

AUTHOR'S NOTE

From the moment I stumbled on the Moltke story eight years ago, I became involved in a never-ending adventure.

One day, as I was doing some routine reference work at Longyear Museum, where I was employed as a researcher and writer, I came across the name Helmuth von Moltke in a number of Christian Science *Journals* and *Sentinels*. Although I had been a halfhearted history student in high school, I vaguely recalled that there was an important player in German history named Moltke, who had been promoted to field marshal by Bismarck after the Franco-Prussian War. And so I went on the Internet to see what the connection was between the Christian Scientist and the great Field Marshal.

It turned out that the Helmuth von Moltke in the church periodicals was indeed the grandnephew of Field Marshal Helmuth Carl Bernhard von Moltke, architect of the Prussian victory over the French in 1871. As I surfed the Internet some more, I discovered that the Christian Scientist had a son named Helmuth James von Moltke, who was a hero of the German Resistance, executed by the Nazis in 1945. I read on and learned that, amazingly, Helmuth James's widow was still living—now aged ninety-four—in Norwich, Vermont.

Next, I read a biography of the Moltkes, *Blood and Iron: From Bismarck to Hitler the von Moltke Family's Impact on German History* by Otto Friedrich. In it I learned that a younger brother of Helmuth James named Wilhelm Viggo von Moltke had left Germany in 1937 for England, ending up in the United States, where he was made an officer in the United States Army. After the war, he studied architecture with Walter Gropius at Harvard's Graduate School of Design, in Cambridge, Massachusetts, later becoming a professor of urban planning there.

As I live in Cambridge, my desk mate, married to a German girl and as fascinated by this story as I was, suggested that I look up the younger brother in the phone book, which I did.

Lo and behold, I found a Mrs. Wilhelm von Moltke living at an address three blocks from my home. I dialed the number. A German-accented voice answered. "Yes, this is Mrs. Wilhelm von Moltke; what can I do for you?" I was astonished. Suddenly, I had stepped into history. I explained my interest in learning more about the Christian Scientist named Helmuth von Moltke whose name appeared in our church periodicals. "Oh," she replied, "you want to talk to my sister-in-law, Freya"—the widow of the German Resistance hero. Mrs. von Moltke—Veronica—then gave me Freya's phone number in Vermont.

When I called, another German-accented but deeper voice answered. It was Freya von Moltke. She invited me to come for an interview, and two weeks later, I was in my Ford Escort headed for the hills of the Green Mountain State.

After a long drive, I arrived at a typical Vermont wooden house, where I was greeted by a very lively lady with a shock of white hair and a friendly smile. I finally got to use a phrase I'd always loved, *Guten Tag, gnädige Frau* (Good day, Madam). She laughed and invited me in.

I turned on my tape recorder and we got down to the interview. It lasted about two hours. Afterwards, as we chatted over tea and pastries, she asked, "And have you been a friend of Veronica for a long time?" I had to explain that, actually, I had never met Veronica and I had spoken with her only over the phone. We had a good laugh.

A few weeks after returning to Cambridge, I received a note from Freya announcing that copies of all of Dorothy von Moltke's letters had arrived at her home. Would I like to come and read them? For the next six months, I made several trips to Norwich, where, seated at a small table in the guest room, I perused the letters of Dorothy von Moltke, wife of Count Helmuth von Moltke. And there began the next chapter in my adventure with the Moltke story, and my love affair with Dorothy's over 750 letters to her parents in South Africa.

When I finished my manuscript about the contributions of

Count and Countess von Moltke to the Christian Science Church (Part II of this book), I gave it to Freya to read. On my next visit, we went over the entire text together, on which she had made corrections, particularly the passages about her husband, Helmuth James.

I recall her sitting beside me at the little writing table with the notebook containing my manuscript in her hands. She turned to me and said softly, "This is beautiful—simple, but beautifully written." She added that over the years since the death of her father-in-law, she had grown to appreciate him more and more. I told her that I felt a warm kinship with Dorothy, to which she replied, "Yes, I can see that you do." She concluded that it was good that this book had been written about them. "They deserve it," she said. Later, in 2007, Freya made the following written statement:

> Dorothy and Helmuth von Moltke would be pleased with this publication. As their daughter-in-law I have witnessed how important Christian Science was in their lives. Using Dorothy's letters, the story has been well and correctly told and represents including the life of my husband in all its details—the past as I knew it.

When I had completed the longer work on Dorothy von Moltke's letters (Part I), I showed it to Freya and her son, Helmuth Caspar von Moltke. Both of them expressed appreciation for the way I had woven the letters together with a continuous narration giving context and background information. "You have built bridges between the letters," Freya said approvingly. Her son agreed.

A couple of years later, Helmuth Caspar read the entire book of Dorothy's letters and made many helpful suggestions and corrections. He wrote me the following in an e-mail:

> Your manuscript has been illuminating even to me. It contains so much more of my grandparents' working and spiritual life that I have never before absorbed as well.

When I applied to Nebbadoon Press to publish the letters, Helmuth Caspar wrote a strong letter of support, part of which is excerpted here.

> Kate Hammond has edited these letters, some of which appeared in translation in Germany in a book entitled "Ein Leben in Deutschland" in 1999. Hers is the commentary on life in a leading German family in a period of great upheaval seen though the eyes of a young woman steeped in the traditions of the Anglo-Saxon democracy.
>
> My family and I would be delighted if her letters became available to an American audience.

When he received the news that my manuscript of his grandmother's letters had been accepted for publication, as well as the shorter one on the Moltkes' involvement in Christian Science, Helmuth Caspar was overjoyed, exclaiming, "Kate, you have hit the ball out of the park!"

Freya von Moltke died on January 1, 2010. A memorial service was held a week later in a packed, white-steepled New England church, with two enormous wreaths from the German Government draped over the altar. The cover of the program included a message that Freya had kept posted on her front door, which on this occasion took on a special meaning.

> To Everybody!
> Please, walk in! Push hard.
> Find me upstairs if I
> don't respond
>
> Freya

The audience chuckled, as they remembered a genuine heroine of the most tragic period in German history. I felt privileged to have known her and to have received so much help and encouragement from her in the writing of this book.

Catherine R. Hammond

October 2, 2013

PUBLISHER'S AND EDITOR'S NOTE

Every extract from Dorothy von Moltke's letters and other source materials have been carefully proofed word-for-word to match the original handwritten documents, which means that misspellings, odd punctuation, and other minor quirks remain for you to see.

We believe that you, as did we, will get to know Dorothy von Moltke as an incisive and caring individual, and will be transported back to her life as a member of Germany's elite society. She describes in these letters, to her parents in South Africa, the idyllic period leading up to World War I; the descent into the chaos of World War I; the effects of the Treaty of Versailles; the Weimar Government's trials, tribulations, and economic hardships; the Depression; and the drama of Hitler's takeover of Germany.

By the time we finished reading aloud (for proofing purposes) the last letter, written in 1934, not long before Dorothy died suddenly, in 1935, at age fifty-one, we both cried, realizing that she did not know what was about to happen to her beloved adopted country and to her five children during World War II.

Part Two of this book gives a glimpse of the Moltke family's spiritual status, including their religious activities, and the values that Dorothy and Helmuth instilled in their eldest son, Helmuth James von Moltke.

The letters reveal how Dorothy and Helmuth taught their children the liberal values that led their most famous son, Helmuth James, to found the anti-Nazi Kreisau Circle, for which he was hanged, in January 1945. The Moltkes' idealism is perpetuated today in the Kreisau Foundation for European Understanding on the family's former estate, where young people now learn the art of waging peace.

George and Jane Spitzer

Germany 1919 to 1937

Germany 1945

Breslau, Scweidnitz, and Kreisau were renamed
Wrocław, Świdnica, and Krzyżowa after World War II.

PART I

THE LETTERS

INTRODUCTION

When a beautiful young South African woman met a German count deep in the countryside of eastern Germany at the beginning of the twentieth century, they began a life together that was to withstand many political and personal upheavals over a period of thirty-three years. Helmuth von Moltke and his South African wife, Dorothy, lived at Kreisau, a large country estate in Silesia, where they raised a family of five children, the eldest of whom, Helmuth James von Moltke, would become the celebrated hero of the German resistance. Count and Countess von Moltke also joined a radical new religion, Christian Science, and served on the committee that translated into German the Christian Science textbook, *Science and Health with Key to the Scriptures* by Mary Baker Eddy.

The story of this remarkable couple is told through over 750 letters that Dorothy wrote to her parents in South Africa from her home in Germany during the first third of the twentieth century. As she was South African, the letters were written in English, with the exception of a few that she wrote in German during the First World War, when sending letters in English abroad was forbidden.

The Moltkes

The family into which the young woman from South Africa married is as historic as it is distinguished. The first Helmuth Count von Moltke (1800-1891)—great-uncle of the Christian Scientist and great-great-uncle of Helmuth James—was one of the most renowned military heroes in German history. As field marshal under Otto von Bismarck and Kaiser Wilhelm I, he led the Prussian armies to victory in the European wars that resulted in the formation of the German Empire in 1871. In gratitude for Moltke's contribution to winning the Battle of Könniggrätz, in 1866, the Kaiser rewarded him with a large sum of money with which to purchase a country estate and, a few years later, conferred on him the title of Count. Moltke bought a large estate with a *Schloss* (usually translated *castle,* but in this case, a *large manor house*) in Kreisau, Silesia, in Eastern Germany, along the Polish border. Kreisau was to remain the Moltkes' home until the end of World War II.

When the great Field Marshal died without heirs in 1891, he left the Kreisau estate to his eldest nephew, Wilhelm von Moltke. Another nephew (Wilhelm's younger brother), also named Helmuth von Moltke, was Chief of the General Staff under Kaiser Wilhelm II during World War I. Lacking the military genius of his illustrious uncle, however, he was blamed for the débacle at the First Battle of the Marne, in 1914, and was soon relieved of his command. Sadly, he died two years later, a broken man.

The meeting

In 1902, Wilhelm Count von Moltke's wife (the Countess Ella, mother of Helmuth, Dorothy's future husband), feeling bored with life in the country and desiring interesting company, placed in a Dresden newspaper an advertisement for paying guests at an aristocratic estate in Silesia, with one requirement: a good hand at bridge. A South African woman, who was traveling with her daughter on an educational tour of Germany, happened to see the notice. Intrigued, they decided to apply. Soon mother and daughter found themselves on the Moltke estate at Kreisau. The mother was Lady Jessie Rose Innes, wife of Sir James Rose Innes, later chief justice of South Africa; her daughter was eighteen-year-old Dorothy Rose Innes.

Before the Rose Inneses arrived at Kreisau, the Countess—known in the family as "Muttel"—had had a premonition that a young woman from abroad wearing a blue necklace and a white dress would bring the family great happiness. And so, when mother and daughter came down to dinner on their first night at the Moltke *Schloss*, it seemed that the prophecy had come true: the eighteen-year-old girl was wearing a white dress with a string of turquoise beads. Events soon confirmed Muttel's prediction. The girl from South Africa and the

3

young heir to the estate, Helmuth von Moltke—eight years her senior and grandnephew of the great Field Marshal—fell in love.

"He sang his way into her heart"

Possessing a magnificent baritone voice[1] and a vast repertoire, young Moltke would occasionally give *Liederabende* (evenings of song), which were described by one family member as *unglaublich aufregend*—unbelievably thrilling.[2] With the lamps burning in the large rooms and on the central staircase of the *Schloss*, Helmuth stood with his back against the end of the grand piano, where, accompanied by his older sister Leno,[3] he poured out his voice in the beautiful melodies of Schubert, Brahms, Puccini, Strauss, Verdi, and Wagner. Perhaps it was in the course of one of these evenings during the summer of 1902 that he, as his future daughter-in-law put it, "sang his way into the heart" of the lovely young woman from abroad.[4]

Soon there was talk of marriage. The girl's mother, however, feeling that her daughter should take more time to consider this important step, whisked Dorothy away to England and later back to their homeland of South Africa.[5] The girl's parents were understandably reluctant to see their beloved daughter married to a man in a country halfway around the world. (The eight-thousand-mile[6] voyage by ship from South Africa to Germany took two to three weeks in those days.) Why couldn't she marry a nice young man from Pretoria or Cape Town?

The Rose Inneses

Dorothy Rose Innes was born in 1884. The only child of Sir James and Lady Jessie Rose Innes, who were both of Scottish descent, she grew up in Pretoria, South Africa.

Like the Moltkes, Dorothy's family was renowned for its distinguished ancestry and accomplishments. Sir James Rose Innes (1855–1942), the descendant of early settlers and the grandson of the first Superintendent-General of Education in the Cape Colony, was attorney general under Cecil Rhodes from 1890 to 1893 and later chief justice of South Africa, from 1914 to 1927.[7] Known for his incorruptible integrity and unflagging industry, Sir James was a visionary with a profound conscience who, at the dawn of the twentieth century, was already advocating the rights of Blacks (then called "Natives") in his country.

In his introduction to Sir James's *Autobiography*, the editor, B. A. Tindall, paraphrases remarks by South African Prime Minister Jan Smuts about his good friend and colleague: "In his public life [Rose Innes] was distinguished by a very high standard of integrity and probity and . . . played an outstanding part in gaining for South Africa a reputation for clean politics." Judges in the Witwatersrand Division of the South African Supreme Court paid this tribute to Sir James: "In his public life he was always a powerful influence for moderation, justice and constitutionalism and zealous to secure fair play and justice for the Native people." And Lord Alfred Milner said of him, "The 'lie in the soul' can effect no lodgment in his clear intellect and absolutely sincere nature."[8]

In 1913, when Mahatma Gandhi, then living in South Africa, had been freed from jail and was under investigation by a commission appointed by the South African government, Sir James was one of the men that Gandhi hoped would be placed on the commission. Gandhi wrote in his autobiography, "We only suggest that some impartial men should be appointed . . . , and in this connection we would mention Sir James Rose Innes and the Hon. Mr W.P. Schreiner, both of them well-known men noted for their sense of justice."[9]

Dorothy's mother, Jessie Rose Innes, came from a prominent South African family named Pringle, whose ancestors had emigrated from Scotland to the farmlands of the Eastern Cape in the early 1800s. She grew up at "Lynedoch," a large farm situated on the Baviaans River near Bedford, and shaded by beautiful groves of large indigenous mimosas and European oaks, willows, ash, and hawthorn trees. She and James were married in 1881, an event of which her husband would later write, "Of the many favours of fortune experienced during a long life, none has been so important as my marriage to Jessie Dods Pringle. . . . No event has so profoundly affected my life."[10]

A strong, practical woman, Lady Rose Innes was active in the promotion of women's rights—a cause that her husband, too, enthusiastically supported. She occasionally travelled abroad to give speeches at conferences on women's suffrage and served for a time as the president of the National Council of Women. Known for her zest for life and a buoyantly optimistic outlook,[11] Jessie was heard to say to her sister-in-law, as she looked out on her flowerless garden one winter, "Minnie, aren't we neat!"[12] This very quality of optimism provided a happy complement to the judge's more pessimistic temperament.

Their shared interest in philanthropic causes, as well as complementary temperaments, may well account for the deep happiness of the marriage of Sir James and Lady Jessie Rose Innes. The distinct individuality and strong character of both her parents would have a profound influence on their beloved daughter in this close-knit family.

Engagement and Marriage

Two years after Dorothy returned with her mother to South Africa, Count Wilhelm died, leaving the estate to his eldest son, Helmuth. The new Count von Moltke and ruler of Kreisau now needed a wife. Although his correspondence with Dorothy had petered out in the interim (he was never a very good letter writer), he learned that the lovely young South African woman he had met a few years earlier was visiting in England, and he immediately rushed over to ask for her hand in marriage. She accepted, and in two weeks the couple became officially engaged. "A dull pale young woman was overnight transformed into a beauty,"[13] commented Helmuth's sister, who had accompanied him to England—

6

revealing the depth of Dorothy's feeling for Helmuth, with whom she had perhaps despaired of ever being reunited.

In the fall of 1905, on October 18 (the same month and day as her parents' wedding twenty-four years earlier), Dorothy Rose Innes and Helmuth von Moltke were married at St. Alban's Cathedral in Pretoria, South Africa. Photographs show a serious-looking young woman in a traditional white wedding dress, with the young Count at her side looking handsome in full military regalia, including a large bearskin helmet.

Their backgrounds differed in language, nationality, and culture, even as the aristocratic string of initials of her husband's multiple names that barely fit on the marriage certificate contrasted with her discreetly penned signature. Yet their social and political ideals, love of family, love of culture, and religion—Christian Science—bound them deeply together, and years later Helmuth would say of their meeting and marriage, *Das war Destiny* (It was destiny).[14] The success of this union would suggest he was right.

After the wedding, the happy couple returned to Germany, to Kreisau, and to the imposing *Schloss* that dominated the estate, surrounded by vast fields stretching out toward the low-lying Eulengebirge—the Owl Mountains—in the distance. There the new Count and Countess of Kreisau were welcomed by family, staff, and many other well-wishers. At the entrance to the *Schloss*, ladies in long white dresses stood on either side of the large stone staircase, holding garlands and baskets of flowers, while a little flower girl in front greeted the couple as they ascended the steps and entered what would be their home for the next twenty-three years. (They would later move to the smaller *Berghaus*—House on the Hill.)

They were in the heart of Silesia, an area with a long history going back to the Stone Age. Over the centuries it was passed back and forth between Poland, Bohemia, Austria, and Prussia, becoming part of Germany in 1909, then coming back under Polish rule at the end of World War II. Its capital, Breslau, now renamed Wrocław (pronounced "Vrōtswaf"), lies beside the great Oder River, the present boundary between Germany and Poland, forty miles northeast of Kreisau. In the tenth century, it had been strategically situated at the crossroads of two major trade routes, one stretching from the Roman Empire to the Baltic Sea, the other from the Black Sea to Western Europe. By the time of Helmuth and Dorothy's marriage, in 1905, Breslau had become a major industrial and cultural center and one of the largest cities in Germany.

The checkered history of Silesia is reflected in the Catholic and Protestant churches in the area, evidence of Catholic and Protestant periods of influence.[15] Four miles (seven kilometers) from Kreisau, in the town of Svidnica (formerly Schweidnitz), is one of the famous *Friedenskirchen* (Churches of Peace) built by the Protestants in the seventeenth century. These churches were built of wood, the material prescribed by the Catholic authorities, who neither wanted nor expected them to last. Yet there they remain, lovingly maintained and used for Christian worship today.[16]

The *Schloss* to which the Moltkes returned in October 1905 was the central feature of the eighteenth-century property bought by the Field Marshal in 1867. The front staircase was flanked by a pair of French cannons, brought back from the Franco-Prussian War. The front doors opened into a large hall with spacious rooms on either side—the family's dining room, library, and bedrooms.

On the walls of the wide stone staircase leading to the second floor were two murals depicting critical events in the Field Marshal's life. One mural portrayed the Napoleonic invasion of Lübeck, in 1806—a traumatic experience that the six-year-old Moltke would never forget and for which he would one day exact retribution. The mural on the opposite wall showed the Germans' victorious entry into Paris at the end of the Franco-Prussian War, with the Field Marshal riding his horse down the Champs-Élysées toward the Arc de Triomphe.[17] The stairs then continued up to the second floor and the Moltkes' music room (*Saal*) and living rooms (*Wohnzimmer*). To the existing structure, the Field Marshal added a third floor, where paying guests, or "PGs" (such as the Rose Inneses), stayed. The kitchens, servants' quarters, and laundry were on the ground floor.[18]

In front of the *Schloss* was the *Hof*, a huge rectangular farmyard surrounded by several outbuildings: stables and cowsheds with red-tiled roofs, housing horses, cows, pigs, oxen, sheep, chickens, and other farm animals. In addition to their riding horses, the Moltkes had eight teams for working the fields. The smell of beasts and fowl sometimes filled the air, especially on hot days, wafting through the open windows into the aristocratic residence. Beyond the *Hof* lay meadows and vast farm fields stretching for miles, where barley, corn, flax, peas, rapeseed, potatoes, and sugar beets were raised.[19]

Tall trees towered over the beautiful long *allées* (walkways) created by the Field Marshal, and lovely gardens surrounded the *Schloss*, with fruit trees that bloomed in the spring, giving off their delicious fragrances. A stream, the Peile, wound its way through the land, reflecting the vast blue sky and clouds overhead. Nestled against a nearby hill was the smaller *Berghaus*, with the *Stoep* (Afrikaans for porch) from which to enjoy views of the surrounding countryside.

There were many workers on the estate: about sixty year-round, with additional laborers at peak times.[20] Nearby lay the village of Kreisau, where the Field Marshal had begun a school for the local children. Under the wing of the estate were two churches—one Protestant, the other Catholic—for which it was the duty of the owner of Kreisau to appoint a pastor and a priest. In short, Kreisau was very much in the feudal tradition, with the lord of the castle looking with a benevolent eye upon the needs, cares, and concerns of his workers and villagers.

It was here in Kreisau, and later also in Berlin, that Helmuth and Dorothy lived out their life together, maintaining the family estate, raising their five children, serving their church, and giving hospitality to family and friends.

Life at Kreisau

Life at Kreisau started out idyllically for the young Count and Countess. There were all manner of pleasant activities to enjoy: large hunting parties followed by dinners in the *Schloss*; frequent visits to other estates nearby and at a distance; charming Silesian holidays and ceremonies, especially at Christmas, when a large Christmas tree stood in the *Saal* as carols were sung on Christmas Eve and gifts lay on each family member's own *Tisch* (table); attendance in 1910 at the "court season" in Berlin, presided over by the Kaiser and Kaiserin; long walks in the forest and rides on horseback through meadows and fields; carriage rides through the countryside on moonlit nights; sleigh rides, skiing, and tobogganing in winter.

Yet, for all the amenities of life on a country estate, the Moltkes' existence was not without its challenges.

Count Helmuth von Moltke came from a society—the conservative German landed aristocracy (*Adel*)—which had little tolerance for anything that deviated from its long-established traditions, both political and religious. His liberal views on politics caused members of his class to regard him as a pariah, and his adoption of Christian Science, which was considered very *undeutsch* (un-German), set him at odds with a society in which one was generally either *Evangelisch* (Lutheran) or Catholic. In the hidebound world of the German *Adel*, how grateful the Count must have been to have at his side a woman who understood and shared his ideals.

The Countess's role at Kreisau was not an easy one, either. At any moment the Moltkes might be descended upon by numerous relatives, to whom the family felt obligated to give hospitality, or by their many friends—even during the lean post-war years. Sometimes Dorothy's homesickness caused her to suffer in a way that even her devoted husband could not comprehend—a suffering she was able to deal with on her own with courage and poise, selflessly reaching out to those around her with deep warmth and affection.

A further complication to Countess von Moltke's existence at Kreisau was that, according to her future daughter-in-law, Freya von Moltke, her parents not only regretted losing her to a country two continents away but "never felt 'Papi' [the Count] was good enough for her."[21] In order to reassure her parents about her life in this distant foreign land, and particularly about her choice of a husband, her letters to them tended to depict her life as "quite a bit rosier" than it actually was. Nevertheless, the letters of Countess von Moltke also reveal a deeply contented woman who had made a commitment to her new life in Germany, with a man she loved, and never looked back.

Freya summed up her mother-in-law's character in this luminous description to me: "She was handsome, but she had sort of a glow from inside, you know, that came out, which was her charm, but charm is too shallow a description. It was an inner strength and loveliness that shone through her and you had to fall in love with her, you had to love her. She was very warm and very intelligent. She really was loved by everybody, and she was a wonderful, warm, understanding center of Kreisau. That's very much in the letters, of course."

"An island of peace"

Dorothy's letters tell the rest of the story of her life with Helmuth von Moltke on their estate at Kreisau, and later also in Berlin, in a world that was at first beautiful and serene, but which later became increasingly fraught with danger and violence as Nazism strengthened its grip on Germany. Yet, in spite of all the political and economic upheavals they were to endure, their home at Kreisau remained for the Moltkes "an 'Island of Peace,' in the ocean of unrest & difficulties around us." [Kreisau, 17.9.1931]

11

1902

Stopover in Berlin

The letters begin in 1902, soon after the Boer War, when Dorothy was traveling with her mother in Germany and had just met the man she would marry, Helmuth von Moltke. After a brief visit to England, the Rose Inneses returned in November to Germany and stayed in Berlin, where they were warmly greeted once again by Helmuth's relatives and friends. Mother and daughter then took a train to Altenburg, to pay a call on Helmuth's grandmother, *Gräfin* (Countess) Bethusy-Huc. Dorothy describes the scene with characteristic warmth and humor.

> We had such a warm welcome from her, and after tea we sat talking until a little after seven, when we went to dress, for she had invited about eight people to meet us;—the Herr Pfarrer (pastor). Excellenz this and Excellenz that, etc etc. Every one was most charming and I enjoyed myself immensely.

> The old lady asked me if I liked Germany when I replied "Yes very much indeed" she was almost childishly delighted and turning to the assembled company she said in a loud voice "Diese liebe Miss [This dear Miss] likes Germany!"!!! Next day we walked about the town which is very old and quaint and sleepy and saw all over the Stift [a home for elderly aristocratic ladies] which was most interesting, and at five o'clock we said adieu and left for Berlin arriving at nine o'clock. [Berlin, 13.11. 1902]

Back in Berlin, the Rose Inneses visited the home of Helmuth's uncle of the same name who was Chief of the General Staff in Berlin. Feeling self-conscious as she came under the gaze of her future husband's relatives, Dorothy was particularly happy to see Helmuth again.

> Today we are going to see something of Berlin and this evening we are going to dine at Frau von Moltkes in order to meet her husband, the General, who at present is away. It is somewhat of an ordeal, for I shall be looked upon with

13

somewhat critical eyes. . . . It is delightful seeing Helmuth once again even for so short a time. It is impossible to describe every ones kindness to me, they all treat me as one of the family, kiss me always as a matter of course, call me "Die Kleine" [the little one] and in a hundred ways welcome me. At Altenburg also the guests we met at dinner wanted to invite us to their houses had we been staying longer, and so it is everywhere,—kindness, kindness and ever kindness. [Berlin, 13.11.1902]

1903

As Dorothy was in South Africa in 1903, there was not much occasion to write her parents. The two letters from that year that exist are relatively inconsequential, containing news mainly about the weather, social visits, and a boring sermon, which hint at the dullness of her existence there. "Dearest Dad," she wrote her father from Wynberg:

> We went to church yesterday at Mr. Vine Halls, and I am sorry to say, I found much amusement in Mr. Arderne's rendering of "Children obey your parents in the Lord," he thoroughly enjoyed reading this lesson, and did so with great pomp, importance and monotony. . . . I hope the heat has not been too trying . [Highclere, Wynberg, 2.3.1903]

1904

Madagascar

Two years after her first trip to Germany, Dorothy was again traveling north to Europe with her mother. They were bound for Italy first, where Lady Innes would be attending a conference on women's suffrage, thence to England to visit relatives and friends. From the ship, the *S. S. Bürgermeister,* she pens colorful descriptions of the East African coast, particularly the beautiful scenery and lush vegetation along the beaches of Mozambique and the island of Madagascar in the Indian Ocean. "Dearest of Dads," she begins:

> Mazambeque [Mozambique], where we posted you a letter, is quite interesting and picturesque, and the approach is really beautiful, the little island set in a lovely sea of blue and green such as I have never before seen, a thin line of white surf and then quaint red, yellow, blue, pink and white houses among the palms. We landed, a partie carrée [a party of four] consisting of Mother, the two Rivitiras and I, and walked about the glarey white streets, utterly deserted they look and all white without a tree so that the glare is even worse than Church Square on a hot summers day. There are no horses, no carts, no women and very few men in this desterled [deserted] town, and yet it is quite attractive in its way; The only conveyance we saw was a rough native made cart, drawn by a lazy tired ox, the load being flour. We had a long walk all along the sea shore and returned to the boat tired but contented sightseers. [*S. S. Bürgermeister*, 1.10.1904]

A few days later they reached Mahajanga in Madagascar, and later the island of Nossi Bé.

> . . . yesterday we reached Nossi Bé, the jewel of the India Ocean I am sure. All day we skirted the coast of Madagasca[r], which is very pretty and rather wild, and at about 4 o'clock we cast anchor in the loveliest bay I have ever seen—mountains all round us, clothed with the most luxuriant vegetation. La bonne mère [the good mother—Dorothy's mother] was so happy! We landed in the most beautiful little village, la Place de la Republic shady with huge mango trees and soft under foot with grass, a fountain playing in the centre, and quite a number of large pretty houses with lovely gardens, everything growing in the greatest abundance, oh so different from Pretoria! The air was heavy with the scent of flowers, such beautiful kinds too. Mother has collected quite a bundle of seeds. Nossi Bé is a lovely tropical island with just a tinge of French charm which is delightful. I have determined to return to this beautiful place some day, for it is really enchanting.

15

It is very noticeable how much cleaner, prettier and more orderly the French places are to any other ports we have visited, and the natives are so superior. [*S. S. Bürgermeister*, 1.10.04]

The only discordant note during their trip was the deafening noise at night of cargo being loaded onto the ship.

When the *Bürgermeister* anchored off Zanzibar, the Rose Inneses unexpectedly met up with an old friend who had learned of the Rose Inneses' presence in the area. In period-film fashion, Sir Owen Morewood surprised Dorothy and her mother when he approached their ship in a cable boat.[22]

> Last Monday morning we arrived at Zanzibar, and who should come on board to look us up but Owen Morewood, to our great surprise. We lunched with him on his cable boat and there Judge Lindsay Smith (another guest) asked us to stay with them while our boat went to Dar-es-salam [*sic*.]. He was so pressing that we could not but accept, said our room was ready for us, that they had been expecting us for some days and so on; but have you ever heard of such kindness? . . . After lunch with Owen we went of a sail the the [*sic*.] cable boat's yatch (yacht!) and then to tea with the Lindsay Smiths as arranged, after a plentiful supply of which we went for a long long drive into the country in the Sultans own carriage, a most gorgeous affair, livery and upholstery in red velvet, a driver in front and a footman standing behind. The drive was beautiful, too beautiful to describe, and such a good road. Mangoe trees larger than English Elms and palm trees everywhere with a delicious green undergrowth making everything look cool and soft. The houses are all old Arab houses, nothing new anywhere, and the streets so narrow that two carriages could not possibly cross, what would happen in such an emergency, I know not, but appar[e]ntly there are so few carriages that they never meet. [S.S. *Bürgermeister*, 9.10.1904]

Next morning—Tuesday—Owen Morewood called for us and we went curio-hunting for the whole morning, such hot,

16

interesting work it is. The streets, crowded with people, narrow, dirty and quaint. Reminding one over and over again of childrens bible pictures, old, bearded men in white turbans and costumes, riding small white donkeys just like Absalom! Donkeys and goats tethered to the house doors, oh so patient and ill-used. Earnest men chanting their prayers and reading the Koran in a loud monotonous voice. And the dirt and colour and picturesqueness of the scene, I wish I could describe it to you or that you could see it! [*S. S. Bürgermeister*, 11.10.1904]

After dinner with the Lindsay Smiths in their house, which was a converted prison ("so quaint and cool and charming"), they attended a reception at the American consulate.

Italy and the Medici villa

Passing through the Suez Canal, the ship finally reached the shores of Italy in early November. After a "disappointing" tour of Naples, Pompeii, and Capri, mother and daughter arrived in Florence, where, comfortably settled in a hotel, they engaged in more sightseeing and studying Italian as they awaited Sir James's arrival. Thanks to some helpful introductions, mother and daughter enjoyed a visit to important art studios and a villa built by Lorenzo de' Medici.

On Thursday, too, Mrs. MacCalmont had a large At Home to which we were bidden. She lives in Villa di Medici, the oldest and most famous villa in Florence, built and inhabited by the famous Lorenzo di Medici in the 15th century, and therefore full, as you may imagine with lovely and historical things. . . . And now goodbye dearest of Dads. We are longing to hear all your news and to tell you of our doings. Have a very happy time in London and come soon to your devoted

Little Girl.

XXXXXX I hope you haven't forgotten what these mean. If you have I will show you when we meet. Adieu. [Florence, 20.11.1904]

1905

Marriage to the Count

After her engagement to the young Count von Molkte, in early 1905, Dorothy returned to South Africa. There the young bride-to-be was deluged with invitations to parties and received congratulations from numerous friends and relatives. "Oh dear," she exclaimed in a letter from Mowbray, a suburb of Cape Town, where she was visiting her grandparents. "I am very lucky to marry into such a charming family and they are all so good to me. I am so happy and the Teuton [Helmuth] is *most* satisfactory!" [Mowbray, 1.3.1905]

Seven months later, on October 18—a sultry South African day—Dorothy Rose Innes and Helmuth Count von Moltke were married at St. Alban's Cathedral in Pretoria. From that day on, Dorothy would live in eastern Germany, making the three-week journey southward every few years for an extended visit. And for the next thirty years, steamships would carry her letters nearly every week to her parents in South Africa.

1906

The *Schloss* at Kreisau

Three months after the wedding, Countess von Moltke, now living with her new husband on the family estate at Kreisau, sent her parents a postcard with a picture of the *Schloss* that had been bought and renovated by her husband's great-uncle forty years before.

> This is my new home. The canon [cannon] in front were captured in 1870 [during the Franco-Prussian War]. Much love and every blessing, eh William![23] [Kreisau, 2.1.1906]

The young Countess's first letter of 1906, written a few days later, contained some important news about her husband's "Onkel Helmuth" (nephew of the great Field Marshal).

18

I suppose you know that Onkel Helmuth has been made "Chef des Generalstabs" [Chief of General Staff] 9the highest post in the Army and the one the Feld Marschal held? [Kreisau, 7.1.1906]

She describes a hunting party with her husband in the magical Silesian forests around Turawa Lake (now in Poland).

The Turawa pine forests are noted even in Germany, the land of forests. I cannot describe their beauty—miles and miles of tall pink-stemmed trees with the most delicious undergrowth of moss and brown bracken and above all this a blue sky and sunshine. Quite delicious. We, that is Anamie and I, were with the shooters all afternoon until 5 o'clock when, in darkness, we returned to tea. I of course went with Helmuth who shot four stags, the best of all. It was delightful walking or standing quite still for hours among these trees. You may imagine how well I am that after being out for four hours I was only pleasantly tired. [Kreisau, 7.1.1906]

Gradually the new Countess von Moltke settled into her new surroundings as she adjusted to the traditions of her new family. Dorothy's sense of humor and proportion helped her to adjust to certain unavoidable aspects of farm life.

We discussed for a whole day the possibility of having my rooms South as you wished, but it simply *wouldn't* go. And really you neednot [*sic*.] worry, Mother dearest, the house is beautifully warm, and in summer one has the Peiler [Peile, nearby stream] odours on one side and the farm yard smells on the other, really not much to choose from and evidently not in the least unhealthy as no one is ever ill. [Kreisau, 7.1.1906]

Several months later, Dorothy gives her father a picture of her busy life at Kreisau. Addressing him as "dear Flen"—a pet name, the origin or exact meaning of which is unknown—she writes:

Of my daily life, dear Flen, I have really little to relate. I am always busy, and absurd though it sounds, every night there is "something left undone." A house as big as this needs much

19

supervision if it is to be well run, and I am stupid at the art of running a house. Then I must walk every day, lie down every day, practice every day, sew, read and write every day, and also find time to be with Helmuth and our guests, without taking into account the many unexpected interruptions and visits. So you see that although I in no way lead the strenuous life, I have quite enough to do to keep me busy, happy, and out of mischief! [Kreisau, 9.10.1906]

Der Jagd (The hunt)

In Germany, there are two kinds of hunts: riders in red jackets flying over fields and hedgerows on horseback, and "shoots," in which the German hunter, walking gun in hand and hiding behind natural blinds of trees and bushes, stalks his prey. Countess von Moltke describes the first kind of hunt.

> Yesterday Helmuth again went a-hunting and Onkel Ludwig (who was spending the week end at the Berghaus) and I drove out to see the finish. They hunt here, not as in England for the excitement or for long, but more than anything else as exercise for the horses, so that it does not last long, but it is a pretty sight to see the horsemen in their red coats riding hard across the green meadows. The hunt is held on Mondays and Thursdays, and this Thursday Helmuth is giving it in Kreisau,[24] after which there will be a big tea here for 30 or 40 people. [Kreisau, 9.10.1906]

Dorothy was touched by the genuine piety of one of the neighboring aristocratic families they visited at this time.

> On Sunday we drove to lunch with the Seidlitz's [*sic*.] who live in a delightful old Schloss, date 10th or so century, quite circular in shape, with a moat still in evidence. They are such nice people; he is Landrat [District Administrator], she a *charming* woman of about 30, with four fascinating children, well brought up and natural. . . . I went with Frau von Seidlitz to hear the children say their prayers in bed; they were very sweet, and much interested in the "Tante's" name—Dorothy—

which they found so difficult to pronounce! The youngest baby, aged 1½, said his little prayer, word for word after his Mother, with folded hands and hushed voice: "Ich bin Klein, mein Herz ist rein, Keiner soll darin wohnen, als Jesus allein." [I am little, my heart is pure, no one may dwell therein save Jesus alone.] [Kreisau, 17.10.1906]

She was still learning to understand German society and the different backgrounds.

I do not yet know Germany, for the class distinctions are so defined that beyond those who are "adlig" [aristocratic], and those who are peasants and servants, I have no idea, except a hazy one of a solid bourgeoisie very trying, and only to be compared to *very* dull middle class Weslyens [Wesleyans] with us. Of the great class to which I belong I know nothing, and yet I suppose it is from this class that the brains and the specialists of Germany are drawn. [Kreisau, 17.10.1906]

On the day before her first wedding anniversary, Countess von Moltke reflected on this occasion with mixed emotions.

I have been thinking so much of all that happened last year on just these days. I can't speak about them, for they were such a mixture of sorrow and joy, the shutting of one door, the opening of another, all unknown. Oh my dear, dear parents, come soon to visit your little bird, that we may all be happy together. [Kreisau, 17.10.1906]

1907

Beginning a family

On March 11, 1907, Dorothy gave birth to her first son, Helmuth James von Moltke—named after her husband, Helmuth, and her father, Sir James Rose Innes. She describes in detail the April christening in the Field Marshal's room at the *Schloss*, with the older generation reverently gathered around.

It was a moving scene—the simple and historic room, the old Moltkes very touched by the memories that crowded in upon them, and this youngest of all Moltkes, unconscious of a past or a future; deeply interested however in the present he certainly was, and as he was placed in the arms of one Godparent after another, he looked up into their faces with large wondering eyes. He wore the cap and dress which Helmuth and his father had worn before him, and in spite of being actively sea sick the little son behaved during the whole ceremony—which lasted about 35 minutes—in the most perfect manner.

First we sang a hymn, then came the Christening service and a short sermon. As text we had chosen: For I am persuaded that neither life nor death, nor principalities nor powers, nor things present nor things to come, nor any other creature, shall be able to separate us from the love of God which is in Christ Jesus. It is one of my favourite texts, and therefore it was chosen. After the sermon, the babe was handed to each Godparent in turn, and finally Monika, the youngest of these, held him while the sign of the Cross was made and his name Helmuth James Ludwig Wilhelm Eugene Heinrich was given him. (Does the length take your breath away? Helmuth and I wanted to call him Louis- James, but the family were so distressed at his not being a "Helmuth" that we had to give in to tradition.) Then the little One was placed on my lap, another hymn was sung, and the Pastor gave us his blessing. Thus was my son baptised. [Kreisau, 5.4.1907]

Retreating to her bedroom, she received a "surprise visit" from the family.

After the christening ceremony congratulations and talk ensued, and then everyone—20 guests in all—went in to dinner, while your little baby with her baby, returned to the nurseries, and after enjoying my little son for a time I went to bed, as it was nearly time to nurse him. However before this took place I had a surprise visit from the whole company, who, champagne in hand, trouped into my room in a body and drank my health; I replying as best I could from among the bed clothes! The speeches, I believe, were charming. Onkel Helmuths I will copy and send you, either this week or next. He was kind enough to write it out for me, as I was not able to hear it. [Kreisau, 5.4.1907]

In her next letter, Dorothy delights in the beauty and sweetness of her little son.

The boy is out on the front stoep [porch] this afternoon, hatless, sleeping peacefully in his p[e]rambulator. His eyes are growing very beautiful, and his skin is deliciously white. . . . You have no idea how sweet he looks sleeping, it really is a joy to look at him. [Kreisau, 28.4.1907]

But soon *Schwester* Marie (Nurse Marie) would be leaving, and the little mite would have to adjust to a new nurse.

His nurse arrived yesterday. I hope she will be satisfactory, at any rate she knows all about small babies, and has had much experience. . . .

It was so pathetic to see the little son yesterday. He knew quite well that a new person had come to look after him and he felt it very much. He would look fixedly at nurse for a few minutes and then with a little sob would look at Schwester.

It made us all quite sad to see it. He has such a sweet nature, and Schwester says he is a *very* good child. [Kreisau, 28.4.1907]

In May Helmuth and Dorothy visited the home of Helmuth's *Onkel* Ludwig, who lived on the estate at Wernersdorf.

On Thursday we went to Wernersdorf for the day, where it was very "gemütlich," as we say in the Fatherland. Onkel Ludwig has bought a piano and naturally Helmuth had to sing, while I, as accompanist, felt inclined to say Don't shoot at the pianist he's doing his best, though as you alas were not there, no one would have understood me! [Kreisau, 4.5.1907]

Meanwhile, the farm at Kreisau was flourishing.

We had the first fresh beans from the green house yesterday—simply delicious! The grapes too are ripening well there.

We are adding to the fowl run and hope in time to have quantities of chickens and ducks. The hens have layed very well this Spring, and we have 17 little chicks already with promise of many more to follow. [Kreisau, 4.5.1907]

In the Archiv Zimmer

The baby ended up in the *Archiv Zimmer* (archive room) where, Dorothy quipped, "in such an atmosphere he will surely be a Field Marschal at an early age!" [Kreisau, 10.6.1907]   She already sees the need for taming his strong will.

> The wee son is developing a will and energy which will need much "pruning" before it can bear good fruit. . . . He will need much discipline during the first years of his little life and firmness too, otherwise his strong will will run riot and bear some bitter fruit. But strong will is a splendid foundation for a character if only the art of obeying is learned thoroughly in early childhood. It is extraordinary how much character this little mite of hardly 3 months shows. He needs a great deal of love, and responds to it at once, but with strangers or comparative strangers he is very reserved, in spite of his friendly smile. [Kreisau, 4.6.1907]

Her life among the German aristocracy brought Dorothy into contact with colorful people, such as a *Gräfin* (Countess) Pückler.

> After a hurried rest Helmuth and I left to dine with the Pücklers, and Hans Adolf[25] went shooting. Our evening at Weisstritz was very pleasant. Gräfin Pückler is a most amusing, downright woman, and exactly as an old Russian princess in fiction always is. And here she was in fact as well! She might have walked out of one of Tolstois [*sic.*] books—the comfortable, conventional dowager, and I had to keep reminding myself, that I was not looking on at a play, but living in one. Truly the worlds a stage! [Kreisau, 4.6.1907]

24

Dorothy surprised people by taking the reigns of a large team of horses.

> It is Onkel Eugene's birthday today, and I am going to Saarau for a few hours this afternoon. You will be amused to hear that I drive the Rappen [stallions] every day myself, and that is one of my chief pleasures. The Y. T. [abbreviation for "Young Teuton"—Sir James's nickname for Helmuth] says I shall end by breaking in young horses! The other day at Herrmanns suggestion I drove "eights" (very large ones!) on a mown clover field, and found it both difficult and amusing. [Kreisau, 4.6.1907]

The Count was taking measures to share his land with the farm workers, although, like the peasants in Tolstoy's *Anna Karenina*, one of them refused his offer.

> Helmuth has given each of his labourers a small piece of garden land for their own, a very good and right thing I think. One however (needless to say a very 2nd rate one) refused his portion; "it was too much work" he declaired [*sic*.]! [Kreisau, 28.4.1907]

The Kuno von Moltke affair

By right of birth, Helmuth was a representative in the *Herrenhaus*, the German government's unelected upper house in Berlin. In June he was asked by the president of the *Herrenhaus* to intervene in a crisis involving Count Kuno von Moltke (1847–1923). Kuno, who came from another branch of the Moltke family and so was not considered a real relative of Helmuth von Moltke, had become involved in a scandal that would soon rock the German nation.

Kuno, adjutant to Kaiser Wilhelm II and military commander of Berlin, and other members of the Kaiser's inner circle had been publicly accused of homosexual behavior by a journalist named Maximilian Harden, editor of *Die Zukunft* (*The Future*).

> Helmuth will probably be called to the Herrenhaus during the

25

next few months, for negociations [*sic*.] are already passing between him and the OberPräsident, on the subject. Graf Kuno Moltke, the beloved of the Kaiser has been dismissed! It is a very unpleasant affair, and will probably lead to a scandal, as there is to be a prosecution for libel against the editor [Harden] of the "Zukunft" ["Future"], and many of the high and mighty are involved. It is said that Kuno is innocent in the matter, and I sincerely hope so. [Kreisau, 4.6.1907]

A passion for politics

As Dorothy and her father shared a passion for politics, her letters often discuss contemporary world events. In his autobiography, her father comments that ". . . she developed a flair for public affairs which, to her parents always a pleasure, became in time, and continued throughout her life, to be a help and encouragement as well."[26]

In the spring of 1907, Dorothy mentions a key figure in the British Empire, Herbert Lord Kitchener (1850–1916), Commander-in-Chief of the Indian Army. At this time there was unrest in India, where a vigorous struggle was being waged against the partition of Bengal by the British. On May 4 Dorothy expresses her confidence in Kitchener's leadership.

> Things do not seem to be very pleasant in India just at present do they? However one feels that Kitchner [*sic*.] is a very capable man and will be able to deal successfully with the situation. [Kreisau, 4.5.1907]

Lala Lajpat Rai, known as the "Lion of the Punjab" and one of the foremost leaders of the fight against British rule, was put in jail for six months, and in June, the United Kingdom declared its refusal to withdraw from India. Rai was released in November 1907.

Sharing her father's liberal views, Countess von Moltke despaired of the conservative and chauvinistic thinking of many of the German landed aristocracy, such as her anti-Semitic brother-in-law, Dietrich von Trotha (married to

26

Helmuth's sister Margarethe).

> Dietrich has been here for a few days, and we had several
> discussions on the Jewish question. He is a violent anti-Semite,
> and I believe in his heart believes that every vice in the
> Fatherland comes either through Jewish or English influence!
> Personally he is very nice, but oh his opinions, political and
> social! Why Onkel Ludwig appears almost in the light of a
> Social Democrat as compared to my honoured brother-in-law.
> [Kreisau, 17.6.1907]

While Dorothy refrained from debate, her intrepid mother-in-law
plunged in.

> I simply sit breathless when he expounds his views. But not so
> Muttel, she enjoys the fight, and shocked him inexpressibly
> yesterday (to her great amusement) by saying that were she
> invited by Herr Belin [Ballin] (the director of the Hamburg-
> America Line, a Jew, distinguished, and a friend of the
> Kaisers) to visit his *Schloss* in Kiel, she would go "mit Wonne"
> [with pleasure]! It is extraordinary to meet a man who knows
> nothing of the dreams and ideals and strivings of the world as it
> is today. [Kreisau, 17.6.1907]

A week of horse races in Breslau (about forty miles from
Kreisau) provided pleasant diversions for the Moltkes.

> There is to be a great racing week at the beginning of July in
> Breslau, which Helmuth and I mean to attend. On Friday 5th,
> races, 6th a ball, 7th races, 8th "Blumen-Corso" [parade of floats
> covered with flowers and drawn by horses], and theatre, and 9th
> races. Isn't that dissipation! Practically everyone in Schlesien
> is taking part, and it will be an amusing and pretty sight.
> Helmuth and I will sleep in Oels, and travel daily to Breslau,
> where we shall have our carriage and horses. [Kreisau,
> 17.6.1907]

Dorothy enjoyed the natural beauty of Kreisau, including her
flourishing garden.

> This is the most wonderful year for accacias [*sic*.], the trees are

white with flowers, and the scent everywhere is almost overpowering in its honey sweetness. The strawberries too are simply glorious—huge and red, juicy and in quantities. The Cosmos look quite nice, but are only about a foot high. However they promise to grow bushy and have just begun to flower. The roses are in full bloom now, and you have no idea what quantities we have, making the garden a veritable rose bower. On the balcony overlooking the Peile we have narrow boxes filled with nasturshiums [sic.] which look very gay, either climbing up the balustrade or hanging down at will. . . .

Last Friday afternoon I drove over to Gorkau to visit Lotte Liers (geb. [born] Kulmiz) and her wee daughter, and returned again after Abendbrod [supper]. The drive both there and back was lovely, by daylight on account of the charming scenery and at night because of the brilliant moonlight. Lotte I found very well and her baby which is so tiny that one can hardly see it (weighing only 5 ½ lbs) was bent on showing us what strong lungs it had. [Kreisau, 17.6.1907]

Christian Science class instruction

In the fall of 1907, the Moltkes went to Hannover to take a course in the art and science of Christian healing known as "class instruction." Their teacher was Bertha Günther-Peterson, who was also a Christian Science practioner—one who heals through consecrated prayer.

Helmuth had met Frau Günther-Peterson eight years earlier, when, experiencing prolonged *schweren Nervenleiden*— severe nervous suffering—he was taken by his mother to Günther-Peterson for Christian Science treatment. Within two weeks, he was completely healed and thereafter became a dedicated Christian Scientist. Learning of this healing religion through Helmuth, Dorothy, too, became a devoted adherent.

At five o'clock in the morning of October 14, Count and Countess von Moltke and their seven-month-old son boarded a train at Kreisau, bound for Hannover. With them were

28

Helmuth's youngest brother, Carl Viggo, Fräulein Horn (the nanny), and a Mademoiselle Mets. Also in the group was Manon Schönberg—known affectionately as "Schönchen"—who was a companion to Helmuth's *Tante* (Aunt) Luise, and much beloved by the Moltke family.[27] She eventually became a Christian Science practitioner.

Arriving in Hannover after the long journey of 350 miles (563 kilometers), the Moltkes and their entourage went to the commodious home of Helmuth's mother, where they stayed for the next two months.

The Moltkes found the course rigorous but interesting. In addition, they managed to fit in music lessons—voice for Helmuth, piano for Dorothy.

> I thought Hannover would be a time in which we should have much leisure, but on the contrary we work from 8 till 8 with the exception of a two hours walk in the afternoon. Our classes generally last three hours, but they are full of interest, and, what is more, full of satisfaction and joy. Then we have a great deal of home work and our music besides to keep us busy all day long. But it is delightful, and we are all very happy. [Hannover, 30.10.1907][28]

They also went to the theater, where they saw Hermann Sudermann's[29] four one-act plays under the title *Rosen*.

> They are quite interesting (though not worth sending to you to read) more as pictures of some aspects of modern life than for their intrinsic value. Of course I stand much too much in the present age to be able to really take an impartial judgment of the life of today, but I do find it intensely interesting to notice the great struggle between idealism and materialism that is taking place. I suppose that for many centuries there has never been so much materialism as now, nor perhaps so much striving after something more spiritual, as the unfolding and popularity of what you call "the newfangled religions" show. The teachings of Christ are, I think most people will admit, the most beautiful and ideal that have ever been given to men. But

what do we see after 1900 years of Christianity? The meek and the poor in Spirit are not considered to be worthy and so it is with most of Christ's injunctions, even when we do not interpret them at all literally. [Kreisau, 26.11.1907]

During the Moltkes' stay in Hannover, the Moltke-Harden case exploded into the greatest social scandal of its day. It became public when Kuno von Moltke sought to defend his honor by bringing a libel suit against Harden. As the scandal involved the highest level of German society—the Kaiser's inner circle—it shocked the German nation and made headlines around the world.

> I don't know whether you have read anything about the Moltke-Harden trial. I hope you have not because it is not pleasant reading. Kuno Moltke though not really a relation has always been regarded as a member of a branch family and you may imagine how all "our" Moltkes feel at having the name they are so proud of thus dragged in the dirt. The whole thing is scandalous and all Germany is sick not only at the revelations but also at the way the whole case has been conducted. [Hannover, 30.10.1907]

The Moltke-Harden trial was evidently of interest to her jurist father.

> You say you would like to know what the German papers say about the Harden-Moltke trial. They are practically all sympathetic towards Kuno Moltke, because he behaved like a gentleman, and they are all sick, not only at Harden's revelations, which are probably not all true, but more especially that such irrelevant dirt is allowed in the Courts of Justice. [Kreisau, 26.11.1907]

Kuno von Moltke's ex-wife, Lili von Elbe, took the stand as a witness against her former husband.

> Kuno Moltke would not allow a word to be said against Frau von Elbe, the chief witness for Harden's case, because she had been his wife, but I hope the truth will be got at now. Frau von Elbe is a miserable creature, clever and unprincipled. Of course

30

I have no idea of the truth or otherwise of the allegations, but even if Kuno Moltke has been weak, I am sure he has not been bad. [Kreisau, 26.11.1907]

Kuno von Moltke was forced to leave the military, but after three trials, he was rehabilitated in the public eye.

A German Christmas

Countess von Moltke's last letter of 1907 depicts the charm of a German Christmas at Kreisau.

You can picture the scene I know—the busy happy people, the excitement of the children, the Christmas trees, the Stollen [German pastry] and nuts and apples and all the other etceteras of a German Christmas. [Kreisau, 23.12.1907]

As part of their feudal duties, the Moltkes provided gifts for the village children.

We had the Einbeschierung [giving out Christmas presents] for the Spielschule [play school] and Dominium Kinder on Saturday. I thought so much of you both! There were over 20 children more than last year, but it all passed off very well indeed, and Baby was enchanted with the people and the Christmas tree. [Kreisau, 23.12.1907]

Sadly, their happiness was marred by a local tragedy.

The whole neighbourhood has been much agitated this week by the death of the Webskys (our neighbours) "Jäger" [gamekeeper] who was shot by poachers last week at the very spot where you and I once were, having lost our way, do you remember? by the wier in Schwengfeld? [Kreisau, 23.12.1907]

Finally, Christmas Day arrived.

Christmas day dear Ones! . . . Baby was delighted with his present and during the singing and reading of the Gosple [*sic*.] talked loudly with us all, saying what seemed to be "Bravo" at the end! He had little silk stockings and white kid shoes on and short sleeves and looked *sweet*. [Kreisau, 23.12.1907]

The gifts bestowed on her and other family members were generous. These included Dresden china, a large fur, a Persian prayer rug, and four silver vegetable spoons. Dorothy concludes, ". . . I was as usual a very lucky and spoiled young woman."

1908

German politics and "the Polish Question"

Early in 1908 Dorothy wrote her father concerning his work in the criminal courts.

> The Crimminal [*sic*.] work especially must be very trying and depressing,—the constant reiteration of evil and evil motives and sordid details cannot tend to enliven one. But now you are away from it all and resting and enjoying life all the more I hope in comparison. [Kreisau,13.1.1908]

She was disheartened by the undemocratic way her adopted land suppressed the Social Democrats through open balloting.

> Sunday, the day we lunched with Onkel Fritz, was the day on which great demonstrations were made against the new ballot law for the Landtag. Onkel Fritz was very worried about it all and finds life as a [government] minister anything but a bed of roses. I must frankly say that I don't understand German politics. To see a great party of people, really composed of many good, able, thinking men, argue in favour of open balloting takes my liberal breath away. They say, of course, that the nation's too young, that if there is no control over the voters the social democrates [*sic*.] would swamp every Parliament, and that would mean ruin for the country; which is no doubt true. But surely something more radical must be done to undermine the power of the social democrates [*sic*.], simply sitting on them can't suffice in the long run, for the principal [*sic*.] is wrong, don't you think so? There must be some way of fighting against the S.D. with *liberal* weapons, which, being the best in their own armoury would turn against them. This constant denying of rights cannot work any permanent good.

[Kreisau,13.1.1908]

At that time the "Polish Question"—how to deal with the large Polish minority within German borders—was an issue hotly debated in Germany, particularly in their area of eastern Germany near the Polish border.

> The "Polenfrage" [Polish question] comes on again in the Herrenhaus on 20th and I am hoping to hear the debate. It is causing naturally a great deal of excitement, and Onkel Ludwig is disgusted with Helmuth for not being in favour of it! It is very interesting to see the awakening, slowly but very surely, of Helmuths own independent judgment. He has a most robust mind and takes an unconventional view of things (ultra-unconventional at any rate in comparison with most of the people he comes in contact with) and I am very glad of the opportunity which the Herrenhaus gives him of coming in contact with other points of view. [Kreisau, 9.2.1908]

Dorothy took an interest in the vital issues confronting her home country, too, especially relations between the South Africans of European descent and the other races.

> What a wrong attitude Natal (the government at least) seems to be taking up as regards the Natives.
>
> I am so glad that such an excellent compromise has been arrived at as regards the Asiatics in the Transvaal; it must have been a relief to everyone. [Kreisau, 9.2.1908]

In February, Dorothy and the Count were in Berlin, where her husband had rented an apartment and had begun taking patients for Christian Science treatment. While there, they enjoyed the city's rich musical offerings.

> Here we are in Berlin enjoying life very much and with the delightful prospect before us of hearing much music. On Sunday we went to a concert given by Scholander, a Swede, who sings to his own accompaniment on a sort of Swedish guitar. He copies in a sense the old troubardours [*sic.*] and stands quite alone in his branch of art; he sings mostly

Volkslieder [folksongs] from all countries and some of his French songs were delightful. [Berlin, 19.2.1908]

In one week they attended an opera—*Tiefland* by Eugen d'Albert[30]—Shakespeare's *As You Like It,* concerts by the famous Belgian violinist Eugène Ysaÿe[31] and renowned soprano Lilli Lehmann,[32] and an exhibition of English art.

For Dorothy, receiving letters, snapshots, and reading material from her parents (to whom she sometimes affectionately refers as "the old birds") helped to bridge the vast geographical distance between them.

> The snaps gave me quite special pleasure, it was so nice to see Uitkijk again and the dear little round fruit trees in the Schoongezicht picture. . . . You cannot think what pleasure it gives me to receive some cutting or paper or book from the two old birds because it is a sign of comradeship in thoughts, a sign that when reading something that specially pleased them they have thought "That will please the daughter too". Which it assuredly does. [Berlin, 19.2.1908]

More news of the Polish situation follows, as well as the baby and his nanny, Fräulein Horn.

> The second reading of the Polish Expatriation Bill comes on on Wednesday 26th and Onkel Fritz is going to speak then. I have a ticket for that day and am looking forward very much to the debate. On Friday we brought the wee son to Saarau and saw him safely deposited there. . . . I really have a treasure in Fräulein Horn who is so absolutely trustworthy and so well educated and nice. . . . I do not know how long we shall remain here, probably until the 5th or 6th of March. We must of course be back for Babys birthday on the 11th. His first year of life in this world, dear little soul! [Berlin, 19.2.1908]

In a few weeks' time the family would be honoring the memory of the great Field Marshal.

> On 24th April, the anniversary of the death of the Feldmarschall, Onkel Helmuth is coming as usual from Berlin

34

with a wreath from the Kaiser, Onkel Ludwig will be here too and in fact it will be a sort of family festivity, Tante Louise[33] however being absent in Holstein where she is visiting the friends and places of her childhood. [Kreisau, 7.4.1908]

Apropos an article her parents had sent to her, Dorothy ponders the pros and cons of socialism.

> Thank you very much for "The Cape" with the Impression of Keir Hardie.[34] I wonder if there would be more freedom and less misery were the ideals of the socialists to be accepted. Somehow the example of Australia, in which the labour party have the power, is not encouraging and I cannot believe that, until human nature has changed and improved, the ideals are very practicable. Talking of reforms, Ellen Key[35] has been lecturing in Berlin before crowded houses and advocating a years compulsory service for girls when they are to learn cooking, housekeeping, parental duties, caring for the sick, etc—not a bad idea is it? [Kreisau, 7.4.1908]

The new flat in Berlin—to which Dorothy and Helmuth planned to "migrate . . . immediately after Christmas!"—was to her liking despite its modest size.

> It is very tiny, consisting of a large room for the boy, a small drawing room, a wee sitting room for the Y. T., as large as Mothers writing room at Bryntirion [in South Africa], a dining room, small bedroom for us, bathroom and kitchen. [Kreisau, 19.4.1908]

She kept well-informed by reading quality newspapers. "I am very pleased with the Westminster and now that we also take Der Tag an excellent Berlin daily paper I feel very well provided for as far as news is concerned. [Kreisau, 7.4.1908]

And she was reading Ibsen's[36] *Rosmersholm* with great interest.

> That *is* dramatic! . . . It took my breath away. Even though I think the end is morbid and unreal, still, it gave me more pleasure than the *reading* of any drama has yet done. [Kreisau,

28.4.1908]

Helmuth's Onkel Helmuth arrived in Kreisau for the
Todestag.

> Friday as you know was the Todestag [death day] of the
> Feldmarschall and Onkel Helmuth arrived in his friend, Dr.
> Öchelshäuser's motor, an hour late for lunch, it need hardly be
> added, for something always does go wrong with a motor when
> one is particularly anxious to arrive somewhere. [Kreisau,
> 28.4.1908]

In response to a request by her parents to assist a young
South African friend intending to study in Germany, Dorothy
offers her views on German higher education.

> Coligny Marchand I remember as a delicate little boy whom
> we looked upon as "effeminate" (at the age of 7!) because he
> played with dolls. I doubt whether I can help him in any way,
> and as one has not the least idea how he has grown up I hardly
> like to risk asking him down here to stay with us, but of course
> it was quite right of Dad to do what he did. Though why he is
> coming to a German University I cannot imagine. It is not
> necessary to work at all there, and the only things you are quite
> sure of learning are to drink enormous quantities of beer, and
> in fencing to have your face slashed without blinking your eyes
> and other such inanities. I suppose people can and do work in
> these illustrious institutions, but I have never heard of them. A
> German Rhodes scholarship boy has just come back to these
> parts and Onkel Ludwig is charmed with what Oxford has done
> for him. [Kreisau, 28.4.1908]

Springtime in Kreisau

The family drove about fifty miles northeast of Kreisau to
Oels, where they attended a funeral, stopping in Breslau on
the way back. The beautiful spring weather of May in
Kreisau made Countess von Moltke almost deliriously happy.

> Oh dearest Mother, the loveliness of Spring! It has all come
> suddenly, the cherry trees are laden with blossoms, the trees

are all, or nearly all a delicate green, and altogether the world is very beautiful. I so often wish that you and Dad were here to enjoy it with us, for it really is an exhilarating time, and one cannot but be happy; when, added to that one has a husband who is *very* satisfactory and very good to one, and a baby who beggars all description, well, happy does not in the least describe what one then is! . . . On our arrival home yesterday at half past six we were so enraptured by the weather that we went driving about until almost 8 o'clock, and then immediately after supper we went for a walk in the moonlight, listening to the birds singing their evening hymns, but hearing alas, no nightingales. [Kreisau, 12.5.1908]

At this time of year, Dorothy enjoyed long rides with her husband over the fields of the estate.

We have been for a long ride this morning already, visiting all the fields were [*sic*.] work was being done. I generally ride a black mare bred in Kreisau from a half bred mother and thorough bred father. . . . She is 10 years old already but has beautiful paces and jumps very well indeed. Helmuth rides Diana whom you knew and who has quite recovered from her accident. . . .[37] We are enjoying fresh vegetables once more, and almost live on asparagus, colrabi, spinach and carrots, for in the Spring we eat very little meat, the vegetables being such a treat and so much nicer. [Kreisau, 12.5.1908]

Her letter ends on a note of sympathy for her father, who had been serving since 1902 as the chief justice of the Transvaal Supreme Court, based in Pretoria.

How relieved the dear Dad must be to be at home once more after his ceaseless journeyings to and fro! But it must have been interesting for him and the tiredness and discomforts one soon forgets, while the pleasant things remain with one. [Kreisau, 12.5.1908]

Two years later, in 1910, Rose Innes was appointed to the Court of Appeals for the newly formed Union of South Africa and relocated to Cape Town.

Historical treasures

One day, the Countess discovered a bit of history in a table drawer.

> A few days ago we sent a writing table, which had belonged to the Feldmarschalls wife, to Schweidnitz to be repolished, as it had stood for a very long time unused in the loft; and in a drawer we discovered a charming miniature, probably of one of the Feldmarschalls brothers, and also six little pencil sketches, one done by the Feldmarschall himself, the others obviously by some better artist. Also an English New Testament belonging to Marie Burt[38] and what was probably her "Brautkranz" [bridal wreath]! There were also a number of newspaper cuttings about the time when Germany annexed Schleswig Holstein, and excitement evidently ran very high, but nevertheless it all sounds very tame when read so many years after, and one felt how history repeats itself, how today, as then, gloomy prophesies are made that the country is going to pieces, and yet nothing of the sort happened or is likely to happen! [Kreisau, 15.5.1908]

Dorothy thanks her parents for sending a paper containing her father's speech and fills them in on her reading.

> Even hashed up as it is by the reporters, it is inspiriting and splendid and so like the dear L.P.,[39] so I can imagine what a fine "few words" it must have been, . . . I hope to read Queen Victoria's Letters in the winter, which everyone tells me are so interesting, for the present I am working furiously at Carlyles Friedrich; . . .[40] [Kreisau, 23.6.1908]

There were more delightful rides on horseback, tennis, and dinner with the Pastor.

> Then yesterday Monika the Y. T. and I went riding immediately after breakfast and did not return until twelve o'clock, having had a glorious ride in the Ludwigsdorf Forst [sic.], sometimes riding straight through the bushes, at others, following a grass grown path, and at one place we had to lead our horses, so slippery was the way. There is hardly anything I

enjoy so much as a ride in the woods among the hills, the beauty and stillness are so invigorating. In the afternoon we as usual played tennis, and the Pastor and his wife came to supper. They are such nice people and you will be glad to hear have quite lost their shyness. [Kreisau, 6.7.1908]

Landowners though they were, the Moltkes had to be careful about money, and Dorothy's parents regularly helped them out financially.

Thank you very much for the Draft, dear Daddy; I have managed rather better this half year and have in consequence saved about £10.[41] Then from 1st June Helmuth has of his own accord given me £10 a month for my daily expenses when I am not with him etc. As however I can get on quite well without it, I mean to put it all in the savings bank, so as to have a fund in hand for emergencies. [Kreisau, 6.7.1908]

Helmuth James was charming not only the whole family but also the Kreisau villagers.

The wonderful boy is blooming and so sweet! He walks quite nicely now when two people hold his hands, and his joy and pride at his feat is really charming to see. Fräulein Horn affirms that on Sunday he saw her bible [sic.] lying on the table and said quite distinctly "Jesus, Lutherle"! ("Le" as you know is a diminutive, used often as a term of affection!) . . . He is loved by the whole village and the children often offer him sweets and give him little pictures, which demands a good deal of self sacrifice on their part. [Kreisau, 6.7.1908]

A day in the life

A typical well-ordered and well-filled day is summed up in this July letter.

Let me give you a résumé of my day just to show you that though I can in no way complain of hard work, I have a very well occupied day. Before breakfast I sewed a little, afterwards played with my son, visited Muttel etc until 10 o'clock, then came my household inspection, flowers etc. At 11 a.m. I sat down to my daily translation which I always do for Helmuth (a piece of Christian Science work) which was finished at noon, when I had an hours music lesson. At one o'clock lunch, then came a woman with laces etc for sale which we inspected, then we played our favourite card game of "Schweinehund", then Leno read aloud to us, Ernsts "Appelschnut" a delightful childrens book, while I sewed. By this time the Boy's play hour had arrived, after which we had tea and immediately afterwards Leno, Helmuth and I drove to Ludwigsdorf and leaving the carriage, walked home. It was delicious walking today, cool and fresh, making one feel very energetic. On arriving home I dressed as quickly as possible and managed to practice half an hour before supper. Afterwards I practiced half an hour more, and here I now am writing to my dear Ones far away and recounting to them a happy and uneventful day, one such as there are many of, happy in every way, uneventful, let us hope, only as regards outward incident. [Kreisau, 21.7.1908]

Guests at the *Schloss* were never lacking.

We are a party of 10 now, at table that is to say, where the two boys [Helmuth James and the Count's much younger brother, Carl Viggo] and the two "Fräuleins" are included. Soon however Fräulein Schorcht [Dorothy's piano teacher] is coming, then at the beginning of August a Fräulein Mullendorff, a C. S. [Christian Scientist] in Breslau is coming to us for a few days, probably Adam Moltke too, Peter [Helmuth's younger brother] is also sure to appear sometime during the next month, then Aunt Annie, and towards the end of August we hope to see Tante Katze [Katze Leonardi, Helmuth's aunt] here, also Ete [Margarethe, Helmuth's sister] with her son. Next week she is coming for a few days but alone. So you see our summer will be a fairly full one, especially for me with my music, for I hope to be very industrious and not to lose any advantage which Frau [*sic*.] Schorchts presence here gives me.

On Saturday a few people are coming to dinner, but otherwise this week is quite uneventful from a social point of view.

[Kreisau, 21.7.1908]

Dorothy describes her sixteen-month-old son's attempts to "read" her parents' letters.

> I wish you could have seen the wee son reading your letters on Monday! I had him sitting by my side on the sofa where I had been reading your letters. Carefully he drew it out of its envelope, spread out a sheet before him and then in a loud and solomn [*sic*.] voice began to read them aloud. When he thought that he had finished with one sheet, he turned to another, and so on till both your letters had been perrused [*sic*.]! [Kreisau, 21.7.1908]

Jan Smuts

Dorothy's father was a personal friend of the illustrious South African leader Jan Smuts (1870–1950).[42] Smuts was a statesman, a military leader, and a philosopher. As Prime Minister of the Union of South Africa (1919–1924 and 1939–1948), Smuts, like Dorothy's father, was a strong opponent of apartheid. Two years before the formation of the Union of South Africa in 1910, Dorothy comments on one of his speeches.

> Thank you very much for the Review of Reviews— . . . [43] Smuts' speech on Closer Union was *splendid*, how I wish that I could have heard him! But I feel proud that it came from a South African and that it was delivered in South Africa. [Kreisau, 21.7.1908]

In August Helmuth was contemplating a trip to England for "a month or two towards the end of the year, in order to study English really thoroughly, and also to see something of the Christian Science work there"—providing a good excuse for the Count to avoid the Junker pastime of shooting game.

> I should be glad for him to learn English well and it would fit in excellently during the time I was in Paris with Mother; also in October, when the shooting begins; for he has given the sport up and being here in this mad-on-shooting land will be a

little difficult then for him, for it is here a matter of the greatest comment and astonishment when one Junker does not do as all the others do. There is no doubt about it, Helmuth is extremely original and individual, he is a "Sonderling", a perfectly wholesome and good one, but you may imagine what an astonishment he is in his class, where individuality is not very often to be found. [Kreisau, 2.8.1908]

Before closing, the Countess mentions the impending flight of an early Zeppelin.

We and the Fatherland are at present very excited about Graf Zepplins [sic.] airship.[44] What a difference it will make, once the air is navigable. [Keisau, 2.8.1908]

The Countess also mentions the family's pastime of reading a play together.

Last week we read Lessings "Nathan der Weise" aloud with divided parts. It was very nice and we enjoyed it immensely. We hope to read another play in the same way this week, Goethe or Schiller I expect, as Helmuth won't hear of anything that is not a classic! [Kreisau, 2.8.1908]

Trip to Bankau

In mid-August the family paid a visit to the country estate of Muttel's family, the Bethusy-Hucs, in Bankau, in Upper Silesia.

We arrived here yesterday to find the house as full as it can be, together with children, governesses and tutors we are a party of 29! You may imagine the talking and fun that goes on. Tante Katze is of course here with her two children, Eddie a splendid boy with a quite exceptional gift for the violin and Madie [*Tante* Katze's daughter and Helmuth's cousin] smaller but very pretty, with her pla[i]ts coiled coiled [sic.] round her head in that becoming German fashion. . . .

This morning about 16 of us were driven in Onkel Heinrichs huge motor to a pond in the woods and there we bathed and swam. It was glorious, and as I had not bathed for years—the

42

last time was at Muizenberg[45]—I enjoyed it immensely. And how we laughed and screamed! We had a raft too, and altogether amuse ourselves splendidly. [Bankau, 11.8.1908]

Dorothy enjoyed a brief respite from her responsibilities at Kreisau. "It is *such* a delightful feeling to have simply nothing to do! Just to wander about, read, talk[,] walk when and as much as one cares to." [Bankau, 11.8.1908]

In October the Moltkes moved back into their apartment in Berlin ("the flat is sweet" [Berlin, 1.11.1908]). Six years before the outbreak of World War I, Dorothy was already apprehensive about relations between Germany and England, and particularly about the attitude of the Kaiser toward the British.

What did you think of the Kaisers reported conversation with an "Englishman of influence"? What I do not understand is, if he really was so friendly towards England, why did he send the telegram to Kruger?[46] [Berlin, 1.11.1908]

Visit to Paris

In December Countess von Moltke rendezvoused with her mother in Paris. Even in 1908, driving in Paris was perilous.

I wish you could see the motor traffic here! Why there hardly seem to be any horses at all, and everyone drives most wildly so that one always crosses a street with ones life in ones hands. [Paris, 12.11.1908]

Mother and daughter visited the Louvre and Luxembourg Gardens, saw an exhibition of watercolors at the Galerie Georges Petit, and went to the theater, where they saw Henri Bernstein's *Israel* ("a very powerful and well acted play dealing with the Jewish question"), *L'Émigré"* by de Meilhan,[47] and Wagner's *Tannhäuser* (she found opera in general to be "'insuportable [*sic*.]' as we say in La belle France.") [Paris, 19.11.1908] Meanwhile, Lady Rose Innes went on a shopping spree.

I wish you could see her at the Bon Marché—as enthusiastic

and pleased as a child, it really was charming to see. I had quite to act the part of a brake and restrain her enthusiasm from going too far!! She really has bought very pretty things and I know you will be very pleased not only at the youthful but at the "chic" appearance of your cara spouse. [Paris, 19.11.1908]

After their Parisian escapade, the Countess and her mother went to the Moltkes' flat in Berlin, where Dorothy introduced her mother to her year-and-a-half-old son.

Then comes Christmas and all its happinesses, and then in January we shall come over to London to you—so you see we have many pleasant things to look forward to this winter. . . . By the time you read this we shall really be almost near to one another. It is a lovely thought! [Berlin, 26.11.1908]

1909

After the visit with her parents in England, their time together inevitably drew to a close. Partings from her mother and father were always difficult for Countess von Moltke, and her parents' return to South Africa in early 1909 was no exception.

Here we are safely back in Berlin and the sweet Boy has arrived, looking oh so bonny, and I can hardly believe that it was only yesterday that I said goodbye to you dearest ones. It *was* hard, and as the train moved out of the station and I knew I had seen Daddys loving eyes for the last time for many months, I began to weep, and saying to the Y. T. "The paper quick" I began reading the Daily Telegraph as hard as I could to distract me, because it was no good thinking about it. Nor is it much good talking about it, Darlings, so I will tell you about our journey instead which was a very pleasant one. We sat up on deck the whole time in a sheltered corner, well wrapped up, and enjoyed the fresh air—I slept most of the time. The crossing was quite smooth, and we were not delayed at all. [Berlin, 3.2.1909]

The pain of separation from her parents was relieved only by her conviction that she was in her "right place" as the wife of Count von Moltke and the mother of one young son (she would eventually have four more children).

> It does seem so strange and sad that I should be living so far away from you and Mother and Africa, and yet—I *am* happy and I do feel that my work and place is here. [Berlin, 4.2.1909]

Helmuth James—to whom Dorothy often referred as "the Boy"—"wrote" a letter to his grandmother.

> The Boy is really delicious. Yesterday he had a pencil and paper and was "drawing" and having seen me some time before writing to "Grannie" he suddenly declared "Gannie write" and forthwith began to scribble to Mother! When asked what picture hung over his bed in Hannover he says "Christus" and then, as if imparting information, "Christus Gut [*sic*.], Gott auch gut"! [Christ is good, God also is good] [Berlin, 4.2.1909]

British royalty in Berlin

Soon after her parents' departure, Dorothy and her husband attended a large reception for King Edward VII and Queen Alexandra in Berlin.

> We found Berlin in pouring rain and for three days it continued, but yesterday and today have been glorious—very cold and a brilliant blue sky—and we are hoping that it will remain so for the festivities tomorrow when the King and Queen arrive. We shall be at the Ministerium and so ought to see very well indeed as the procession will pass up the Linden to the Schloss. Everything is quite charmingly decorated and tomorrow is to be a sort of public holiday, so great excitement prevails. [Berlin, 8.2.1909]

In spite of the festive atmosphere, the tensions between the United Kingdom and Germany were hard to ignore and are reflected in Countess von Moltke's description of the Berliners' cool reception of the British royals.

> We have just returned from greeting the King. We had very

45

good places at the Ministerium and altogether it was quite nice, though I always think that it is rather a case of tant de bruit— pour un moment [so much noise—for a moment], on these occasions, everything is so soon over. King Edward looked nice and cheerful and everyone was cordial and friendly, though one could not call the crowd "wildly enthusiastic", which was after all hardly to be expected. [Berlin, 8.2.1909]

While her husband was learning to speak English, Dorothy was learning to teach it.

This morning I am going to my series of lectures on the "Musikalische Romantiker" which ought to be very interesting and this evening I take my English class for the first time alone—a mighty task, for teaching is not easy and I have to follow Schultzchen[48] who has a really great gift for teaching. Helmuth had his first English lesson this afternoon; I hope his new teacher will be good. [Berlin, 8.2.1909]

On the occasion of her twenty-fifth birthday, the young mother was touched by her little son's birthday offering.

Baby came in to me this morning with a huge bunch of violets in his hand and with help now and then from Nana said in a low but worthy-of-the-occasion voice the following little verse. *Too* sweet it was!

"Mein kleines Herz, mein kleiner Mund,

Wünscht Dir viel Glück zu jeder Stund'.

Hab' ferner mich von Herzen lieb,

Ein Küsschen Deinem Kinde gieb."

[My little heart, my little mouth,

Wishes you much happiness at every hour.

And, furthermore,

It gives your child a little kiss.]

That I am thinking much of you both today, I need hardly say, darlings, need I? Your thoughts must be wandering back over

46

the 25 years to the day when the little baby came into your midst and brought with her (although she did not know it) a heart *full* of love for you both.

> Goodbye and God bless you
>
> Your
>
> Twenty-five-years-old Baby [Kreisau, 20.4.1909]

A letter written in late March, more than four years before the beginning of the First World War, shows that the danger of war was already present in people's minds. As a British woman living in Germany, Dorothy sees both sides of the question.

> Here we still are in uncertainty as to the outcome of the Balkan Crisis. Tante Katze writes that in Austria every preparation for war has been made; it is very trying living thus on the qui vive. The second great topic of conversation is the English naval programe [*sic*]. Here people think the English quite mad, though I must say I do see that it is a life question for the British Empire, but at the same time it is a good thing that the French do not get as excited every time the Germans make some improvement in their military arrangements! [Berlin, 24.3.1909]

She sees the impracticality of Germany's ambitions to expand its colonies.

> And what possible advantage could Germany gain by fighting England? Colonies, you say; but as she can't even manage to "colonize" Poland, Schleswig Holstein and A.-Lorraine with any conspicuous success, and her faraway possessions cost her a great deal, I am sure she has absolutely no desire to acquire Canada or South Africa whose inhabitants she knows would never consent to the change and would give her endless trouble, national and economical. [Berlin, 24.3.1909]

Count von Moltke's healing work

By this time the Count was spending one or two days a week

in Berlin, attending sessions at the *Herrenhaus*, and seeing his patients the rest of the time. Some especially good news Dorothy is able to report is her husband's successful healing work as a Christian Science practitioner—cures of several illnesses, including "an awful skin disease," asthma, and atrophy of the leg muscles in a young boy. [Berlin, 24.3.1909]

A particularly dramatic healing is recounted in *Helmuth James von Moltke: Geschichte einer Kindheit und Jugend*, by Jochen Köhler. The Moltkes' *Stellmachermeister* (master wheelwright), Herr Herford, had been experiencing servere kidney pains and went to the Count for help. His daughter, Ellie Herford, whose mother had been lady's maid to Countess von Moltke, told Köhler the story.

> "My father always had very bad kidney pains. Once, the pains were so bad, he jumped up almost all the way to the ceiling, then my mother, who worked in the Schloss, asked permission to speak about it to the Count."
>
> "What happened then?"
>
> "He came immediately."
>
> "And then?"
>
> "He went into the room where my father was lying, and we all had to get out. It didn't take long, then the Count came back out."
>
> "And? What happened?"
>
> "After that, my father never had any more trouble with his kidneys."
>
> "Did you hear any more about this event?"
>
> "Yes. In the coachman's quarters. It was over the horse stall. There they all sang."[49]

A letter Dorothy wrote to her father in May 1909 reveals how deeply committed she, too, was to this religion.

If it was merely a religion of healing what use would it be to me do you think? I always have been well and strong. But in Christian Science I have found a rational answer to all my questionings and I am only one among many thousands, I have found the most wonderful peace, the panacea for all fear, and the greatest incentive not only to pure and right living, but to pure and right thinking too. . . . I really am almost ashamed of this dissertation, and you must not please think that it is written in a "converting" or dogmatic spirit. As you know I don't talk much about these things, and it is only because you wrote about it and because I so appreciated your interest that I have written as I have done. . . . let me only add that it is *not* a new sect or religion, but simply the teachings of Jesus Christ. [Kreisau, 4.5.1909]

In her next letters, Dorothy writes on another subject of interest, the rights of women, as well as her ongoing concern about the military buildup in the United Kingdom and Germany.

It is extraordinary how public opinion is changing in regard to womans position; and especially in Germany I notice a great change for the better.

. . . I realize that it is absolutely necessary for England to "rule the waves", and it was not *that* which seemed hysterical to me; but all these phantoms of airships, troups [*sic*.] landing at night on the east coast etc, are not worthy of a great nation; it really is a mental illness on its part. . . . And yet there is no doubt that the situation is serious, for even if Germanys intentions are entirely peaceful (as I am convinced they are) still her navy presents a constant menace to England, for at any moment she may be dominated by more bellicose ideas. [Kreisau, 19.5.1909]

Kurz, Sembrich, and Culp

While in Berlin, Dorothy and the Count heard three of the most celebrated singers of the day: the Austrian soprano Selma Kurz[50] ("really magnificent, though without much personal charm") [Berlin, 10.3.1909]; the Polish coloratura Marcella Sembrich; and the Dutch mezzo-soprano Julia Culp.

Dorothy began teaching English to German students of Christian Science in Berlin who wanted to be able to read *Science and Health with Key to the Scriptures* by Mary Baker Eddy, which had not yet been translated into German. She gave regular lessons to people from all walks of life, including electricians, seamstresses, and policemen.

> My English class grows continually, and I have 12 pupils though all do not come quite regularly, being prevented often by their work. They are all getting on *so* nicely, and it is really touching to see the trouble they take and the pleasure it gives them to learn English. They have just learnt a little verse by heart and are so proud and pleased! [Berlin, 10.3.1909]

> Countess von Moltke gives a charming account of her two-year-old son's attempt to pay his respects to a queen at a park in Berlin.

> Yesterday it being Königin [Queen] Louise's birthday, and Klein [little] Helmuth being a frequent visitor to her statue in the Tiergarten, the wee son went off with a bunch of violets to lay on the pedistale [*sic*.]. He was charmed with the idea and felt very important. Alas however, everything was most beautifully decorated, and as is so often the case in the Vaterland, policemen abounded and no one was allowed to approach quite near. So he came home very disappointed, still carrying his violets. [Berlin, 10.3.1909]

She notes that her son is ". . . beginning to understand and talk English now, but he always looks upon the language of his Mama as a huge joke." She also observes the emergence of a strong character.

> The son grows in many ways more like his Father every day— that is to say he has the same sturdiness, fearlessness, energy and masterfulness, but I have no fear for his upbringing, though there are many battles to be fought with him, for he is *very* affectionate and loving, not at all obstinate and very

50

susceptible to logical reasoning. [Kreisau, 22.8.1909]

Helmuth James's emerging spirituality

One December evening, Countess von Moltke was pleasantly surprised when the English nanny, Miss Chalmers, who was a Christian Scientist, overheard her young charge trying to recite a prayer written by Mary Baker Eddy for little children.

> Miss Chalmers and I had several times repeated a little prayer to him but he had never seemed to take the least notice of our recitals. Yesterday after supper Miss Chalmers went into the nursery and found him trying to say this prayer to himself
>
> Father-Mother God, loving me,
>
>> Guard me when I sleep
>> Guide my little feet
>> Up to Thee.[51]
>
> He could only remember a few of the words but said it after Miss Chalmers and at the end quite of his own accord he said "Ganz bis oben" [Way up high] and then "dass [sic.] muss ich immer sagen wenn es ganz dunkel ist. *Ganz* leise muss ich es sagen." [I must always say that when it's very dark. I must say it very softly.] [Berlin, 6.12.1909]

Dorothy was touched by the child's natural desire to pray, without any pressure from Miss Chalmers or herself.

> Isn't that sweet for no one had ever told him a word about praying, it simply came naturally to him and is to me another proof that each human being has or had in the depths of his heart a longing for some sort of spiritual life. [Berlin, 6.12.1909]

Another of Dorothy's letters at this time testifies to the sweetness of Helmuth James's character, and of the close bond between mother and son.

> Today I had to scold the Boy rather severely, and after listening seriously to what I said he began playing with his toys, but after a few moments he turned to me and said "Does

Mami love das Kind [the child] now?" "Yes I replied, Mami always loves the child, only when he is naughty it makes her sad." "The child loves Mami very much too" he then said, was that not sweet? [12.9.1909]

At the age of two, Helmuth James was already winning the hearts of the people of Kreisau.

The Boys decided views on everything is a constant amusement to everyone. . . . When "Papi" [Count von Moltke] returns from his early morning ride, he is allowed to ride too, and it is a pretty sight to see the two Helmuths perched up on Diana, who, conscious of the little mite sitting almost on her neck, walks with great dignity round the house. The Boy has a kind and loving heart, and gives freely, from cake to pats. . . . He is the greatest joy in the world to us both, and in fact to the whole of Creisau. It is really quite touching to see the pride and devotion of all the farm people to him. He knows most of them by name and calls out loudly to his different acquaintances when he sees them "Maier", or "Rüster" etc as the case may be. [Kreisau, 1.6.1909]

Similar passages depicting rides in the Silesian countryside display Dorothy's gift for description.

It is a most lovely Spring morning and I have been revelling in the sunshine and budding life all around me. Even before breakfast the Y. T. Klein [little] Helmuth and I went driving over the fields, and I do not know which of us enjoyed it most; certainly it was very delicious, with skylarks bubbling over with song everywhere and a faint green shimmer showing on all sides. [Kreisau, 20.4.1909]

Countess von Moltke made sure the small child knew of the accomplishments of the great Field Marshal whose name he bore.

The other day we went into the Feld Marschalls room to look at the barometer and he suddenly said to me "Mami, wie heisst das Zimmer" [Mummy, what is this room called?] "Opapas Zimmer" [Great-grandfather's room] I replied "Wo ist denn der Opapa?" [Where is Great-grandfather?] was the next question. Then I told him a little about the Feld Marschall, that he was a great man and a great soldier and that was why people, anxious to remember him always, had put up a great "picture" to him in Berlin[52]. All this interested the little fellow immensely, but he did not think that I was honouring his "Papi" enough, so in the middle he broke in with "Papi ist *auch* Soldat und *auch* gross" [Papa is also a soldier and also great] quite sure that his beloved Papi was as great as any "Opapa" could ever be! [Keisau, 29.6.1909]

That summer, the boy took an interest in a much earlier hero from the Bible stories his mother was reading to him.

His mind is extraordinarily active and he takes a really burning interest in all he sees and hears, forming too an independent opinion about most things for himself.... He loves being told stories, and when I told him about Daniel and the lions the other day he was intensely interested and of course ended up by saying "noch mal" [again]. [Kreisau, 10.8.1909]

Birthday parties, which are very important in German culture, were frequent events in the Moltke family. Present at the one for *Tante* Luise was a Herr Listermans, "Helmuths terribly-expensive-but-ever-so-excellent singing master," [Kreisau, 15.6.1909] who would remain at Kreisau to give the Count singing lessons for the month of July—and who had known two of the greatest geniuses in music.

How often do I wish that you were both here to enjoy the music in which we are revelling just now. . . . As Listermans knew and worked much with Grieg and Brahms, he is able to tell us many interesting little things about both these great men, and altogether I am enjoying having him here, especially as he is a guest who is never in the way and never a bother. [Kreisau, 13.7.1909]

In one of her letters, Dorothy refers to a German preacher who was in China at the time of the Boxer Uprising, when, in the summer of 1900, a Chinese secret society known as the

Boxers, fiercely angry with the presence of the European powers and missionaries in China, attacked the European and American legations in Beijing, killing thousands of people, most of whom were Chinese, including some Chinese Christians.

> Our missionary festival on Sunday was really not bad at all. The "Prediger" [preacher] had been 25 [years] in China, and told us much of the horrors of the Boxer risings and the heroism of the christianised Chinamen. It was like a chapter from the history of the early Christians and martyrs. [Kreisau, 15.6.1909]

At the end of her letter, Dorothy mentions an important historic step toward the formation of the Union of South Africa, which came about one year later.

> I forgot to say how glad I am that Natal has accepted Union, & with such a big majority. [Kreisau, 15.6.1909]

A few months later she writes of being ". . . very impressed by the enormous step forwards that South Africa has taken in the last few years; it is really wonderful." Her next paragraph describes watching with her husband the military maneuvers of an army that in a few years would be at war with her homeland.

> We saw everything beautifully and in fact were in the middle of a cavellry [*sic*.] charge, but it eventually was so late that we turned in at Stephanshain for lunch at 2 o'clock, . . . The Boy was of course enchanted at the whole thing and kept asking if the Kaiser was not there. For a short time he even watched the manoevres on horseback, sitting proudly on Diana in front of his father. [Kreisau, 12. 9.1909]

Birth of second son

In September 1909 the Moltkes rejoiced in the arrival of their second son, Johann Wolfgang ("Jowo"), and in his harmonious delivery under the care of a Christian Science midwife and a Christian Science practitioner. The practitioner was Ulla Schultz (later Oldenbourg), who was not only Dorothy's practitioner but also a very close friend of the entire family, including the children, and a frequent guest of the Moltkes at Kreisau.

Toward the end of 1909, Dorothy expressed the satisfaction she was finding in her work as a teacher of English (". . . they began a year ago and did not know one word of English. Now they can read Science and Health quite decently, just looking up the most difficult words.") [Kreisau, 12.12.1909] as well as her deep sense of fulfillment.

> I feel so strongly that I am in my right place, doing my right work, and it is this feeling that gives me such supreme contentment. Do you understand dear ones? Of course apart from all this I am very happy anyhow, but it is this feeling of being in my right place and doing the work which it is mine to do that prevents me from having regrets or even moments of depression and homesickness, that, and my religion. [Kreisau, 12.12.1909]

1910

Making their *Knicks* [curtsies] to *Seine Majestät*, the Kaiser

In the winter of 1910, Count and Countess von Moltke were presented at court—an imperative for people in their social position. In January they attended the court ball hosted by the Kaiser in Berlin, also the many dinner parties and smaller balls of the court season. There the Moltkes were presented to the Kaiser and Kaiserin, and met royals from other countries as well.

> Prince Oskar—one of the Kaisers Sons—and the young Crown Prince of Greece were there. And after I had been engaged for the Cotillion and had danced about 10 minutes, I discovered that my partner was the latter! I attempted one sentence in the 3rd person and then boldly asked him to talk English which of

course he speaks perfectly. After that we got on much better. But it was rather a bomb shell when I discovered who he was, for I thought him just a very young officer—which he is—and was not exerting myself overmuch in the matter of conversation. I was taken in to supper by a young attaché who had been a Rhodes Scholar at Oxford and loved England, as indeed all those who have been there seem to do. [Berlin, 9.1.1910]

Helmuth had to strike a balance between these worldly duties and his Christian Science practice in Berlin.

Helmuth has a good many patients and that makes it rather difficult for him when going out so much as we are at present. But it won't last so very long and we shall then have done it once and made our knix [*sic*][curtsies] to S. M. [Seine Majestät—His Majesty] and the world in general. [Berlin, 9.1.1910]

Dorothy describes this time with characteristic humor and a sense of perspective.

I wanted to know how to address royalties in English as they *may* talk to me in that language (the Erbprincess [sister of the emperor] did) and anyway the 3rd person, which is the German custom, is so complicated that I am sure to come a cropper if I attempt it! [Kreisau, 1.1.1910]

She observed many royals close at hand, some of whom did not make a good impression.

Tomorrow is Tanz Probe [dance rehearsal] at Tante Julie's, as it was on Tuesday, when both the Eitel Fritzes were there and the August Wilhelms. Princess Eitel Fritz is very good looking, but is bad mannered, arrogant and very unpopular. The little Princess August Wilhelm seems sweet and her husband is said to be the cleverest of the lot. . . . It is interesting to see once, but it is necessarily very superficial and the outward things play a very large part in the whole, and it is not a bit my life or the things that I care for. . . . My court dress, that is *your* dress, is an Irish lace tunic over gold, the lower part being heavy

56

white chiffon over the same gold underskirt; the lace is finished off at the knees with brown fur. The train is soft salmon-coloured velvet with a broad edge of brown fur all round and a few big roses in the same shade at the bottom. It really looks very lovely. . . . The tiara is really magnificent, and it makes me feel quite queer to think that I am to wear anything so regal. We never dreamed that anything so lovely could be made from the stones in the orders.[53] But enough of these most worldly matters! [Berlin, 16.1.1910]

In late January, the Moltkes attended an elegant evening at *Schloss* Bellevue, an opulent candlelit ball at which the Kaiser and Kaiserin were present.

Schloss Bellvue [*sic*.] lies buried in the Tier Garten [a large park in Berlin] and is very old. Most beautifully furnished is it too, and everything looks so lived in and used and individual. The whole palace is lit by candle light, with here and there an oil lamp and the light is wonderfully soft and pretty. The ball room is oval and white with some marble pillars of a beautiful greeny blue colour. There were about 100 to 150 present, and among other [*sic*.] the Kaiser and the Kaiserin, The Crown Princess of Roumania—a famous beauty—Prince and Princess August Wilhelm, two of the unmarried princess [*sic*.] and the little princess who is going out for the first time. Then Princess Friedrich Leopold with her daughter, the Crown Prince of Greece, and a number of smaller royalties as well. Princess Pless was also there, but I was disappointed in her looks. I was presented to the Kaiserin who spoke a few words in English to me and I also shook hands with the Kaiser, but I don't think he knew who I was. At supper I sat at the table next to his and so had a good opportunity of seeing him. He is a fine looking man with a black moustache, iron grey hair and such "alive" eyes. The Kaiserin has beautiful white hair and looks sweet, friendly and rather stupid. English seems to be the international speech, the Crown Princess of Roumania, the Crown Prince of Greece speak almost always in that language and one heard it all round one, the daughters of the Italian Ambassador spoke it too, and quite a number of others; it is evidently "chic"! . . . We eat off silver plates, and altogether it was a very interesting experience. I wore my green Boulmier christening dress and I hope did the authors of my being justice! [Berlin, 30.1.1910]

Diamonds glittered, and gowns and uniforms and pages dressed in red swirled in a mass of brilliant color.

The royal ball last night was a wonderful sight, but so tiring, for one stood nearly all the time, and there was so much to look at. The jewels were wonderful. One woman had real diamonds sewn on her dress, right down the sides of the skirt and many had the front of their bodices entirely decorated with precious stones. And then the uniforms, Chinese, Japanese and Turkish as well as all the European representatives, and the dozens of pages in red with front and sleeve ruffles who lined the walls. Indeed it was almost blinding in its gorgeousness and colour and from the gallery above the Saal [ballroom] looked like an exquisite Persian carpet. [Berlin, 30.1.1910]

By this time, however, Dorothy was beginning to feel a little overwhelmed by the endless parties.

. . . this afternoon I am going to Cécile Lauru's Causerie[54] on the Femmes illustrées [illustrious women] and this evening we are asked to a dinner Mrs. Merrill is giving at the Hotel Bristol. Tomorrow we have a lunch party, some people to tea in the afternoon, and my English class in the evening. As a matter of fact it is really too much dissipation and I do not enjoy it as I should if there was just half as much, for one has absolutely no leisure. But it is a good thing to have done it once. [Berlin, 30.1.1910]

A subplot to the Moltkes' participation in the court season concerned Helmuth's younger sister Monika. Prior to one of the balls, Dorothy's mother-in-law had warned her about the parsimony of the rich.

On Saturday Monika is going with the Eitel Fritz's [sic.] to a ball near Kiel to which the Kaiserin and nearly all the royal family are going. It will be a very nice and amusing experience for her. Muttel writes to tell her to take plenty of money with her for "Prinzen bezahlen selten für ihre Gäste"! [Princes seldom pay for their guests!] As Monika must travel 1st Class this is rather hard on her! Anyhow we hope for the best. [Berlin, 15.2.1910]

As it happened, Monika fell in love with the Kaiser's son, Prince Oskar. Dorothy laments this doomed attachment and describes the ball.

It really was a great success, especially as, it being about the last dance of the season, everyone danced with much spirit. The cotillion was charming, nothing but yellow and white tulips and narcissus, & daffodils, yellow roses and white lilac (yellow and white are the Silesian colours.) The supper was excellent. Clear oxtail soup in cups, turbot with champignons [mushrooms], turnedeaux [sic.] aux artichocks [sic.] with green beans + potatoes, cold turkey (cold roasts are very much the fashion this winter) and salads, Pêches à la Melba and cheese straws. All the princes were ill with different things except Prince Oskar who of course was there. I say "of course" because, unfortunately, Monika and he are much too fond of one another. It is a great pity, because nothing can possibly come of it, but it makes it very difficult for her to leave Berlin and take up her old life again when all her thoughts are here. [Berlin, 27.2.1910]

Sadly, this fairy tale romance came to an inevitable end.

Monika left early this morning; poor dear it was rather a wrench for her, but she has had a glorious time and played a leading part in social things, for she is a first class dancer and rider besides being a charming girl. [Berlin, 27.2.1910]

Amidst the whirl of dinners and balls, the Moltkes attended two operas, thanks to the Count's persistence.

On Sunday evening we went to the Opera and heard Humperdincks new work "Die Königskinder" [The King's Children]. He wrote Hänsel und Gretel you know, and this new opera, after years of silence, is creating a great sensation. It is simply charming and I hardly ever remember having spent a more delightful evening. On the next evening we were there again, this time to hear Mozarts "Zauberflöte" which has been "neu einstudiert" [given a new production] with marvelous scenic effects, I think to please the Kaiser who loves all such shows. I find them rather dull, and they do not in any way add to the art of the whole; but the singing was very good and the music very delightful, though too much drawn out. These are the two musical "events" of this winter, and we were considered extremely lucky to get seats at all, as everything is sold out days before the performance. Indeed only through the Y. T.s persistency did we do so, he standing for more than half an hour before the ticket office opened to procure the last two tickets in the whole opera house! [Berlin, 21.2.1910]

"Yesterday I saw God and the angels"

Helmuth James, now almost three, continued to astonish his mother with his spiritual insights. "The spiritual side of him is developing so beautifully, it is sometimes quite overwhelming," she wrote in late January, "and yet he is very manly and really quite wild, with a marked sense of humour (such an invaluable gift!).

> The other day he said to me, looking terribly serious "Wenn das Kind unartig ist, dann sind Keine Engeln da, Kein Gott, Kein Weihnachtsmann, dann ist das Kind ganz allein." [When the Boy is naughty, then no angels are there, no God, no Father Christmas, then the Boy is all alone.] The spiritual side of him is developing so beautifully, it is sometimes quite overwhelming; and yet he is very manly and really quite wild, with a marked sense of humour (such an invaluable gift!) [Berlin, 30.1.1910]

The following summer, the three-year-old boy spoke to her of God and angels.

> The other evening I had said goodnight [sic.] to little Helmuth and was just saying a few words to Miss Chalmers, when the Boy called me back and asked "Warum ist Gott immer bei

mir?" [Why is God always with me?] I told him because he was Gods child and God loved him and protected him. "Gestern habe ich Gott und die Engel und der Mond und Sterne gesehen im Himmel" [Yesterday I saw God and the angels and the moon and the stars in Heaven.] . . . . On my inquiring which he liked best, he replied "alles [*sic*.] im Himmel ist sehr schön." [Everything in Heaven is very beautiful.] [Kreisau, 27.6.1910]

"It is so delightful to see how a childs mind opens and develops," his mother commented [Kreisau, 27.6.1910]. Weeks later Dorothy observed Helmuth James praying for his younger brother, Jowo.

After I have prayed with little Helmuth he likes me to go over to Bruders [Brother's] bed and then we "pray for Bruder" that is to say we repeat the same little verse. It is touching to see the unconscious baby sleeping peacefully while his 3 year old brother says his prayer for him. [Kreisau, 26.7.1910]

The boy was already acquiring gracious manners.

Yesterday the three little Belknap girls came to tea with him, aged 7, 5 and 3. They live just below us and are very nice indeed. He was delighted at having them and made a dear little host, handing them cakes with a serious face and "Hier hast du, Mädel." [This is for you, little girl.] They spent most of their time swinging on the rings which was part of your Christmas present to him. [Berlin, 15.2.1910]

Jowo

The younger son, Jowo, too, impressed everyone with his good behavior and sunny disposition.

He is *such* a merry laughing little fellow and is always trying to talk or sing. He knows me quite well and always welcomes me with a broad grin and a war whoop. . . . Jo-Wo is growing very pretty, and though I thought little Helmuth much more beautiful at the same age, many people (who do not flatter!) say that he is the prettiest baby they have ever seen. He certainly is the best behaved in every way. . . . Little darling!

[Berlin, 27.3.1910]

Although Dorothy was not perturbed by them, demonstrations in her adopted country were striking fear into the hearts of many Germans.

I am glad to notice that the Germans have a silly bogy that makes them jump quite as much as the English. Where the word "German invasion" sends a shiver down every true Britons back, the words "Social Democrats" and "Revolution" have the same effect on their cousins in the Fatherland. Last Sunday there were great demonstrations to protest against the new Reform Bill and everywhere people spoke as if something equal to the French Revolution was about to happen! Whereas it was all really rather harmless; in one place the police drew blank revolvers just to keep the crowd from pressing too much, but otherwise it was all as orderly as any demonstration in London. I wanted very much to hear the speeches in the Abgeordneten Haus[55] on this new Bill, but it was quite impossible to get tickets. [Berlin, 15.2.1910]

The Count's two worlds

Count von Moltke was now dividing his time between running the estate in Kreisau and maintaining his Christian Science practice in Berlin.

Helmuth has a great deal to do for he has about 15 patients and that takes up a great deal of time. I have three English classes now, so you see we are neither of us very idle. . . . Helmuth (the big one) is . . . altogether much with the children, which is good for them and him. [Berlin, 15.2.1910]

He was also using his beautiful baritone voice as a church soloist.

Helmuth is singing a good deal just now and learning a lot of new things and we are just starting playing duets for piano and harmonium together! . . . As Helmuth has about 20 patients you may imagine what a lot he has to do. [Berlin, 27.2.1910]

In mid-March, the Count suddenly boarded a ship in

Liverpool and sailed to Boston. For the last three years, on behalf of thousands of German students of Christian Science, he had been urging Mary Baker Eddy to allow her great work, *Science and Health with Key to the Scriptures*, to be translated into German. Because she wanted to make sure that the textbook would be translated by expert translators who also had an understanding of Christian Science, Eddy had waited for several years before granting permission for its translation into any foreign languages. Now the Count felt spiritually impelled to go to Boston to urge Eddy to authorize a German translation.

The trip was successful. Although Moltke was not able to obtain a personal interview with the leader of the Christian Science Church, it was during his visit, on March 31, that Eddy finally gave her approval for a German translation of *Science and Health*.

This was an historic moment for the Church of Christ, Scientist, signalling the initiation not only of the German translation but of translations of the text into many other languages. The following year, Helmuth and Dorothy would give seven months of their lives to this important work. (The translation work is discussed in detail in Part II.)

Sir James's autobiography

Throughout her life, Countess von Moltke was interested in her father's career, often expressing her desire that he write his autobiography.

> All that Daddy told me about his political fights with Rhodes, Sauer[56] etc interested me intensely. It must need great courage to stand quite alone. I wish Daddy would write a mémoir of his public life, even if only for me, for so much of it took place when I was too small to understand and I should so love to know something about the inner workings of those exciting days. Perhaps when he retires? He must think about it. [Hannover, 10.4.1910]

Sir James, of course, did eventually write his *Autobiography,* which was published in 1949.

In May, the Count's liberal political views caused a stir among his reactionary peers in the *Herrenhaus*.

> When he was at the Herrenhaus last week he listened to the debates but abstained from voting as he felt he could not honestly do so. In every way he has rather an isolated and difficult position here, for he is in many ways so different to the men of his class and no one is used to surprises of that sort in this country. . . . And the Y. T. is developing very liberal opinions which make him looked upon as rather a fool and a pariah! [Kreisau, 3.5.1910]

As the daughter of liberals, the young Countess was able to offer moral support to her husband.

> Of course it does not really matter to us for we know that there are crowds of intelligent good people to whom such views seem the most natural in the world instead of, as here, being considered quite treasonable. And someone has to break the wall of traditions and prejudice and let the air of freedom in so that *individualities* (a thing much lacking in the "Adel" [nobility] in Germany) may have room to develop. But it is sometimes not very pleasant work! [Kreisau, 3.5.1910]

Helmuth's progressive ideas shocked some members of his family, too, such as his archconservative brother-in-law, Dietrich von Trotha.

> Dietrich gets terribly shocked and disgusted sometimes! Luckily in all these struggles (and there are a good many in our life) we really are of one mind which is perhaps the greatest help of all. [Kreisau, 3.5.1910]

When Edward VII died, on May 6, 1910, and his son George V ascended the British throne, Dorothy took an optimistic view of the new monarch's prospects.

> Somehow I have great hopes of the new King and believe that he may do much more than we expect. God grant it may be so. . . . Curiously enough politically I am absolutely South

African. That is to say I have no enthusiasm or even regard for anything to do with German politics, and that side of me has not changed one bit since the day I left Africa nearly 5 years ago.   [Kreisau, 30.5.1910]

She was particularly heartened by the creation of the South African Union.

Yesterday Union was announced as an accomplished fact in South Africa! I thought much of you and sent my country the warmest wishes and love. What a fine country it will be! God bless it. [Kreisau, 30.5.1910]

In June, Countess von Moltke rejoiced that her father had moved to a less pressured post and accepted the Appeal Court judgeship.

I am sure you will never regret it, and you will live a long and happy and not too overworked life, congratulating yourself all the time on the step you have taken. [Kreisau, 7.6.1910]

She shared her father's admiration for Abraham Lincoln, a biography of whom he had been reading.

I was so interested in all Daddy wrote to me about Lincoln. What a wonderful man he must have been! . . . It is so refreshing to know that a man can play a great part in politics and history and yet remain simple and a lover of Truth. [Kreisau, 7.6.1910]

German-American veterans at Kreisau

In July, a group of Germans who had emigrated to the United States came to pay their respects to the great Field Marshal. Dorothy described the visit to her mother.

On Saturday as I told you . . . we had the deputation of the Deutscher Krieger Verein [German Veterans Association] in here and were about 30 all told. We met them at the Kapellen Berg[57] and after the "president" had made a speech and a wreath had been laid on the grave we drove home to lunch with them all. They were all simple people, of the better sort of workman and most of them had not been home to the "Heimat" [homeland] for 20 or 30 years and it was curious to see the blending of German and American. As long as they marry Germans they remain Teutons but let their wife be American and they become complete Yankees. There are 14000 members of the Verein in American [*sic*.] and only those may join who have served in the army or navy here. [Kreisau, 4.7.1910]

Future of the Church of Christ, Scientist

Countess von Moltke's last letter of 1910 included some thoughtful observations.

> Are not people who only talk about *persons* trying and tyring [*sic*.] after a time? I find that so much here, where in general society the conversation almost always revolves round individuals and their doings, and abstract questions are seldom broached. [Kreisau, 29.12.1910]

On December 3, 1910, Mary Baker Eddy died at her home in Chestnut Hill, Massachusetts. In answer to her father's inquiry as to how this would affect the future of the Church of Christ, Scientist, Dorothy expresses her confidence that the five directors of the church would ably "carry on affairs, so everything will continue as before." She concludes by praising Eddy's accomplishments.

> It will be interesting to know what place history will accord her in the annals of great women; but she certainly did accomplish much (I speak only of outward things)—a church which in 40 years has branches in every Protestant and some Catholic countries, a daily paper which, standing for clean journalism, has, in 2 years time, a larger list of subscribers than any other paper in America, and a publishing house in which three other religious magazines are printed. And she was nearly 50 when she began! [Kreisau, 29.12.1910]

1911

While Kreisau was being renovated in preparation for the

new baby Dorothy was expecting, the Moltke family once again went to Hannover, where they stayed for the first several weeks of 1911. As she prepared for the birth of her third child, she welcomed the opportunity for quietude and reading.

> Never have I found so much time for reflection and the cultivation of the inward man, also for intellectual studies as the months before Motherhood. [Hannover, 23.1.1911]

She was enjoying Matthew Arnold's book of essays, *Culture and Anarchy*[58] ("His objections to the aristocracy taking a leading part in the work of regeneration, also to 'Jacobinism and Philistinism' were a delight, and so true."), and a biography of Bismarck's wife ("It is not good or normal for any human being to be adored in the way she adored her husband. . . ."[59] [Hannover, 23.1.1911]

While in Hannover, the Moltkes attended a concert by Spanish violinist Joan Manén[60] and, on another evening, heard Humperdinck's masterpiece, *Hänsel und Gretel*.

> . . . it made me think so much of the time we heard it together in Berlin, the first Christmas you and Daddy were with us, do you remember? Helmuth still weeps at the scene where the guardian angels come! [Hannover, 18.1.1911]

The Trothas

A few days later, while her husband was in Berlin, Dorothy took a trip to Düsseldorf to visit her in-laws, the Trothas.

> I arrived here safely yesterday afternoon, the journey only taking a little over four hours; but the country is very different to our more Eastern part, nothing but factories everywhere and slate roofs and different architecture, most people living in houses as in England, instead of flats. Düsseldorf is noted for the way it is laid out, and certainly the trees and grass and water are wonderfully pretty even in winter while in summer it must be lovely. The Trothas have a large house looking straight onto the park and as I write I only see trees, grass and rhododendron bushes which for a town is rather an unusual

view. Dietrich [von Trotha] had just had a slight operation to his nose and was rather piano [quiet] when I arrived, but Ete[61] and the two boys were blooming. [Hannover, 23.1.1911]

Much as she appreciated the good qualities of her brother-in-law, she found his ultraconservative views archaic and stultifying.

> How Dietrich Trotha would amuse you! So kind, such good manners, such a gentleman, and with the opinions of the middle ages. One can't even argue with him. It is to me always a little sad to see Ete married to him, for so much of her must perforce sleep with him as her lifes companion. Luckily she has her children and is the most charming mother I know or could even imagine. But it is a little tragic to see her, like so many of the "Adel [aristocracy]", groping half-blindly in a world the currants [sic.] of which they no longer know how to cope with, half angry, half puzzled, totally at a loss. And what is to take their place at the helm of the State? At present there is nothing but the Social Democratic party, full of hate and fury, and as Matthew Arnold says, "where bitter envying and strife are, there is confusion and every evil work".[62] [Hannover, 23.1.1911]

"Mami is my best friend"

A conversation between mother and son at this time reveals the close spiritual bond between Dorothy and Helmuth James. She had asked the boy to write a card to his little cousin, Carl Didi,[63] to which he had responded, "Nein" [No].

> "Oh, said I, but he is your best friend." Nein was again the answer. "Who is your best friend" then asked the Y. T. "Mami is my best friend" was the prompt answer. Need I tell you that I felt very proud and yet very humble and extremely happy.[64] [Berlin, 7.3.1911]

The four-year-old son's discovery of God's ever-presence was a significant indication of his spiritual awakening.

> The other night, for the first time for a year or more, he slept

68

with his door shut and the room quite dark,—all his own wish, and when I came a little later to tell him how glad I was that he was brave enough to sleep in the dark, he said "Ja, Mami, ich habe jetzt gelernt dass [*sic*.] Gott überall ist." [Yes, Mummy, I have now learned that God is everywhere.] Rather sweet is it not? . . . He . . . seems to have an excellent sense for the fitness of things. [Kreisau, 16.4.1911]

A few months later, Dorothy shared with her parents a dialogue overheard between young Helmuth, now four, and a Russian boy named Gert. The two mites were discussing theology.

Gert made some absurd remark, to which Helmuth replied ich glaube es aber nicht [I don't believe it][.]

G[ert]. "Wenn Du nicht glaubst kannst Du nicht in den Himmel kommen[.] [If you don't believe, you can't enter Heaven.]

H[elmuth]. Ja aber doch. [Yes, I can.]

G[ert]. Nein gewiss nicht[.] [No, certainly not.]

H[elmuth]. "Ja aber im Himmel macht der lieber Gott alle Menschen wieder gut[.] [Yes, but in Heaven the loving God makes all men good again.]

G[ert]. Woher weisst Du es dann. [How do you know that?]

H[elmuth]. Das ist die Wissenschaft (C.S.)!! [That is (Christian) Science.][65] [Boston, 26.11.1911]

When the chilren disagreed over a second metaphysical point, Schönchen, *Tante* Luise's companion and a Christian Scientist, came to the rescue.

. . . Gert maintained that God had arms, hands and feet and Helmuth knew that was not so, so they both came to ask Schönchen about it. She explained as best she could that God is Love. [Boston, 26.11.1911]

Count and Countess von Moltke found the traditional lifestyle of idleness enjoyed by the German country nobility empty and unsatisfying.

> This "country gentleman" life is not "the real thing" for people as young as we, and especially for Helmuth there is not half enough outlet for his energy,—a woman generally manages to occupy herself more easily than a man, which makes many things easier for her.—.[sic.] And I should not be surprised if some day or other Helmuth took up work in a town and used Creisau just as a summer holiday home. His uncles and relations would be terribly shocked, but each generation differs, more or less, from the other as regards ideals (though I never feel that with you dear Flen) and certainly in Germany at least the present generation is more strenuous though perhaps on the whole not with such strength of character as the older. [Kreisau, 21.3.1911]

Helmuth found his work for the Christian Science Church much more meaningful and satisfying than the traditional pursuits of the landed aristocracy.

> At present Helmuth has the work he is doing for the C. S. [Christian Science] Directors in Boston and is therefore fully occupied, but I shudder to think what I should do with him if that were not the case! And even when the house is full of guests the problem is not solved for it is not the proper life for people of our age to spend our time simply in riding, driving, games and talk. These are delightful as a relaxation, but not as the days work, more or less; delightful for the summer holidays but not when it becomes the chief occupation of the year. This must not make you think that I am in any way discontented, for on the contrary I am very happy, only I can see that we cannot go on living all our lives like this. A few people make their country life really active and interesting and busy (not many) but one can't make a man take an interest in party politics when he just *won't*, or do any of the other "usual" things that don't appeal to him. On the other hand come such considerations as the social (in the big sense of the word) influence one has with the peasants and the evils of absentee landlords and many other things, to be weighed in the scale,

and it is quite difficult to know what is right. Be thankful dear Flen, that you never inherited an estate, it complicates life considerably! Helmuth often says quite wistfully "If only my name was Mayer!" [Kreisau, 21.3.1911]

The Moltkes were enjoying some of the thoughtful writings of the great Field Marshal.

We have been reading some "Trost Gedanken" ["Comforting Thoughts"] written by the Feld Marschall when he was 90 years old. They are really beautiful thoughts on the immortality of man, and the relation of reason to religion and morality, written in a very clear style . . . and are a really remarkable product for a man of that age. [Kreisau, 21.3.1911]

Lord Milner and his "Kindergarten"

A letter written in April discusses a group of young British intellectuals who had been brought to South Africa by Alfred Lord Milner, High Commissioner of the Union of South Africa, to serve in the South African Civil Service after the Boer War, which ended in 1902. Known as "Lord Milner's Kindergarten," they were instrumental in preparing the way for the formation of the Union of South Africa, in 1910, and later favored an imperial federation of the British Empire itself.

I need hardly say what a joy your letters were yesterday and I was especially interested in hearing what the different members of the Kindergarten were doing—how strange that so many of them have drifted away from South Africa, and it really seems a pity that their enthusiasm and gifts could not have been better utilized by her, though of course, looked at from a broader standpoint, they are working for the Empire, and incidentally for one of the biggest ideals, wherever they may be. [Kreisau, 4.4.1911]

Willo

The Moltkes, a family that seemed to produce mainly sons, were always hopeful that the next child would be a girl.

However, when a third son, Wilhelm Viggo ("Willo"), appeared on May 8, they were delighted.

> It is a very happy and healthy and hale and hearty young woman who writes to you this week, and I hardly know where to begin in my tale. . . . we were all very cheerful in spite of "It" being a boy. The Y. T. at once had visions of the five of us riding together and we were soon consoled—even Muttel! . . . The babe is very fat and has heaps of black hair and dark eyes, and seems more like little Helmuth than JoWo. The two elder boys are vastly interested in him, especially when he drinks, and "der allerkleinster Bruder" [smallest brother] is a subject on which little Helmuth enjoys talking. [Kreisau, 16.5.1911]

Two weeks later, Dorothy was enjoying being alone with her new son.

> Miss Flower [the Christian Science midwife] left this morning and we now have full charge of the baby; he sleeps with me, but otherwise Miss Chalmers looks after him. He has an extraordinarily energetic face and seems to know and think a great deal, not having at all the usual artless look babies have. My three little sons—I dream that some day they may prove a blessing to the world. [Kreisau, 30.5.1911]

Indeed, all three of these boys would grow up to make major contributions to society, which are discussed in the Epilogue.

Schwester Ida

"As you know," Dorothy wrote, "I help Helmuth with his work, and that, with my other duties and occupations, fills up my time pretty well." [Kreisau, 12.6.1911] In addition, she took an interest in the village people and educating them in important practical ways. One of the most helpful things Dorothy did for the village was to appoint Ida Hübner as kindergarten teacher in Kreisau. Although *Schwester* Ida," as she was known, had had no formal education and was illiterate, she was a woman of unusually high character, with a gift for teaching small children, balancing a loving approach with firm discipline. The children, including

Dorothy's own children, who also attended *Schwester*'s kindergarten, all loved *Schwester* Ida.

The golden mill in the forest

One day *Schwester* and two others took the village women to see the "golden mill in the forest." As the means of transportation was provided by the Moltke family, one suspects that the Countess was behind this fairy-tale expedition.

> On Sunday all the women of Creisau who belong to a "Flick Verein" [sewing circle] started by the Schwester, went on an excursion in two of our waggons, with Schwester, the Pastor and the Lehrer [teacher] in command. The happiness was unclouded. One woman said, she had been 27 years in Creisau, but such a lovely day she had never had! Another, about 80 years old, also went saying it had been the greatest wish of her life to go to the "Goldener Waldmühle" [golden mill in the forest] and at last it was to be realized! It was quite touching. This winter Frau Lorenz is going to start cooking classes in the evening, to give some of the very ignorant housewives an idea of how to do better. And I also hope to arrange for two or three lectures on the care of children for the Creisau women, some of whom are appallingly ignorant on the subject. [12.6.1911]

Dorothy took heart at the German news reports of the recent coronation of King George V.

> *What* festivities there have been in England! The German papers have all been most friendly and flattering in their accounts of the Coronation and it really seems as if things were improving between the two countries. [27.6.1911]

In July, the new baby was christened.

> The third little son has been christened and is called "Wilhelm Viggo, Friederich Eduard," the first name after Vatel [grandfather], the second because I like it so much, and the other two after two of the Godfathers; we think of calling him "Willo" which is a combination of the first two names. He

behaved beautifully, being wide awake and cooing every now and then in the prettiest way. The other two boys sat on little white chairs on either side of me, and were quite still until the end of the address when JoWo started to walk about a little and little Helmuth, after examining the baby, gravely took him by the hand and brought him back. JoWo wore a white silk smock, and little Helmuth a white Kittel [smock] with pink, and I a white spangled dress with a pale mauve tunic. [Kreisau, 11.7.1911]

The passage from First John (I John 3:1-3) that they selected for the christening was one that is read every Sunday in Christian Science church services.

We chose the text: Behold what manner of love the Father hath for us that we should be called the sons of God"[66] for the sermon and our nice little Pastor preached most excellently. I am sending you a copy of the hymns. You were mentioned in the address, and were not forgotten in our hearts, Dear Ones. [Kreisau, 11.7.1911]

Trip to Boston

That summer, Count von Moltke was making plans to travel to the United States to serve on the committee that would be translating *Science and Health* into German. He was one of three Germans selected for this monumental task; one of the other two was the Moltkes' good friend Ulla Schultz.

Meanwhile, Dorothy was preparing for a trip with her young brood to South Africa for an extended visit with her parents. She decided, upon further consideration, to accompany her husband to Boston instead. As she explained to her parents, "As the time for our departure drew nearer the thought of being separated so long weighed on us dreadfully and I felt that Helmuth needed me greatly." [Kreisau, 25.7.1911] This meant leaving her three young children with family and nannies, and delaying her trip to South Africa for a couple of months.

I really feel that it is right to go with Helmuth, and if, feeling that, I still persisted in coming to you now, I fear I should feel unhappy all the time. . . . The Y. T. cabled to Boston to ask if I could take part in the work there and they have replied in the affirmative, so that it will be very interesting for me there. [Kreisau, 25.7.1911]

And so, in August, Count and Countess von Moltke and Ulla Schultz set sail for America on the S.S. *George Washington*. Leaving the German shores, the ship passed through the English Channel.

Early this morning we reached Cherburg [*sic*.], and it was curious to note the difference between the English & French coasts—the latter dotted with white friendly houses, the former much sterner looking with grey walls and roofs. We sailed up the Solent at about 7 on Sunday evening, a pretty sight, with the white cliffs of old England shining in the light of the setting sun. I was very excited at seeing the first English men of war I have seen for years, and the King of Spains ship together with numberless yachts and other boats were stationed at Cowes. We passed very close to them and the usual salutes were made. Then we anchored close to the Union Castle boats and you may guess with what pleasure I looked at their red funnels. Then the tender came with passengers, and such a jabbering of English—it *did* sound so nice! And then away again past the ships and houses all lighted up and twinkling cheerily to us, into the vast darkness of the night. . . . One of the loveliest sights is the rising of the full moon every evening. "That orbed maiden with white fire laden."[67] She rises majestically out of the black sea, first one only sees a bright line and gradually she appears in all her beauty, it is really imposing, & the sight quiets practically the whole ship, everyone silently watching the growing beauty. [S.S. *George Washington*, 7.8.1911]

Finally, the ship sailed into New York Harbor, and before long, the Moltkes arrived in Boston.

Translating *Science and Health* into German

Almost immediately the Moltkes were deeply engaged in the translation work. Serving with them on the committee were two other Germans, Ulla Schultz and Renate Hermes King; Theodor Stanger, a German-American who was editor of the German-language periodical, *Der Herold der Christian Science*; and Adam Dickey, a member of the Christian Science Board of Directors whom Eddy had personally appointed to serve on the translation committee, to ensure that the German translation accurately conveyed the spiritual concepts in *Science and Health*.

Dorothy explains the importance of the work:

> This is extremely difficult and it has to be most thoroughly done because about 5000 people will study it daily, more than any other book except the Bible, and the number is increasing rapidly. [Boston, 10.9.1911]

The Moltkes' involvement in the translation of the Christian Science textbook is discussed more fully in Part II.

America

Countess von Moltke gave her first impressions of American life and the many ways in which it contrasted with South African life, particularly in relation to the black population.

> One sees many natives about, great numbers seemingly very well-to-do and as smartly dressed as can be. There is very little feeling against them in Boston and they have equal rights with the white man I am told. [Boston, 4.9.1911]

Dorothy was as appalled by the yellow journalism then prevalent in Boston as she was impressed by the signs of property among blacks and immigrants.

> How the newspapers would amuse you! *Nothing* but local news, and of this sort "Stork expected by Mrs. X, the 30,000 dollar bride". "Beatty condemned to death but still unmoved." "Mrs. Z. obtains devorce [*sic*], says wealth is vulgar." And so

on, one more weird than the other. The headlines fascinate me and I try to gather as many as possible while sitting in the tram [subway].

It is wonderful what America makes out of the immigrants who come to her shores. They are often the outcasts, the n'er do wells in their own country, but after a few years they develop into free American citizens. Every one here seems well dressed, even the butchers boy is not to be recognized by his clothes and the blacks are as fashionably dressed as I am, their teeth glistening with gold stoppings! Things seem done on the assumption that everyone "plays fair." Motors are left alone for hours in the street, peoples flower gardens merge into the thoroughfare yet not a flower is touched, the tram conductor gives you no ticket but relies on your own right feeling to pay him, and so on. And then, the reverse of this picture is the corruption in public life. I can only think it is explainable by the theory that the American separates public and private life entirely and is as unscrupulous in the one as he is scrupulous in the other. [Boston, 19.9.1911]

She was astonished at the number of cars ("over 30000 in Massachusetts alone") and at the noise and darkness of the train stations ("the trains are dirty and terribly noisy, for they go extremely fast") [Boston, 19.9.1911]. She was also astonished by the modern labor-saving applicances, which enabled "nearly 9 tenths of the people [to] do without servants, . . ." [Boston, 22.9.1911]

Rumors of war

As far away as Dorothy and Helmuth were from Europe, they were still troubled by the rumblings of war.

Last night Helmuth heard some talk in the tram about "War" and "Germany" and for a moment we got a great fright, for of course we should have to try and get home at once if such a terrible thing should happen, and the only route would be [via] Siberia—a long and very costly journey. Luckily however there is no reason to think that the Morocco question[68] will not

77

be soon peaceably settled, it would be an outrageous thing to fight about the sand hills of North Africa, anyway. . . . there does seem great unrest everywhere in Europe. [Boston, 30.9.1911]

While the Moltkes missed their loved ones, they were sustained by the knowledge of the transcendent importance of the work they were doing. Obviously feeling the pressure of her parents' mounting impatience with the delays to her trip to South Africa, Dorothy felt compelled to defend her decision to accompany her husband to Boston for the translation work. "In the meantime Darlings," she added, "you must possess your souls in patience and know that as soon as it is possible we will come to you." [Boston, 30.9.1911]

Dorothy and Ulla took a trip to Marblehead and Lynn on Boston's North Shore, and enjoyed New England's spectacular fall foliage as they canoed on the Charles River in Cambridge ("the tints of the oaks and maples were glorious, and gliding noiselessly along one could easily imagine the Indians life among these woods"). And the Moltkes enjoyed touring the country roads in a rented Cadillac ("an old and not very pretty affair but it goes well and was the best we could get"). That evening they dined with the first managing editor of *The Christian Science Monitor,* Alexander Dodds. [Boston, 30.9.1911]

John Hays Hammond

While in Boston, the Moltkes reconnected with John Hays Hammond[69] and his wife, Natalie. They had become good friends in South Africa, where the prominent American engineer and entrepreneur had mining interests. The part that Dorothy's father had played in rescuing the American from prison after the Jameson Raid in South Africa undoubtedly contributed to the warmth of affection between the two families.

In 1895 there was an ill-planned attempt by Leander Starr

Jameson and other English South Africans to overthrow the Boer government in Transvaal. The attempt failed, and Hammond, who had been associated with the leaders of the raid, was placed in jail under horrific conditions and sentenced to death. Fortunately, Sir James was able to use some of his connections with Afrikaaner officials to bring about the deliverance of the accused from prison, and Hammond and all but two of the others were released. After that, Hammond relocated to England, returning eventually to the United States.[70]

Dorothy describes their visit to the Hammonds' gracious residence in the seaside town of Gloucester, Massachusetts.

> Our rooms are gorgeous and we have been wandering round like little children looking at everything and laughing outrageously at ourselves. Our bedrooms are very pretty and overwhelmingly elegant,—heaps of silver, fine linen, the latest magazines and needless to say pretty furniture, curtains and so on. . . . Oh my Darlings, I can't tell you how delightful the Hammonds have been! Just the same warmhearted people as of old. It really has been a joy to see them. They both look as young as ever, except that he has a white moustache; and she has all her old vivacity, the same beautiful hair, the same charm. "Uncle Jack" as I am to call him, embraced me right away, . . . [Boston, 14.10.1911]

At the Hammonds' house, they met the Hammonds' son, John Hays Hammond Jr. (1888–1965), later to become the world-famous inventor of radio remote control, which served as the basis for modern missile guidance systems, and the builder of the Hammond Castle, now a tourist attraction and arts venue in Gloucester. Dorothy describes "Jackie" as a young man.

> Jackie, aged 22, is a dear and seems to be a very remarkable fellow, doing good research work already. . . . It has been a perfectly lovely visit and done me good, for they really are splendid people. . . . It was delightful to find them so unchanged by success, just as simple and warmhearted as ever.

79

[Boston, 14.10.1911]

In early November, the Moltkes went to New York to attend the annual meeting held by Christian Science teacher Laura Lathrop for her students, who had taken Christian Science class instruction with her. Lathrop had taught the Moltkes' teacher, Frau Günther-Peterson. Although they enjoyed the meeting, they were disappointed by the noise and dirty streets of the city. They marveled, however, at the George Washington Bridge and the skyscrapers, the architecture of the New York Public Library ("their libraries are always their most beautiful buildings and are very popular and frequented by the very poorest as well as those who have more leisure"), and the women riding "straddle legs" in Central Park. [Boston, 5.11.1911]

Yeats, de Pachmann and Saint-Saens

In Boston, the Moltkes took advantage of the city's cultural attractions, attending plays by Irish playwrights W. B. Yeats[71] and Lady Gregory,[72] who were in Boston at the same time as the Moltkes. [Boston, 30.9.1911] A few weeks later they saw J.M. Synge's *The Playboy of the Western World*.[73]

> A good deal of resentment and bad feeling towards England is displayed in them all. Strange is it not that England can deal so justly and wisely with every other dependency, Ireland alone remains a step-child. [Boston, 21.10.1911]

The Moltkes went to the opera and concerts, too, including by the famous pianist, Vladimir de Pachmann, called "the Chopinzee."[74]

> We all thought it the most perfect playing we had ever heard. But Pachmann himself is the funniest little man you have ever seen, taking the audience into his confidence in the middle of a piece, gesticulating, and insisting on the people clapping! [Boston, 21.10.1911]

A little over a month later, the Moltkes heard Pachmann play again.

> . . . the little funny old man played most beautifully. He kept on telling us (while he was playing) C'est un génie, Chopin, C'est magnifique, ça [What a genius Chopin is, really magnificent] and so on. And then he got up and told us he could not play any encores as he had to catch a train for New York and anyway he was not "disposé [in the mood]." He is delightful in his utter naturalness. [Boston, 1.12.1911]

With the John Munro Longyears,[75] they attended a performance of Saint-Saëns's *Samson and Delilah*.[76] Later they heard the famous tenor Leo Slezak,[77] and a concert of Wagner arias sung by the great Austrian contralto, Ernestine Schumann-Heink,[78] who "was as splendid as ever. She sang parts of Rheingold and Götterdämmerung in a truly masterly way." [Boston, 26.11.1911]

1912

In March, after seven months of intense labor, the translation of *Science and Health* was finally completed. The Moltkes immediately boarded the *Mauretania* and headed for Southampton, England. There they picked up their children and the rest of the family entourage and, at last, set sail for South Africa, where they would remain for the next several months.

"Onkel Helmuth thinks there may be war"

By October, the family was back at Kreisau and enjoying life in the country again. Peaceful as the world seemed at the beautiful Silesian estate, however, the Count's uncle, who was Chief of General Staff, warned the family of the possibility of war between England and Germany.

> I really got into contact with Onkel Helmuth for the first time. He was almost prevented from coming by the Balkan War,[79] for though I don't think they expect war, yet awhile at any rate,

he has to have everything absolutely ready. Onkel Helmuth thinks there may be war for the simple reason that everyone has prepared for it for so long and such tremendous armaments are always a danger, but he too thinks there is absolutely no reason for going to war and he said "If only England and Germany would go together they would lead the world; this whole "Spannung" [tension] is the work of King Edward." he [sic.] thinks the feeling in England against Germany is manufactured by politicians, the press and the diplomats, though I don't quite agree with him there. He has of course a very great responsibility and remarked "if war is coming I hope it will come soon before I am too old to cope with things satisfactorily." As a matter of fact everyone is so afraid of war that I think that will keep them from breaking the peace. Anyway I comfort myself thus. [Berlin, 22.10.1912]

In December, Dorothy was still feeling "on edge."

The European situation seems a little bit easier, but of course an eruption can occur at any time. Let us hope it will be avoided for it would be *awful*. It certainly was touch and go a week ago, and the General Staff people have been working day and night. [Berlin, 2.12.1912]

Silesian Christmas

Christmas was around the corner once again, and the people in the village prepared for the approaching holiday with its charming Silesian traditions.

At 2 o'clock Schwesters "Frau Oberin" arrived to lunch and at 3:30 we all assembled in the Spielschule [play school] which was most charmingly decorated. The rooms were packed, the schoolchildren sang and recited and the Pastor held an appropriate sermon on "Die Liebe höret nimmer auf" [Love never faileth] which text is to be read on the outside of the crèche with my monograme [sic.] above it. It really was very touching to notice the pleasure and appreciation of all. The mason who planned and built the crèche added a small entrance room as his gift and the carpenter presented the window necessary. Was that not charming? Afterwards we all adjourned for tea at the Berghaus and at about 7 o'clock the several guests departed. [Berlin, 2.12.1912]

Helmuth James was pleased with books sent by his grandmother from South Africa.

The little books for the Boy have come and we are reading Joan of Arc. They are rather difficult for him and I have to explain a good deal but he loves the story all the same and has been busy all the afternoon building Orleans, the English camps, a certain bridge etc. Joan is represented by an Indian horseman with some white paper tied round him to hide discrepancies! [Berlin, 2.12.1912]

In Munich, the Moltkes attended a wedding that was unusual (for them) in that the bride was Jewish.

Ellen made a perfectly charming bride. The relations on her side are all immensely wealthy financiers of a distinctly Jewish type, people with plenty of interests, very artistic, quite a new type for me. It was all very interesting. We went to the opera and hear [*sic*.] Aubers "Des Teufels Anteil" [*The Devil's Portion*][80] but it was nothing striking.

. . . tomorrow I must sally forth early to buy the toys for the village children. [Berlin, 2.12.1912]

Preparations for war

By mid-December, the threat of war was hard to ignore.

The situation in Austria seems to be still rather strained. Tante Katze [Helmuth's aunt, Katze Leonardi] is to remain alone with Madi [Tante Katze's daughter and Helmuth's cousin] in Wien [Vienna] for Christmas, which of course means that things are mobilised in Lemberg [German name for Lvov, now part of Ukraine] and Toto [Toto Leonardi, Helmuth's Cousin][81] is not free. Here in the General Staff they look upon war as pretty certain, but then of course it is the business of the General Staff to think war. [Berlin, 17.12.1912]

A letter from Kreisau describes actual preparations for war.

> The great topic of conversation here is war. Everything is ready, which of course does not mean that it is sure to come, but still shows that it is very possible. All the officers have their orders and Prince Oskar who was coming to Monikas wedding has written to say that "owing to an important work which he has been given but about which he is not at liberty to speak" he is unable to be present, which of course means that he will be given some position, should war be declared, which needs preparation. Every officer has his box and has had a trial packing of his things. In fact the way everything is prepared is wonderful, but it would be a crime to go to war on such slight provocation. Austria's mobilization costs her ½ million marks daily and the danger is that to get the money back she might provocate things and force Germanys hand. [Kreisau, 23.12.1912]

Many German soldiers were eager to go to war in order not to "waste" the expensive uniforms they had just purchased.

> The German people as a whole don't want war, though the soldiers do, especially as the service outfits they have all invested in (the officers I mean) has cost them about £25 and they don't like to see that of no use. The great danger to my mind lies in the fact that the Conservatives look upon war as the only means of checking the S.[Social] Democrats (just as Napoleon III did) and want it for that reason; they look upon it, too, as inevitable (so childish!) [Kreisau, 23.12.1912]

War would mean a loss of help on the farm, which posed a serious threat to Helmuth's Uncle Ludwig.

> Already Onkel Ludwig is considering whether or not to plant beet this year as there will be no men to cultivate the beet fields if war is declared. The S. Democrats have said, I believe, that if there is war, they will show "Herr von Moltke who is Herr", which means that he will not have a very pleasant time if left alone in Wernersdorf without coachman or driver. I write all these details, as I know it will interest you to learn of all the

84

"Stimmungen" [moods] we are going through. Thank heavens that there are other people in Germany besides Conservatives and Soldiers! [Kreisau, 23.12.1912]

Dorothy reassures her parents that they are well supplied.

We have killed 2 pigs one calf, 8 hares and 8 pheasants so you can imagine how full my larder is. [Kreisau, 23.12.1912]

1913

When Helmuth James turned seven, he began his "first lessons" with a tutor, who came every Wednesday and Saturday. Dorothy describes the boy's deeply serious approach to learning.

It was quite a touching sight that met my eyes when I went in to visit Helmuth at his first lesson. With a kind of religious expression he sat with folded hands, bent on not missing a word, like a shy youth being initiated into his first sacred and all-important practices. May that feeling not disappear all too quickly!

Meanwhile, she was enjoying the writings of Austrian writer Hugo von Hofmannsthal [82] and American author Mary Antin's autobiographical work *The Promised Land* (1912).

It is the story of a Russian Jews experiences first in Russia and then as an immigrant, in America. It is interesting especially as being a true account of how aliens are "Americanized", but what I enjoyed almost most was the picture the book gave of the life of Jews in Russia—incredible! [Kreisau, 7.4.1913]

Lady Rose Innes comes for a visit

In late February 1913, Dorothy's mother was on her way to England, en route to Kreisau. Dorothy urged her to stop at Budapest on her way "for the Womans International Congress.... She would meet many interesting women and would revel in the whole thing." [Kreisau, 27.2.1913]

Finally, at the end of April, Lady Rose Innes arrived in

Berlin.

> She has such a wonderful power of enjoying things which is so splendid. . . . The chicks were *so* excited about Mother and remembered her at once I think, even Willo [then aged two] having a sort of "I think I've met you before" air about him! [Berlin 24.4.1913]

Together they went for "a lovely motor run . . . in among the mountains" [Berlin, 24.4.1913] and, in beautiful spring weather, picked lilies of the valley on the farm. Dorothy's mother entertained Helmuth James by reading to him the English classic, *Alice's Adventures in Wonderland* by Lewis Carroll.

In her letters to her father, who was still in South Africa, Dorothy discusses the local government elections as well as national politics.

> I am enclosing a copy of an election paper for the Landtag [provincial government] elections next month. It *is* sad that you and I belong to the "schaumschlägerischen Liberalismus" [hot-air liberalism]! A miserable performance the whole leaflet is— and the Y. T. is supposed to disperse some dozens of these among his workmen—I am curious to know what he will do— conveniently forget them I expect! [Kreisau, 30.4.1913]

> Almost a year before the Archduke of Austria was assassinated (on June 28, 1914), setting off World War I, Dorothy preseciently observed:

> I do wish Germany was not allied so closely to Austria, for the advantage to the former country is small indeed and through Austria we seem constantly to be "almost" involved in war. [Kreisau, 7.5.1913]

Kaiser Maneuvers

In spite of their antiwar position, Dorothy writes in May that her husband was "very keen" to show his father-in-law the "Kaiser Manoevres [*sic*.]" that would be taking place in their area in September, during Sir James's forthcoming visit to

86

Germany. [Kreisau, 7.5.1913] These maneuvers turned out to be of great interest to Sir James, who recorded his impressions of them in his *Autobiography*.

Amid the patriotic fervour which prevailed the autumn manoeuvres of 1913 began. They opened with a review of an army corps at Breslau; for an hour and a half the serried ranks went by. As the infantry approached the saluting post where their War Lord, surrounded by a brilliant staff, was stationed, they swung into the goosestep which was maintained for a like distance beyond. To the uninstructed eye it seemed an exaggerated and unpractical gesture, though it may have been valuable as a test of fitness. The physique of the men was excellent; the artillery and cavalry swept past in fine style. Afterwards the Kaiser inspected his white cuirassiers, a crack regiment, officered for the most part by Silesian junkers. A significant feature of the review was the presence of numbers of men who had completed their army service. They were members of clubs (Kriegs Vereinen), and were lined up immediately behind the seated spectators; their presence emphasized the strength of the military spirit which prevailed. The manoeuvres proper, which lasted several days, terminated in the neighbourhood of Kreisau. So that we were well inside the area of operations, which was swarming with troops. Billeting was freely resorted to and cheerfully endured; all classes were ready to inconvenience themselves in order to accommodate the soldiers.[83]

In October, after her parents had returned to South Africa, the Moltkes hosted a successful shoot, followed by a dinner with royalty—Crown Prince and Princess Friedrich Wilhelm, son and daughter-in-law of the Kaiser.[84]

Our dinner last night was quite nice, only 16 people. The Princess is charmingly pretty & very fresh & natural. At 10 o'clock she disappeared for 20 minutes to nurse her baby (just as I did the evening before!) and then came back. He is clever & has many interests, he is "Landrat" [Prussian title for a regional administrator] & has a great deal to do & is one of the best dilitante [*sic.*] musicians in Germany, but I like Friedrich Heinrich[85] (Lenos friend) better, he has more heart. It was the first time I had ever dined with royalties & it was rather amusing. They are very natural members of their species. The Prince & Princess went into dinner together (but sat opposite one another) and the rest of us just sauntered in after them, not being "taken in" at all. [Kreisau, 28.10.1913]

C.B.

The end of 1913 brought the arrival of yet another son in the Moltke family: Carl Bernhard (later shortened to Carl Bernd), known as "C.B." The family bought a new pony for the children, and plans were made for young Helmuth James to begin school in the neighboring town of Schweidnitz (now Swidnica, in Poland). Dorothy ends her last letter of 1913 as follows:

And now goodbye. I have still much to do for we have not even begun the servants [Christmas] tables. Whatever may separate us outwardly, inwardly we are very near, & I owe you an immense debt of gratitude now & through all time for all you have given me in thought, in outlook, in example & in love. [Kreisau, 22.12.1913]

1914

World War I

As the year 1914 opened, Dorothy gloried in the winter snow, her husband and four young sons, "a lovely new book on Goethe," and work for house, church, and village.

We tobogganed for several hours during the morning, 6° of cold but windless & perfectly heavenly. Then I went in the sleigh with the three children. . . . I could not help thinking how very rich my life is. There was Carl Bernhard looking up at me with wonderful, expressive eyes & 3 other little lives being moulded at my side. I thought of you two & how you enrich my life, my C.S. [Christian Science] work & interests which brings me in to touch with problems & people otherwise remote from my sphere of life, beside me lay a lovely new book on Goethe which is waiting to be read, I thought of my husband, the work that awaits me in house & garden, in village & round about & I felt that I was an abundantly blessed woman, living and working & dealing with realities, & I felt very grateful about it all.   [Kreisau, 1.1.1914]

Except for a concert by legendary pianist and composer Ferruccio Busoni,[86] whom they considered "an even greater pianist than Pachmann" [Berlin, 17.2.1914], the cultural offerings during that season were not to the Moltkes' taste. For the cheerful, optimistic Count, the dark theatrical works of the Scandinavian writers had little appeal.

There is nothing very wonderful going on at the theatres, Strindberg[87] & Ibsen, which the Y. T. doesn't care to see & Shakespeare. [Kreisau, 1.1.1914]

She was grateful for the political progress in her homeland, in contrast with the political style of Germany at that time, which she found "sickening."

I read about the Bloemfontein Memorial with much interest, it must have been a touching and dignified celebration. But what a triumph for the British *and* the Dutch peoples that, after all that had happened,[88] such tolerant speeches & such sympathetic feelings were possible. Truly, I come of a great people! Here politics are sickening. Neither side has the least sense of proportion or humour, and has a torrent of invective for the opposition which borders on the ludicrous. . . . Helmuth spent some very interesting hours in the Herrenhaus. On Saturday Graf Yorck attacked the Chancellor on his supposed indifference to Prussias place in the Empire. . . . The whole event created *great* interest as it is the nearest approach to a "Vote of censure" that the Herrenhaus has ever ventured on. [Kreisau, 12.1.1914]

On Dorothy's birthday in February, celebrated with the usual fanfare of gifts and speeches, "Onkel Ludwig made a charming little speech, he, Tante Louise & the Y. T. weeping copiously!" [Kreisau, 23.2.1914]

War looms on the horizon

By July, war was in the air, and the English nanny was returning to her homeland.

> Martial law has been declared & the army in East Prussia has mobilised. It looks uncommonly like war & already no letters or telegrams are allowed to be sent abroad. Miss Chalmers leaves tonight & is taking this letter & a cable with her, for I do not know how long it may be before you hear from me again. Anyway don't worry about us, we are sure to pull through alright. [Kreisau, 31.7.1914]

As the Moltkes reorganized their lives in preparation for the impending conflict, Dorothy's faith sustained her.

> Onkel Helmuth telegraphed today advising us to stay quietly in Creisau, so the Trothas, the Berghaus & I remain here, Muttel[,] the boys (the 2 big ones I mean) & Leno go to Hannover & the Y. T. for the present is in Schweidnitz. All the horses & the motor will be commandeered & Hermann & our man servant have to leave at once. Tomorrow (unless things look much brighter) we will pack away the silver & all the entailed & valuable things, & then await events. There will be plenty of work for us all to do & I am so sure of Gods protection that I do not feel a bit anxious, only very sober. We have bought plenty of provisions & on Monday will make Sausage & "Poekelfleisch" [corned beef]. . . . The telephone service here is interrupted & nothing of a private nature is allowed to pass. . . . And now Beloved Ones, goodbye. Don't worry. We are all well & with Gods help will keep so. [Kreisau, 31.7.1914]

Finally, on August 7, the German army invaded Belgium. Immediately, the United Kingdom and France declared war: World War I had begun. The Count was immediately called up and soon left Kreisau.

90

Helmuth James vividly remembered the day "Papi" went away and recorded it many years later in a letter to his own two young sons, Helmuth Caspar and Konrad, then six and two years old. In January 1944, writing from the main Gestapo prison in Berlin, where he was detained prior to being sent to Ravensbrück, Helmuth James recalled the day his father left for the front.

> Everyone stood downstairs on the front steps; all the servant girls and Mamsell [the Moltkes' cook and housekeeper, Mrs. Ida Märkert] also appeared. He got into the automobile that we had at that time, an open gray wagon, I think it was a Mercedes. Mami embraced him, then he drove off, and with that the war began.[89]

With the outbreak of war, correspondence in English was forbidden, and so Dorothy was obliged to write to her parents in German—translated here:

> Beloved Parents,
>
> I am writing in German, because we are actually not allowed to write letters in any foreign languages. Miss Halma [the Moltkes' American governess], who is going back to America, will send this letter to you from there. We are all doing well. I hear from Helmuth almost daily. He is very cheerful and we [are] all hopeful, in spite of the tremendously overwhelming power against us. . . . All the people are united, every personal advantage or quarrel is forgotten, everyone is living only for one thing—Germany's victory, which is synonymous with Germany's existence. . . . I work a lot in the garden and have to take care that there should be no want in the village, etc. . . . May God grant that the Russians do not come here, for then all would be lost for us, but I don't believe that it's possible. . . . [Kreisau, 25.8.1914]

Countess von Moltke now found herself caught in the middle of a conflict between the country of her birth and the country of her husband and four sons. Much as she loved South Africa, however, her loyalty was to her adopted land—a position from which she never swerved—and she stoutly defended its honor. In his letter to his children, Helmuth James describes his mother's steadfast allegiance to Germany.

> When the war came and Mami's parents and her childhood friends were on the side of the enemy, Mami never doubted for an instant that her loyalty must be for her new homeland. She stomached the pain, and with all the love she had for the land of her birth, as a German she nevertheless accepted the fate that had been imposed upon us.[90]

Helmuth James also recalls some of the practical measures Countess von Moltke took on behalf of the German people around her. One of these was to provide protection for the women of Kreisau in the form of a wartime homeland organization. He remembered some of the activities at Kreisau during that time.

> Twice a week, all the women on the estate came to the *Schloss*, and in the living room sang patriotic and spiritual songs. They shared the news of their men, they also knitted, and we children helped wind wool and do other similar things.[91]

> Thus, to these Kreisau women, who could have taken offense because she was an Englishwoman, she was a support and a help in difficult times.[92]

Treatment of prisoners

In her letters to her parents during the war (the originals are in German), Dorothy took care to correct rumors that her parents might have heard about the treatment of the enemy (the British, French, South Africans, et al.) by the Germans.

> It has occurred to me that you have probably heard the most dreadful stories about the German treatment of the enemy, etc. The discipline is wonderful, but the civilian population were so horribly shot, and such horrors have been inflicted on the wounded, that, out of self-preservation, very harsh things went on, but *only* where snipers were concerned, or where horrors

had occurred. At first I simply did not believe any of it, but now I have received letters from relatives who were eye-witnesses, and they confirm it. One can understand now how it was possible that so many horrors in the Belgian Congo were reported. I am sending you an article about the General Staff, which will certainly interest you. It is all true. The order and moral elevation of the people is the most fantastic. Mobilization completely without alcohol. And all without chauvinism. One hears people talk only about the horrors and (unfortunately) about England not having remained neutral. Otherwise one hears only "the poor boys" who "can't help it" and so forth. It is all so dignified. Never have I been so enthusiastic about Germany as now. It means the rebirth of Germany. I wish I knew how it looks in England. And my good friends who will be fighting there. It is dreadful! Hopefully this letter will reach you soon.

In my thoughts I am much with you, you know that.

1,000 thoughts of faithfulness and love from your daughter. [Kreisau, 27.8.1914]

Russian Coral Bells

From Herr Eulig, the gardener on the estate, who was stationed in Russia, the Moltkes received "pressed Russian Coral Bells." As soldiers and officers—friends and relatives—were dying for their country daily, Dorothy wrote her last letter of 1914[93] in German.

> I am completely beside myself with joy, for even I have just received your dear, dear, dear letters. I have wept terribly over them, but it did me good. Apparently I have not received your telegram either, which you intended to send via Miss Chalmers. The times are endlessly difficult and it weighs upon one day and night. But it is nevertheless very grand and inspiring. The unity [of the Germans] is overwhelming, and the best side of everyone comes to light. From Helmuth I have, thank God, good news and now and then, although he is not in Germany. He recently wrote, "the sacrifices that the war

demands are terrible. But the beauty of it is that one does not mourn the fallen soldiers. They have done their duty. That is all that enters our consciousness." All our loved ones and acquaintances are away, and every day one hears of someone or other who is dead. It is a frightful time. Please don't believe that the Germans are unnecessarily cruel. They don't do anything that they wouldn't do to the civil population. 24 officers in Friedel Ploetz's cavalry division were killed in two weeks by murder or by snipers—many acquaintances among them. Thus you can see that strong measures must be taken to stop all this.

Here we live outwardly very peacefully. The inspector remains until the nineteenth, then I take over the financial part, and an old uncle from Jungnitsch will help with the business. Only old men and old horses have remained, but we will get things done very well. Georg is our main support in the house! For the present, everything here is very peaceful. If the Russians come into these parts the children will have to go immediately to Schleinitz, and all the people to the mountains. But may God protect us from that! The children are very cheerful. Helmuth James gets himself out of all difficulties by saying, "My Mami is African." And recently he said to Tante Louise, "Isn't it true that the English are better than the Russians and French"! Helmuth and Carl Didi spend many hours together and play wonderfully with each other. Baby has even celebrated his birthday. I have thought so much about you and think about you constantly. [Kreisau, 11.9.1914]

1915

"From the Y. T. I continue to have good news," Dorothy wrote in March 1915.

> . . . his work . . . includes organizing part singing among his men to pass away the time & keep them occupied. He rides over the fields just as if he were at home, inspecting the work, and yet what a difference. [Kreisau, 3.3.1915]

94

"Now it is deadly earnest"

The poignancy of Dorothy's situation as an English-Scottish South African woman living in a country at war with the United Kingdom and South Africa is brought out in a letter in which she recalls the day, two years earlier, when her parents had watched the Kaiser's maneuvers at Kreisau.

> It is Carl Bernhards birthday & my thoughts have been much in the past. Two years ago today, do you remember, your expedition to the manuevres [*sic*.] & return (passing the gloomy occupants of the Berghaus Wagen on the way!) & your sitting next my bed. And the little red morsel of humanity [Carl Bernhard] who is now such a sunny, self-willed little elf. And the aeroplanes & other evidences of war. Then it was only play, now it is deadly earnest. . . .

> Do you remember Wilhelm, the 2nd coachman? He died in Kurland a few weeks ago. Carl Viggo writes that it is already very cold & wet. Toto Leonhardi [*sic*.] was in Bankau for a day—just as bright & enthusiastic as ever. It is very interesting to notice how differently the war affects different people. [Kreisau, 8.9.1915]

Asta Maria

In 1915, a daughter was added at long last to the Moltke family. Their fifth child and only daughter, Asta Maria, was born on August 9. "Asta is enchanting & so good," Dorothy wrote in December. [Kreisau, 14.12.1915]

Dorothy observed the unfolding of each son's unique personality.

> He [Jowo] is developing fast now & is growing very keen about his lessons. He is very unselfish & especially sweet with the little ones. Willo, on the contrary, thinks no one so interesting and important as "ich" [I], but he is *so* funny in his pronounced individuality, & goes generally by the name of "Professor." The Boy [Helmuth James] is wonderfully mature for his 8 little years & yet is quite a baby. He is necessarily a

95

little spoilt, being the eldest, & is rather masterful, but with such a loving little heart. [Kreisau, 15.9.1915]

They were learning important life lessons.

The other day, JoWo did something not quite right, & on being asked if he had been the culprit he at once said "ja." So Lydia did not scold him but only told him not to do it again. Thereupon Helmuth took Lydia aside & said: "I see how much better it is to tell the truth *at once* & not beat about the bush & I'll do the same next time too." Rather sweet isn't it, for the boy always tries to find excuses *why* he has done a thing. [Kreisau, 15.9.1915]

War work

In addition to caring for her expanding family and her involvement with church services, Dorothy became deeply involved in war work.

Of course the five little ones take up a good deal of time & still more thought, & I find much to direct and arrange in the village as well as in the "Hof" & house, especially now that so many of the men are away. Then the work in Schweidnitz, C.S. [Christian Science] work I mean, & knitting, & comforts for the hospitals & troops are also a very important part of ones present life. . . . The country is putting on its Autumn dress once more & one is doubly sad to think that summer is over with the prospect of winter in the trenches & in the sad, lonely homes before one. [Kreisau, 15.9.1915]

The Moltke family also gave hospitality to the wounded.

We often invite wounded from the hospitals in Schweidnitz to come here for tea & supper, which they of course love doing. We play games with them, sing, & talk, & it is most interesting hearing of their experiences. Helmuth James always picks out the sorriest of the lot & looks after him as a hen does its chickens. [Kreisau, 14.12.1915]

Christmas Day

On Christmas Day, the Count arrived home in time for the family's festive celebrations, "looking very well & in excellent spirits."

> We had a very nice "Einbescherung", the children were wild with excitement (JoWo had not slept for two nights for pure joy!) & we were as happy & contented as is possible at the present time . . . . Even Bobby, the bulldog, had "Wurst" & the ponies sugar, so everyone, even the animals, were happy. [Kreisau, Christmas Day, 1915]

1916

"What will the New Year bring us all?" Dorothy asked hopefully on New Year's Day, 1916. "Surely never did we so long to know. God grant that it bring us peace & reunion." [Kreisau, 1.1.1916]

Schönchen

Tante Luise and her companion, Schönchen, were much loved members of the Moltke household, and are affectionately described in Helmuth James's letter to his sons.

> Tante Luise, the sister of my grandfather, Wilhelm Moltke . . . was a marvelous aunt. She adored all her nephews and nieces; all the old uncles always came to visit her, there was always wonderful food; and she was always shaking her head full of short white hair. . . . The house was run by Schönchen, who tirelessly worked all day to make it pleasant for everyone. . . .
>
> In 1911 I often went to work, doing handicrafts in the Berghaus, but in 1912 I moved in when Mami and Papi went away, and for me that was a marvelous time. Everyone spoiled me, and Schönchen did handicrafts with me whenever she had the time.[94]

This included working with Schönchen to prepare for Christmas—decorating the Christmas tree with beautiful

ornaments and assembling gifts of apples, nuts, and
Pfefferkuchen in colorfully decorated bags for the poor
people of the parish and for the family.

During the war, Schönchen was engaged in nursing the
wounded.

> Schönchen is nursing on a hospital train plying between the
> west front & the inland hospitals. She is splendid at her
> work. . . . Helmuth & Carl Viggo, both very well, are in the
> east. [Kreisau, 8.3.1916]

In September, Dorothy's husband returned from the front in
time for Jowo's birthday.

> Last Saturday the Y. T. arrived, . . . He is in Berlin on business
> just now, but we expect him back today for 24 hours before
> going to his post in Russia again. We celebrated JoWo's
> birthday on Sunday, we were 18 to dinner, his father "liess ihm
> Hochleben" [gave three cheers, "long live Jowo"] the 8 boys
> roared "Hoch", JoWo loudest of all & we felt that a long life
> was insured for him![95] [Kreisau, 27.9.1916]

Daughter Asta was already giving evidence of personal
charm.

> Asta is cute & very imitative, very amusing in fact & *so*
> cheerful, by the time you two old birds see her she will be
> perfectly bewitching & I can easily picture Dads state of
> subjection! [Kreisau, 27.9.1916]

In October, Dorothy updates her parents on her husband's
service in Russia.

> Helmuth is splendidly well, brown as a nut, & in very good
> spirits. He is Commandant in a little town & has lots of
> farming besides, & has a good deal to do with the inhabitants.
> He rides a lot & is extremely fit. He has taken a pointer out
> with him this time as he always "shoots" his own dinner.
> [Kreisau, 8.10.1916]

> The Y. T. has an ammunition column now & is not far off from

Carl Viggo, though they have not met yet. He is very pleased with his new work. That he is "Rittmeister" [cavalry officer] you know, don't you? [Kreisau, 17.10.1916]

The Moltkes' kindness to prisoners was deeply appreciated by two Russian soldiers.

Two of our Russian prisoners had to leave a few weeks ago in order to work in a sugar factory & when they heard that they had to leave Creisau they wept! They are very well looked after naturally, & are nice, hard-working fellows. Every week they are weighed to see that they are being fed properly (that is orders) & Frau Jungnitsch & the Stellmacherin [wife of the wheelright] cook for them. The things they like best they ask to have often such as salad etc. [Kreisau, 17.10.1916]

In the next letters, there is more on the sadness of war.

Yesterday I went to a very nice musical tea in Schweidnitz, lots of nice people & good music, but what a tragedy life is now-a-days. Nearly everyone had a son or a husband fighting by Verdun or at the Somme. . . .[96] Monika now has English & French prisoners working for her. The Russians used to give a concert every Sunday in the "Hof" [manor] & she gave them cigarettes in return! I expect the English arrange races & sports instead!! [Kreisau, 28.10.1916]

Dorothy was especially busy this year preparing Christmas gifts.

I have 70 "Hof Kinder" [children of the farm workers] this year for Christmas & 45 parcels for soldiers at the front to send off, so that means quite a lot of thought & manual work. Then about 25 "family" & 20 servants to give presents to, so that I shall be kept busy for the next few weeks. [Kreisau, 12.11.1916]

In spite of its being the first one without the Y. T., the Moltkes enjoyed a happy Christmas Day as the year 1916 drew to a close.

1917

With February temperatures at twenty degrees below zero, Countess von Moltke writes, "The world looks very beautiful, but it is cruel for the troops & for the poor." [Kreisau, 9.2.1917] The weather was, however, good for skating.

> We have done a good deal of skating in Schweidnitz this week. The Boy gets on very well, JoWo staggers about & I am just beginning to skate alone. With Ete[']s helping hand I am getting on quite nicely, but of course have had some hard bumps, which is quite as it should be. [Kreisau, 9.2.1917]

The departure of a nanny in April saddened little Jowo.

> Tilla left us yesterday, Jowo especially was heartbroken, I have never seen the little man so moved, it really was most touching. He wept while saying his prayers, & first thing this morning went into her empty room, saying today he couldn't really enjoy his holidays if Tilla wasn't there. [Kreisau, 3.4.1917]

Monika, Dorothy's sister-in-law, was doing her part for the war effort.

> Monika has taken 6 city infants under a year into her house, a tremendous work & responsibility for her, . . . [Kreisau, 3.4.1917]

Helmuth James was doing well in school, where he ranked eighth in a class of thirty-three, and was showing signs of maturity in other ways, too. The ten-year-old boy took charge when Dorothy drove to a town in deep snow and got stuck on an "utterly lonely bit of road at 8 p.m.!"

> The Boy was splendid, full of sense & spirits, looking after JoWo & me, wrapping us up etc as if he were our father! I kept thinking how Dad would approve of his fortitude & care, for it really was a rather unpleasant situation, which I shall never get into again if I can help it. [Kreisau, 8.4.1917]

100

Coupled with a feeling of contentment with life at Kreisau was a painful awareness of the realities of war.

> Here the days pass in a very pleasant way, & it is hard to realize *what* awful struggles are going on in the West. The sum total of human misery seems sometimes more than can be born [*sic*.] & yet one lives on & laughs & forgets & is interested in a thousand things—what a strange mixture human nature is! [Kreisau, 14.6.1917]

As much as possible was done for the South Africans prisoners—including supplies sent by Dorothy's parents.

> How splendid that you are able to send all the S. Africans prisoners food & clothing; it must be a tremendous work. [Kreisau, 3.4.1917]

A Fräulein von Held helped out as interpreter.

> Frl. v. Held is interpreter in a prisoners camp at Cassel. She is very kind to all S. Africans, so let us hope for their sakes that there are a number of them there. [Kreisau, 14.6.1917]

Fräulein von Held was also involved in "looking after the womens [*sic*.] welfare" in the mines and factories. [Kreisau, 1.12.1917]

Countess von Moltke was virtually running a wartime hotel at Kreisau.

> We have practically no flowers this year & one misses them dreadfully, but all the beds are taken up with vegetables to feed all the hungry little & big people in the Schloss. [Kreisau, 12.8.1917]

> My war work in summer consists in offering an [asylum] to people where they can rest & get enough to eat. At present I have a household of 30 to provide for & next week we shall be even more. [Kreisau, 25.8.1917]

Fortunately, the war had little or no negative impact on the Moltke children.

101

The chicks are all very flourishing & leave me no time to be lonely or indulge in sad thoughts. It *is* a work to bring up 5 young ideas! Each one needs separate attention, but they are worth it. [Kreisau, 5.10.1917]

The Count came home to Kreisau in October for a few days ("such a joy"), before returning to Berlin for a session at the Herrenhaus. [Kreisau, 13.10.17] Dorothy writes in December, ". . . he leads an exceedingly uneventful & solitary life in Russia, filling in his spare time briefly with reading: Our talks were chiefly about the future, near & distant, & he as usual is very full of plans." [Kreisau, 12.12.1917]

And so the world rolls on, & the babies become schoolchildren & they in their turn men & women moulding destinies. [Kreisau, 1.12.1917]

1918

The news for January was a new convenience: electric lights were being installed at Kreisau. The children were "all well & wonderfully good, the Boy is doing well at school & has an extraordinary sense of duty. Asta is a rascal but a most adorable one.... Astar is a born Hausfrau; before she is out of her cot she calls out in a comanding [*sic*.] tone 'Bett lüften!' [Air out the bed!] She is perfectly sure in her own mind that she is meant to rule & she acts accordingly." [Kreisau, 11.2.1918]

By March, the house was lit by electricity for the first time.

The children went almost mad for joy, raced about the house switching on the lights & dancing Indian dances in the intervals.... it is so nice that the installation should just coincide with the Y.T.s visit. The whole house will be illuminated this evening when the dear person arrives. [Kreisau, 8.3.1918]

The children enjoyed singing English nursery rhymes sent by their attentive South African grandmother.

The Nursery Rymes [*sic*.] have arrived safely & we have begun singing them; Hey diddle, diddle goes splendidly already & the chicks are enraptured. . . . Carl Bernd is quite puffed up by the thought of "singing English." [Kreisau, 16.3.1918]

More hard war news follows.

On Wednesday I am going to hear Bachs "Johannis Passion" in Breslau, spend the night there & then go on Thursday to Conradswaldau where I hope to see Friedel Ploetz who is home at last after over 3 years imprisonment—you may imagine his joy. [Kreisau, 24.3.1918]

Bill Moltke is in a sanatorium growing strong & young again after the last frightful 4 years & Trude is going to him next week, so is sending her two children to me for 6 or 8 weeks. . . . I do wish I had news of my English friends who are involved in the gigantic struggle going on in France. [Balfanz, Pomerania, 14.4.1918]

Poor Mrs Scholtz! I am trying to make enquiries about her boy & if I hear anything definite will let you know at once. I suppose he belonged to the Royal Flying Corps? [Kreisau, 24.4.1918]

Her visit to the Eye Hospital brings home the terrible effects of the fighting.

I also spent 2 hours in Schönchen's Eye Hospital,—so touching. Some blind & the rest with one eye shot out or wounded. [Kreisau, 24.4.1918]

Dorothy received some good news at about this time—the advent of women's suffrage in England.

How glad you must all be at the franchise being given to women in England! What a new outlet of energy & enthusiasm it will be. [Kreisau, 8.3.1918]

When Lady Rose Innes was commended for her war work in Pretoria, where she had worked with other women to equip a

South African hospital ship, Dorothy rejoiced over "the splendid news of Mother's decoration. . . . I am sure never was an honour better deserved ."[97] [Kreisau, 19.5.1918]

In May, the Count returned to the front, this time to the Ukraine. In bittersweet mode, Dorothy reflects, "Never was the Spring so beautiful as this year, & the world so troubled."

> The poor Y. T. is puffing away in the train at present to the uttermost ends of the Ukraine—an awful journey which I fear will put an end to his many unexpected & pleasant visits. [Kreisau, 19.5.1918]

She continued her hospitality at the *Schloss* as part of her war work. Little Asta, too, did war work in her own way.

> The other day Asta was standing at the window upstairs & seeing one of the prisoners passing by, the little mite yelled out "Leo", Leo looked up & nodded to her & she called out "guten Abend", you can imagine how pleased he was! [Kreisau, 2.6.1918]

As always, separation from her parents tugged at Dorothy's heartstrings.

> . . . here we are separated as completely as if you lived on another planet, the faithful William is dead & our hearts are sore at the loss of many friends. [Kreisau, 21.6.1918]

In July, Helmuth was reassigned to work "as agricultural officer nearer home, though still in occupied country." [Kreisau, 18.7.18]

Gilchrist

A South African family friend named Gilchrist was taken prisoner in the area. Young Helmuth took a keen interest in him.

> The Boy was very excited about young Gilchrist & as the prisoners often come to the Kapellenberg he is constantly wondering whether this or that one may not be he! [Kreisau, 18.7.1918]

104

While giving hospitality to German soldiers, Dorothy received news of Scholtz, the South African airman whose mother had been anxiously asking for news of him. It seems that a German friend of the Moltkes, Wolfgang Websky, had met Scholtz in the Officers Camp in Freiburg and was going to "try & find out for me where he is." She also received news of Gilchrist.

> Young Gilchrist, to whom I wrote, made an attempt to escape, but was captured again in Austria & is to be sent back to Schweidnitz. There are over a dozen S. Africans in Schweidnitz, but none whom I know. . . . I have had a full house & much to do & am glad that there is to be a fortnight's pause before a fresh relay arrives. [Kreisau, 1.8.1918]

Her German friends, however, were not so fortunate in acquiring information about their soldiers in Africa.

> . . . none of the Germans get news of those in East or West Africa & that of course is very torturing. [Kreisau, 1.8.1918]

Countess von Moltke derived strength and comfort from her husband's presence during his leaves from the front, writing, "It is a wonderful refreshment to have a 'good mans shoulder to lean on' for a while & not to bear the war burdens quite alone." [Kreisau, 10.8.1918]

The prospect of meeting her parents in one of the Scandinavian countries at some point also cheered Dorothy's spirits. She could not then know that the war was almost over.

> The longer the war lasts the more intense my longing for you becomes. Should it go on still for years, which God forbid, do you think there is the least possibility of your coming to Danemark or Sweden? Because I think it might be possible for me to get a passport for those countries, especially for the former; but I am terribly afraid of submarines for you & implore you not to think of coming unless it can be accomplished without danger. [Kreisau, 26.8.1918]

The more tragic the war news, the more she strove to rise above it, as in this letter written after learning of the death of a South African friend.

> Poor Bobby Lindley, I remember so well the rejoicings when he was born. It is frightfully sad, & such cases meet one on every side. . . . One must keep ones mind on essentials now-a-days, & not let the nonessentials which are mostly trying get the upper hand in one's consciousness. [Kreisau, 11.10.1918]

Armistice

At last, the long struggle was over, and on November 11, the Armistice was signed in Compiègne, France.

> It seems impossible to express a thousandth part of what one is feeling. . . . The changes for us will come later I expect, when peace is signed & somebody has to pay; that "somebody" probably will be us. But *nothing* matters if we only once reach the stage of living in a world in which peace & order reigns. [Kreisau, 19.11.1918]

> Anyway I know you will be glad to here [*sic*.] that up to the present everything is quiet & orderly here & one hardly notices any signs of the new régime. But what a time this is! You can hardly imagine what a state of upheaval we are experiencing. [Kreisau, 27.11.1918]

She found solace, however, in her warm relationship with her husband's sister, Margarethe von Trotha, who was also a Christian Scientist.

> My greatest comfort is Ete who has a point of view beyond the typical conservative. We have grown very near to one another during these hard years of warfare. [Kreisau, 27.11.1918]

Another consequence of the war was a severe food shortage, which caused social unrest.

> There is great probability that in the early Spring, February till June, there will be much unrest & strikes etc., on account of the scarcity of food. Now I should be *most* unwilling to leave

106

Creisau, for the more difficult the situation the more necessary it is that the "Herrschaft" [owners of the estate] should be on the spot. It is simply a question of duty. . . . The food question is a very serious one. [Kreisau, 28.11.1918]

One positive result of the war was the establishment of women's suffrage in Germany.

It seems very funny to think of the German women having the vote; I am trying to get a lecturer to speak to the women here on the subject of their responsibilities & duties regarding the franchise & hope to succeed. Women are on all boards & "Vereins" [societies] already—when the Teuton does anything he is very thorough!! [Kreisau, 27.11.1918]

1919

Aftermath of World War I

In the beginning of 1919, Dorothy reassured her parents, "For the present all is quiet here," adding cautiously, "though no one knows of course how long it will last" [Kreisau, 7.1.1919]. Although the *Schloss* was full of German soldiers at this time, the *Einquartierung* (quartering) brought with it many blessings for the Moltke family.

We are quite safe for the next few weeks at any rate as we have heavy "Einquartierung" here, the house is full to overflowing with officers & men, all very nice which is a great thing. How long they will remain it is naturally impossible to say, but I expect they will be here well into February, perhaps even until the Spring. Through them we have got enough coal to heat the house & so feel ourselves in clover. They bring a good deal of food with them, so that it is possible to cater for them without ruining oneself. [Kreisau, 7.1.1919]

The children especially enjoyed the attention of the officers.

The children are all very well & happy & enjoy the "Einquartierung" immensely, for the officers romp & play with them a great deal & they are having the time of their lives. The other evening seven of the officers came to hear her [Asta] say her prayers, & she was enchanted. [Kreisau, 7.1.1919]

In the spring, the Moltke family was able to get away from the misery of postwar Germany and take refuge in The Hague, Netherlands, for a two-month visit with Dorothy's parents, who had travelled from South Africa. In his *Autobiography*, Sir James describes the effect of the war on his daughter's family.

We arrived at the Hague early in April; Dorothy and her children were already there, and we spent two delightful months together. They were all rather fine-drawn; the blockade had left its mark upon them, in spite of the fact that they had all along resided in the country. The children were peaked and sallow, and their mother declared that she felt as if she never wanted to look at mangoldwurzel [Swiss chard] or potatoes again. The younger children had never seen an orange. We had brought a store of 'goodies' from the Cape, and the process of making up for lost time was a pleasure to all concerned. To our little war-sundered family the Hague was a charming trysting-place. The leisurely unfolding of a European spring is in strong contrast with the brief interlude between the seasons which prevails in most parts of South Africa. And we were in the middle of the bulb country; wherever we travelled, acres of colour were splashed upon the verdant landscape. Dutch bulbs are renowned the world over, and the industry is a valuable one. It has the advantage of being carried on in beautiful surroundings and of yielding a lovely by-product.[98]

Unbeknownst to Sir James, the Moltkes' visit to the Netherlands had been facilitated by an old friend of the Rose Inneses', William P. Schreiner, High Commissioner for the Union of South Africa in London. Having learned of his friend's benevolence toward his beloved daughter, Sir James wrote of his meeting with Schreiner in London.

There had been a touching conversation at our first meeting; I had corresponded with him about Dorothy's welfare, and he

108

handed me the office file to read. I found that every cable and letter had been drafted by himself, and the instructions at every stage had been written in his own hand. Deeply grateful though I was, I pointed out that if he insisted upon giving personal attention to every detail of the papers that came before him, he would kill himself in the end. 'I dealt with your daughter's case as if she were my own child', was his reply. It was the crown of well-nigh fifty years of friendship, and the fragrance of it is with me still. There are some things that are unforgettable.[99]

Two months later, the Moltkes returned to Germany and the punishing economic conditions of the postwar period. Writing in late fall, Dorothy describes the heavy snowstorms that were causing shortages of potatoes and beets.

> . . . no fodder for the cattle; that means no butter & milk! . . . it needs all ones courage & ones strength to keep going. . . . The chief thing however is for Germany to get through this winter without a catastrophe of some sort. . . . [Kreisau, 16.11.1919]

Out-of-control inflation plagued them and all Germans, as did the Allies' delay in returning German prisoners of war.

> The poor Y. T. it really is most trying for him. . . . Confusion on every side! Added to this he like everyone else here is dreadfully depressed at the endless postponement of the prisoners of wars return. And of course the feeling of impotence, so very new to Germans, is exceedingly galling to them. How far we have failed to keep our promises I may not able to judge, but it is a cruel thing to keep these thousands of men from their homes, especially as you have such endless means of turning the thumbscrew should we need it. [Kreisau, 28.11.1919]

As early as 1919, Dorothy foresaw the consequences of all this humiliation and suffering.

> There remain only two possibilities for the world: a real League of Nations, or a constant plotting on the part of Germany to regain her old power, & there can be no doubt as to which course is the wisest & best for all mankind. I belong

to the League of Nations league which is very active in the Fatherland. [Kreisau, 28.11.1919]

She notes, too, the treatment of German prisoners by the British and Americans in contrast to that of the French.

The poor Bankauer[100] are expecting French or English Einquartierung, after having had German soldiers there for a year. We all hope the English will come, though of course any billeting & especially any enemy soldiers are most trying. Wolf has returned from France having pretended he was mad & being in consequence sent home. He, like all others coming from France have had a cruel & appalling experience. I have only heard of one man up till now who has been decently treated in France, whereas all those in American camps & nearly all those in English camps speak well of their treatment, although in England they had very scanty food in many cases (not officers) but the treatment was humane. Whereas the French in many cases are sadists. But enough of these horrid subjects, only our hearts are very full just now about the poor German fellows languishing in France. [Kreisau, 28.11.1919]

It was now mid-December, and another German (i.e., elaborate and magical) Christmas was just around the corner. Countess von Moltke thanks her parents for Christmas gifts of cocoa and coffee sent from South Africa and looks forward to a family visit to Cape Town planned for 1921. [Kreisau, 17.12.1919] Asta, now aged four, was already preparing for the trip.

Asta declared in her high little voice the other day "Wenn ich zu Grannie und Daddy gehe, nehme ich meine Schippe (trowel) mit." [When I go to Granny and Daddy's, I will take my trowel with me.] She is always planning for the journey. [Kreisau, 28.11.1919]

In spite of the shortages, the Moltkes managed to continue the family tradition of entertaining a large number of people—mainly relatives—with a sumptuous holiday dinner, for which the estate's farm was able to supply the food, at the

110

Schloss.

> I have an enormous amount to get through before Christmas & will be glad when everything has gone off well & happily. We shall be 20 at table and 12 downstairs, so it needs some contriving to make everything nice. We shall have a good supply of meat for the holiday week which is a great help, for on Saturday we are killing a pig, & we have geese & ducks too to fill the hungry mouths. [Kreisau, 17.12.1919]

The Count strained every muscle and nerve to manage the estate farm and to carry out other duties as well.

> The Y.T. is truly splendid, works untiringly, & in spite of his many worries & difficulties is always cheerful & harmonious. Sometimes only rather silent, that is the only sign he gives. He often works from 4 a.m. & is at it all day long. As he is "Amtsvorsteher" [administrative head] he has a lot of clerical work as well. We are in great straits for fodder for our cattle, as the Rüben [sugar beets] are still to a large extent in the ground (the Beet leaves & "Schnitzel" are excellent fodder) & yesterday our milk output fell within 24 hours 30 liters! In our butter & milkless country that is very serious. The Y.T. was able to buy some Schnitzel yesterday, enough for a few weeks, but for an enormous price naturally. We have not only not been able to sell a single potatoe [*sic*.], but have had to *buy* some for 12,000 M. (£600) to feed our people & ourselves! So you see life isn't all roses! But it might be much worse so we are cheerful & hopeful in spite of it all & are thankful for our really warm house. [Kreisau, 17.12.1919]

1920

Hope for a better world

By 1920, there is a tone of desperation mixed with optimism in Dorothy's letters.

> Everyone has instinctively the feeling just now, that the world is so depressing, that one cultivates domestic happiness &

unity to a much greater degree than ever before. [Kreisau, 1.1.1920]

Her hopes for the promises of the new League of Nations were already faltering.

Dear Dad, *what* has become of our League of Nations on which we staked all our hopes for the future of the world? I fear it is stillborn. Anyway the policy of the Allies is strengthening the hands of reaction & Conservatism here enormously, & one can't be surprised at it. I think Wilson's[101] failure one of the great tragedies of history. Such high ideals, & not the strength, ability or force to see them through or else withdraw. The breach of faith is what distresses me most. [Kreisau, 1.1.1920]

She deplores the harsh terms of the Treaty of Versailles, with its demands for huge reparations to be paid by the defeated Germans.

The Germans did many frightful things, nay unpardonable things no doubt, but they were done during a life & death struggle, while the present acts [of the Allies], just as cruel though more civilized, are committed on countries that are completely vanquished. [Kreisau, 1.1.1920]

She describes the chaos created by inflation and its effect on the food situation.

A great famine is expected in March till June owing to our having no money to buy food (our mark is now worth a little more than a farthing!) but things so often turn out better than one expects, that I don't really think it will come to a general upheaval, though doubtless thousands of unfortunates will be near starving. . . . The Y. T. is wonderful, developing a thoroughness & industry which is quite amazing, and in spite of everything always cheerful & kindly. [Kreisau, 31.1.1920]

Treatment of the war criminals by the Allies loomed, as Germans struggled to rise above poverty and inflation.

The question naturally which is uppermost in all our thoughts

112

is the "war-criminals" list, & I fear stormy days are ahead of us. . . . The Allied Commissions are here. The British very correct, the French beastly. Even the English are disgusted & have removed the French from the Chairmanship. . . . Berlin has much improved during the last year or so, much cleaner & more orderly. The prices are terrific. People well dressed, but selling their household goods to make it possible. . . . [Berlin, 7.2.1920]

To her parents, concerned about the burdens Dorothy was bearing as hostess of Kreisau, she explains the rationale for the Moltkes' custom of regularly serving dinner to fifteen or twenty, sometimes as many as thirty, people.

I know you sometimes think the family impose too much on us, but then, you see, the Y. T. inherited *everything* with the unwritten obligation of keeping up the "home" in Creisau for all. . . . It would be considered very queer to live alone when the distress round about one is so very great. . . . The whole of the Creisau income is swallowed up by the peoples wages. One wonders how it is going to end. The Y. T. is splendid, never depressed or downhearted & yet not taking things too lightly. [Kreisau, 1.9.1920]

The Count joined the relatively liberal *Deutsche Volkspartei* [German People's Party].

Last Wednesday a branch of the "Deutsche Volkspartei" (used to be national-liberal & corresponds to the moderate liberals in England) was formed here. . . . The Y. T. is the only man of his class who has joined it, in Silesia, the home of Junkers! . . . it is a "right" party, but much more broadminded than the conservatives. [Kreisau, 14.9.1920]

His new allegiance was in strong contrast to the thinking of the military class from which he came.

The military mind is the most unimaginative, stupid & narrow imaginable. I know so many "military minds" here, dear people, . . . but heaven forbid them talking politics, war, or any "big" subjects. [Kreisau, 3.10.1920]

113

A bright note for Dorothy was South Africa's part in the First Assembly of the League of Nations in Geneva, November 15 through December 18, 1920.

> I have been following the Society [League] of Nations Conference in Geneva with much interest. What a fine representative South Africa has. I do hope some good will come of it all in time. [Kreisau, 29.11.1920]

On the last day of December, Dorothy sailed to South Africa with two of her children—probably the two youngest, Asta and Carl Bernd—for another extended visit with her parents.

1921

"Most dearly Beloveds," Dorothy wrote in May as her ship passed Walvis Bay (now in Namibia), on the west coast of Africa, en route to Germany. "Did you see me waving from the other side of the ship long after you had left the quay? I saw your dear handkerchiefs for quite a long time." [Walvis Bay, 9.5.1921]

Arriving in Germany, she received a festive Silesian welcome as members of the family wept tears of joy.

> Surprise to say that the Y. T. met me at Hamburg & my return to Creisau was quite touching. The 3 boys met us at Königszelt, Helmuth James a young man, a child no longer, with a deep voice, a very good slender figure, and quite a head taller than his father, it is simply unbelievable. In Creisau village there were 2 archways of green with "Willkommen", one at the entrance to the Hof & the steps & columns of the *Schloss* decorated likewise. Schwester & the schoolchildren sang as we arrived, Muttel, T. [Tante–Aunt] Louise & T. Viola wept & we were all very happy!! . . . The Schwester has just been with another series of children who sang a song about Frau Gräfin [Countess], Africa, etc., to the melody of the Wacht am Rhein! It was extremely funny. [Kreisau, 13.6.1921]

114

The Little War

In addition to the residual effects of World War I, the little war with the Poles, who were fighting against the Germans in Upper Silesia, continued to plague the country. The family learned that Carl Viggo and his nephew Hans Carl were "both fighting in Oberschlesien [Upper Silesia] & at one time there was fighting every night in Bankau. The conditions are *much* worse than the papers admit there." [Kreisau, 13.6.1921]

> At present OberSchlesien [*sic*.] is occupying all our thoughts. We all hoped the English troops would reestablish order, but they say their hands are bound, which means, I suppose, that the French have made concessions in the East in order to be allowed to dominate in Europe. The sufferings of the inhabitants are great, & terrible cruelties are perpetrated. The "Selbstschutz" [self-defense] consists of students mostly with ci-devant officers in command, for the Reichswehr [army] is not allowed to go there. . . . The nation is growing terribly bitter, which is so bad for the soul of a people & the Allies are simply recreating German militarism. Meanwhile, the Upper Silesians are suffering terribly. O. [Onkel] Heinrichs inspector at his 2nd estate was carried off by the Poles who of course are quite out of hand. [Kreisau, 18.6.1921]

> The Poles are simply bandits, not regular forces at all, with proper French & Polish officers. . . . A wretched state of affairs. . . . This little "war" has already cost Germany as much as the Franco-German war did!! [Kreisau, 3.7.1921]

Adding to the Germans' misery were the sanctions imposed by the Treaty of Versailles.

> And the sanctions! What do you say to the sanctions being continued, although Germany has signed & is fulfilling the ultimatum? No one ought to be surprised when the Germans refuse to trust fine words after the experience of the last 2 years. [Kreisau, 3.7.1921]

Countess von Moltke took refuge in the positive, uplifting

115

teachings of Christian Science and, rising early, fled to Schweidnitz to catch the Sunday church service at "the impossible hour of 8:30 a.m." [Kreisau, 3.7.1921]

Dorothy hoped that the family's good friend Jan Smuts, who was on his way to Europe, where he was instrumental in the founding of the League of Nations, might help with the crisis in Upper Silesia.

> I wrote to Smuts a little while ago, asking him, if he did come on to the Continent, to come to Creisau as I wanted him to see a little of the Upper Silesian question, but alas, as was to be expected, he hasn't the time. [Kreisau, 18.7.1921]

Inflation and drought

The rest of the world, including the Moltkes, endured yet another deprivation—severe drought. With the wells so low that "no baths can be taken," there was no place in which to wash dirty linen, and the plants were dying. [Kreisau, 30.7.1921]

During this period of wild inflation and economic chaos in Germany, Dorothy's parents came to the family's rescue with generous allowances, which they cabled from South Africa. Upon receiving a cheque for £315, Dorothy writes that she intends to keep the money outside the country, in Rotterdam, "for the present, until the mark falls again as it is sure to do in January when the reparations are due."

> . . . the mere fact of having money in Rotterdam that, at a crisis, could be used, takes a great deal of strain off the Y. T.'s shoulders. The farm is *very* well stocked & in very good repair, but the difficulty is to find ready money. . . . If we hadn't had (& still have) that awful drought we should have got through so much better. [Kreisau, 13.12.1921]

In late December, the Countess once again set about preparing for a German Christmas, with theatricals by the children. [Kreisau, 24.12.1921]

1922

Strikes and a "Russian" winter

In February 1922, a paralyzing railway strike caused a reduction in postal and train services, while inflation reached absurd proportions. Taking advantage of the English pound's value relative to the depressed German mark, the Count used the check from South Africa to pay off some large debts that he had inherited from his father.

> It will be a great comfort to have them got rid of & I know you will be pleased. It was a debt in pre-war times of £12,500,— just fancy that being covered by £315! [Kreisau, 6.1.1922]

The winter of 1922 was bitterly cold ("Oh my Darlings, Such cold; quite Russian." [Kreisau, 25.1.1922]), with freezing temperatures, which made it especially expensive to heat the *Schloss*. Yet the snowy weather had its poetic aspect and afforded the family an opportunity to enjoy winter sports.

> On Tuesday the Y. T. had to go to Dittersbach on business & we sleighed over, through the mountains, 6 hours there & back in *warm* sunshine through beautiful winter forest scenery. It was lovely. [Kreisau, 16.2.1922]

> . . . all the world is sleighing, skating, tobogganing & skiing. . . . The thermometer has been, for some weeks, 5° below Zero (Fahrenheit) and when one blows ones nose the handkerchief freezes at once—verra arkkard! [Letter to Aunt Annie, Kreisau, 8.2.1922]

The animals, too, struggled with the extreme cold.

> Even the poor fowls have had the combs frozen in the fowl house! And the pheasants fly into the garden to look for food. [Kreisau, 11.2.1922]

Watching over her brood with the tender care of a mother hen for her chicks, Dorothy appreciated the individuality of her husband and each one of her children.

> The Y. T. is very capable & busy & silent & kind, just as he

117

always was, really a dear. And the babes are all very sweet, each in their different ways. . . . It is all so interesting, & one sees how little one really can do, how each is born with his own tastes, weaknesses & strengths, & at best, one can but prune & encourage & shape a little. [Kreisau, 8.2.1922]

I wish you could see the wriggles & squeaks of joy that daily are indulged in by Carl Bernd on account of his bantam fowls, . . . We gave him a ducky little fowl house for Christmas & the bantams, 3 hens & a cock, laid their first egg yesterday. . . . He has already invested in a note book to keep accounts in, & can think of nothing but his fowls. Altogether he is developing so nicely, all his naughty, tearful ways have been outgrown & he is *so* delightfully active, capable & independent, whereas I can't imagine *how* Willo is ever to get on in the world, being so unpracticable [*sic*.], forgetful, easily influenced, & hopeless at school. Poor little fellow, one can only help him to overcome his weaknesses as much as one can, & the rest he must do himself, but it won't be easy for him.[102] [Kreisau, 24.2.1922]

The family, in turn, showed their love for Dorothy with a large birthday dinner for forty-eight, including the usual toasts.

Herr v. Portatius made a charming little speech, on account of my birthday, asking the assembled guests to raise their glasses to the "Sonne von Creisau" [Sun of Kreisau] (!! who can that be I wonder?). [Kreisau, 24.2.1922]

"By the way, you will be amused to hear that Muttel reads nothing but English novels, (German books bore her she says!)," Dorothy wrote her parents in March. To accommodate her mother-in-law's new literary enthusiasm, she asked her parents to send over some old-fashioned novels with "plenty of love interest."

She started reading English (with a dictionary when she can't make head or tail of a thing) while I was in Africa, as it made her feel more connected with me—rather touching isn't it?—&

118

the habit has grown. [Kreisau, 10.3.1922]

Now that Helmuth James had reached the age of fifteen, the family decided to send him to a boarding school in Schondorf, near Munich, approximately 300 miles (500 kilometers) from Kreisau. Dorothy was deeply affected by this change.

> Tomorrow it will be 15 years since Helmuth James was born— & it seems like yesterday. They have been quite unclouded years as far as he is concerned, dear boy, & now the great step of leaving home is drawing very near. His last birthday at home. It makes me feel rather solemn. He is such a dear fellow, with all his instincts right, the best type of normal human being, so capable & hardworking & affectionate, & entirely reliable. [Kreisau, 10.3.1922]

Before leaving for Schondorf, Helmuth James was confirmed in the Lutheran Church in a ceremony at Kreisau—"such a stupid event, but, in the end, he wanted it done because of tradition & being the eldest etc" [Kreisau, 11.2.1922].

> The Boy was confirmed on 3rd, here in the *Schloss*, in the Fieldmarshals room which is preserved as a sort of place for family functions. I am enclosing a photo of the Boy in his Tyrolese [Tyrolean] dress which is what is worn at his new school in Bavaria. [Letter to Aunt Minnie, Kreisau, 8.4.1922]

The separation was difficult for both mother and son. "I miss the Boy very much & he suffers a good deal from homesickness, poor fellow," she writes, "but it is good for him, as is so much that is unpleasant." [Letter to Aunts Annie and Minnie, Kreisau, 6.11.1922].

The Treaty of Versailles and reparations

The Countess was philosophical about a larger issue as well: Germany's ongoing struggle to pay the reparations imposed by the Treaty of Versailles.

> The Y. T. returned from Berlin on Monday morning, having heard nothing but pessimistic utterances from every side. It

seems neither the Government nor anyone else knows what to do next, how to pay the reparations every ten days, keep money in the country & steady the prices. . . . it is an unwholesome state of things, & everything is in a thorough muddle. . . . it is the old order that is changing, & most men are mere insects compared to the all-compelling, logical and unerring course of the worlds development. [Kreisau, 24.2.1922]

Like most people in Germany, she deplored the terms of the Treaty.

The news of the demands the Reparations Commission have formulated will be a great shock to everyone in Germany. . . . they mean a new & heavy burden of taxation. . . . The state is almost bankrupt, & its citizens *who are able to earn* are many of them in a flourishing way, & there is plenty of money about, no unemployment & overworked factories. (For widdows [*sic*.], penshoners [*sic*.] & old people living on the interest of their investments the situation is pitiful.)   [Kreisau, 23.3.1922]

Summer Sunday

In March, the village children performed a medieval ritual at the *Schloss*.

Tomorrow is "Sommer Sonntag" [Summer Sunday] i.e. the village children come & sing songs & get a special kind of cake in return. It is an old custom, dating from the middle ages, & is sometimes ushered in by a tussel [tussle] between winter & sommer [*sic*.] (personified) in which the Summer is victorious. [Kreisau, 23.3.1922]

Perhaps this allegory of the warmth and light of summer triumphing over the cold and dark of winter held special meaning for the Countess and her family in these dark days.

As summer turned into late fall, the economic situation remained dire.

    . . . paper money hasn't anything like the real purchasing
120

power of metallic coinage. . . . we rub along, but when raw materials become prohibitive, as is beginning to be the case, the people simply can't help plundering if they want to live. But we all hope that somehow or other the worst will be avoided, though nothing constructive can be done in Europe till the Treaty of Versailles is revised. That is the corner stone. [Kreisau, 6.11.1922]

1923

Women' Congress in Rome

In March 1923, Dorothy's mother was once again on her way to Europe for a visit with her daughter's family. The plan was for mother and daughter to meet in Rome, where Lady Rose Innes would be addressing the Congress of the International Woman Suffrage Alliance. Dorothy wrote to her father in South Africa.

We are really *very* happy here, enjoying everything except that part of the Congress which is presided over by a Latin, for they seem to have had very little training in chairmanship & do it badly. [Rome, 13.5.1923]

One can easily picture Dorothy's warm-hearted, outgoing Scottish-South African mother getting along in the Eternal City.

She picks up Italian with her usual thoroughness, talks to all the cabdrivers, concierges etc & makes a friend of each one, & just *hates* it when a situation arises which is beyond her vocabulary! [Rome, 13.5.1923]

Tea with Mussolini

The Congress included a garden party at which Benito Mussolini was present.

The Congress has been a disappointment, . . . but of course it has been interesting to see & meet so many well-known women, be it ever so superficially. . . . Mother spoke *very* nicely a few evenings' ago for S. Africa, just a 4 Minutes speech. . . . Picture Mother & I eating an ice on a peice [*sic*.] of *paper* (no plates available) with *one* spoon & this at a Government Garden party on the Palatine!! Musolini [*sic*.] looks dreadfully insolent & second class, rather like a third rate film hero. [Rome, 18.5.1923]

From 1923 to 1925, the industrial Ruhr valley region in Germany was occupied by French and Belgian troops. This action was provoked by Germany's failure to make the coal and coke deliveries to France required by the terms of the Treaty of Versailles. Dorothy was appalled at the attitude of the French.

Stresemann [German Chancellor and Foreign Minister in 1923][103] has retired. I think he had great courage & ability, but *nobody* can really improve matters as long as France refuses to settle the Ruhr problem. The factories are closing everywhere, which of course is frightfully serious. . . . During the last 3 weeks all the villages & farms have organized & have firearms with the consent of the government (you better say nothing about this as it may be contrary to the Treaty) in order to protect themselves against marauding bands or communistic putsches. [Kreisau, 5.10.1923]

A bad potato crop in most of Germany added to the misery caused by the foundering economy and rampant inflation.

. . . the unfortunate townsfolk walk from one farm to another trying to buy some sacks for the winter, & generally meeting with a refusal. The shops are nearly empty, . . . The peasants won't sell for paper money, it is so worthless. . . . I think it is simply wonderful that order is being so well maintained in the Reich. . . . the worst fears of bloodshed etc seem to have been overcome owing to the energetic measures of the government,—martial law etc, so that things look a *little* brighter, if only we can get food, coal & work for everyone, all will be well. [Kreisau, 10.10.1923]

Inflation and hunger

The Countess describes the plight of the banks and the lack of available credit.

> The banks are in a perfectly hopeless muddle. One can't pay by cheque any longer, for it takes a fortnight for the bank to place the sum to the other mans credit, & by that time the money is valueless! Hence everything is paid in cash or barter, & there is no credit given anywhere. [Kreisau, 25.10.1923]

Everywhere, the people were desperate for food.

> It is a great nuisance. . . . The towns are in a terrible plight for there is practically no food to be had. . . . Soup kitchens are being organized everywhere for the townsfolk. . . . People come all day long asking for food or potatoes or wood, it is both heartrending & a pest. My astonishment is that things are still so orderly. The Germans are certainly a very disciplined & quiet people, . . . The riots, unrest & misery are all around, but up till now Schweidnitz & the surrounding country are perfectly quiet. [Kreisau, 25.10.1923]

The Count did his best to alleviate the hunger and suffering of the people of Schweidnitz.

> The Y. T. is trying all over the country to buy some loads of potatoes for the Schweidnitz people, but up till now has not succeeded. . . . life is difficult enough even for us, especially as everything & everybody depends on us, & for the townsfolk it is simply devasting [*sic*]. [Kreisau, 25.10.23]

> The Y. T. spends his mornings almost daily in driving about trying to sell something or get enough money to pay for some necessity. The banks are hardly used by the farmer any longer, though of course the rest of the public who only deal in paper money must. . . . We have formed a "Not Gemeinschaft"[Society for the Needy] in Schweidnitz, & all the farmers give of their produce, & this is given in turn to the most needy, also milk & sugar for the babies, but even that is not adequate to meet all the needs of so many unfortunates.

[Kreisau, 2.11.1923]

Measures were taken for the protection of the people in Kreisau.

> We have formed a Heimat Schutz [Homeland Protection] in Creisau, as most other villages & towns have, & every night 2 men patrol the village from 9–1 a.m. & 2 others from 1–4, to prevent stealing & incendiarism. [Kreisau, 15.11.1923]

In these difficult times, the teachings of Christian Science were a source of strength and courage to Dorothy and Helmuth.

Inflation and Nazism

As inflation continued to soar, Adolf Hitler began to make some bold moves in Bavaria.

> . . . the mark has reached fantastic numbers; we all reckon in "goldmarks" but still pay in paper billions & trillions. . . . The keeping of accounts has become well nigh impossible. . . . By todays paper I see that Hitler has declared a dictatorship in Bavaria. I don't trust him or the Bavarians either, though I feel sure they don't want to sever their connection with the Reich, but they have no foresight or political sense, which indeed is a most rare gift in this country. [Kreisau, 9.11.1923]

For Germany's troubles, Dorothy places particular blame on the French Government's punitive attitude toward Germany.

> It really is a horrible muddle, & unless Europe & America can rid themselves of French influence, & act in a broad statesmanlike way, I can't see how Germany is to recover. The privations are infinitely worse than they were during the blockade, & the wonder is, that order is maintained at all. . . . It is strange how one goes on living ones ordinary life, in spite of all the momentous happenings around one, happenings moreover which may have very serious consequences for each one of us. [Kreisau, 9.11.1923]

The Countess's next letter traces the fast-moving events in

Germany and Hitler's attempted putsch.

> History marches apace in the Fatherland these days, & since last I wrote, there have been all sorts of ups & downs in Bavaria, the Crown Prince [Wilhelm] has returned, & the Government is working without a majority. I don't suppose anyone out of the country can follow the quick march of events, even we find it very complicated. That Hitlers Putsch has failed so entirely is a great gain, though no one quite understands Kahr['s] [Bavarian right-wing conservative politican] change of tactics.[104] The Crown Prince's return has evoked very little comment, most people are glad that he has been able to rejoin his family, but, for the moment at least, no political role is assigned to him. The great battle of the moment is being waged with unstable currency. If we can evolve a stable currency. . . . If we shall be able to pull through, if not, chaos will result. [Kreisau, 15.11.1923]

Despite these economic challenges, many German Christian Scientists found reasons to give thanks at their annual Thanksgiving services.

> Yesterday we had our C. S. Thanksgiving Service. We had hired a good sized hall which was quite full, about 400 people, & it really was a great success. It is touching to hear people giving thanks & praising God in these days of stress & want. [Kreisau, 15.11.1923]

In late 1923, the German government embarked on a program of economic recovery based on the introduction of a new and stable currency, the Rentenmark.

> The outlook is just a wee bit brighter, owing to the new currency which really looks as if it means to be steady. Prices have gone down too a little (mostly agricultural products only unfortunately!) & the Separatist Movement in the Rheinland has failed signally, in spite of all the help France gave it. We also once more have a constitutional government,—it is indeed practically the same Stresemann government with another less compromising figure head. [Kreisau, 6.12.1923]

125

Her comments on the future of Germany were prophetic.

> Smuts' speech on arriving in Cape Town was cabled over here yesterday, & I quite agree with him that once Germany gets on her feet, she will recover quickly. The difficulty & problem will then be, to keep her from starting a war of revenge, & through her exaggerated industriousness, from becoming a menance [menace] by ousting others from the market. However its a long way before these questions become serious, & at present we shall all be thankful if not too many die of hunger & cold this winter. [Kreisau, 6.12.1923]

> The vital question just now is: can the government carry on with these few millions of "Renten mark"? They are dismissing crowds of officials & in every way trying to economize & it is said that gigantic taxes are being prepared once more. Nothing matters if only we can pull through & save the currency, but it must be frightfully difficult to find a way. . . . Later, in years to come, when Germany is on her feet again, some wise Statesman (perhaps the Boy!) will have to evolve an arrangement so that English & German commercial competition don't clash unnecessary [unnecessarily], "spheres of influence" or something of the sort, because otherwise German industry will again become a most unpleasing trait, & quite rightly so. [Kreisau, 13.12.1923]

> But the chief thing is that we don't go under, either the family or the nation, & about that I am quite optimistic, how could I be otherwise with all the dear children who are such a joy & promise for the future? [Kreisau, 21.12.1923]

A miracle play and the fox trot

The family attended a medieval Christmas celebration in an ancient church—probably the Church of Peace in nearby Schweidnitz.

> On Sunday we all . . . went to a really beautiful "Advents Feier" (1ˢᵗ Sunday in Advent) in the FriedensKirche [Church of Peace]. It was done as these things were done in the Middle Ages, Mary & Joseph, the shephards [sic.] & many angels, all

126

acting & singing in front of the altar. Beautiful choirs & music, & selections from the Bible in between. It was a sort of miracle play, & most moving especially in that strange & beautiful old church. [Kreisau, 6.12.1923]

As the year 1923 drew to a close, Count and Countess von Moltke enjoyed learning some new dances.

The Boy . . . has been teaching us all dancing & every evening now after supper we all dance, even the Y. T.—fox trott [sic.], & all the rest of the modern dances!   [Kreisau, 28.12.1923]

1924

Winter at Kreisau

Owing to the heavy snows and slow trains in January 1924, the family at Kreisau felt "practically cut off from the world" [Kreisau, 3.1.1924]. Dorothy describes a comical moment with her sons and Muttel.

. . . the children have been ski-ing [sic.] & driving on their toboggans with the pony inspanned [harnessed] in front (a row of them, one behind the other) & the Boy skiing with the pony too, all very happy & enjoying their holidays immensely. . . . On Sunday we all supped at the Berghaus, & 4 boys pulled & shoved Muttel who sat crunched up in the little handsledge we had for the Boy when he was 2 years old! . . . It was most comical, Muttel thoroughly frightened, but not wanting to stay at home alone, & so willing to suffer greatly, with her whole head, face & all done up in cloths & mufflers! You may imagine the jokes & laughter! [Kreisau, 3.1.1924]

Dorothy's fortieth birthday celebration included hilarious performances by the children.

. . . the Frauleins, pretending to be a troupe of wandering English players, acted, sang & danced & amused us generally for more than an hour. Jowo is an extraordinarily clever comic actor, & Asta & C. B. [Carl Bernd] were perfectly ducky as

127

peasant children, dancing & singing together. Willo as a dry-as-dust Professor with spectacles was indescribably funny, but the "clou" [highlight] was a butterfly dance by Jowo, dressed in black gauze with an apricot coloured sash, who danced quite as well as Joseph in the "Legende" we saw together in Breslau. Everyone was most impressed & much entertained. [Kreisau, 5.3.1924]

In the evenings, the Count read *Adventures of Huckleberry Finn* by Mark Twain aloud to the children—"in German of course" [Kreisau, 28.2.1924]. Meanwhile, Dorothy pondered the future.

> If we lived 30 years later we should no doubt be able to go back & forth to one another by aeroplane, in the shortest time (though I fear it is more probable that "patriots" by that time will have wiped out European civilisation altogether, in which case it is better that we live at the beginning of the century.) A dismal ending to a letter, but I really aren't dismal, au contraire; man is a pathetically hopeful animal, isn't he? And somehow one always hopes reason may triumph over blindness after all. There *is* a leaven at work. [Kreisau, 28.2.1924]

The German economy and politics

Although Germany continued to be plagued by massive unemployment, Dorothy was encouraged by the stabilization of currency through the introduction of the Rentenmark. "Our Rentenmark," she writes, "has made an incredible difference in everything, political, commercial, social & moral. . . . Altogether there is a glimmer of hope everywhere" [Kreisau, 17.1.1924].

> I wonder whether you know that Germany without any trumpet blowing has become, at least as far as food is concerned, a free trade country? . . . it is simply heavenly having a stable currency once more, . . . [Kreisau, 30.1.1924]

There were still difficult problems for agrarians and landowners, but the German economy was reviving in general, a sign of which was the availability of oranges.

> At present the Fatherland is being flooded with oranges, . . .
> after doing without them for 10 years, people seem to be
> almost living on oranges, it is quite touching to see with what
> eagerness old & young participate in this novelty. [Kreisau,
> 23.1.1924]

Political developments abroad also were, to Dorothy, signs of
an improvement in the state of the world. As a liberal, she
was heartened by the recent success of the Labour Party in
the United Kingdom, which, she wrote, was "sure to be sound
on foreign affairs too" [Kreisau, 17.1.1924] and commends
the new British Prime Minister, Labour Party Leader Ramsay
MacDonald.

> We are all watching Ramsay MacDonald with great interest.
> His foreign policy is sure to be good and courageous. . . . If it
> weren't for all the suspicions, & barbarous traditions &
> phrases, what a much happier place the world would be.
> [Kreisau, 7.2.1924]

Hitler's trial

From February 26 to April 1, Adolf Hitler, retired general
Erich Ludendorff, and others[105] were tried for treason after
Hitler's attempt to grab power in the Beer Hall Putsch the
previous November.

> We are all very interested in the Ludendorf[f]-Hitler trial. I
> could weep over the lack of comprehension all these worthy &
> patriotic German conservatives show; they learn nothing & are
> quite hopeless; it is tragic to think of a big & in very many
> ways most excellent nation being governed i.e. misgoverned by
> these men. I don't think any other country possesses such a
> large number as Germany, who having eyes see not. [Kreisau,
> 5.3.1924]

When the case was decided, Hitler was given a light sentence
and Ludendorff was acquitted. Dorothy was dismayed at the
leniency of the *Volksgericht* (People's Court). [106]

> We were all very interested of course in the judgement given in

129

the Hitler Ludendorf[f] case. In my opinion it was much too mild. The truth is, it wasn't the proper Court that tried the case (that would have been in Leipzig) but a "Volks Gericht"—an institution which was dissolved on 1st April & which Bavaria had called into being in order to deal leniently with "Right" Putsches & hardly with Communists; laymen & judges sat in it. Leipzig would have dealt much more impartially with the case. But the difficulty of course is that a large part of the nation are in sympathy with these men. I wonder what the elections will bring forth. [Bresa, 2.4.1924]

Before ending her letter, Dorothy expressed her deep appreciation for her close relationship with her father.

... what a precious gift it is to be such friends with ones father as I am with mine. I really think one very seldom comes across such a perfect relationship, & I am very thankful for it. . . . I hate missing so much of you, *To* which the boy will reply "you ought to have thought of that earlier" ah me, as the Y. T. wisely remarked the other day on the same subject: "das war destiny"! [It was destiny!] I fold you in my arms & love you very, very dearly. [Bresa, 2.4.1924]

Eugenics

During this period, the German government instituted the policy of eugenics, an attempt to improve the human race through genetics.

I think it a very wise step, & will prevent a number of incurables being born, but I must confess I was astonished that Eugenics had made such strides, for, after all we in Silesia are I suppose the most Eastern part of Western Europe, i.e. in many ways the least progressive. [Kreisau, 26.3.1924]

With elections looming, Dorothy became concerned about the growing influence of the *Deutschvölkische Freiheitspartei* (The German People's Freedom Party).

We in the country notice very little election excitement. Everyone takes it for granted that the Right Parties will gain

130

greatly, until having proved that they too are unable to really greatly improve conditions, they will lose much of their influence. . . . The Deutsch Völkische Freiheits-Partei (a sort of Right Bolshevism) are gaining ground everywhere & are very dangerous. [Kreisau, 24.4.1924]

When the election was over, she felt somewhat pacified by the results.

The elections have come & gone, & (secretly) I am relieved that we haven't gone more reactionary than we have done. Everything passed off quite quietly, & there was very little visible excitement & no violence which was surprising. . . . I must say, I think it quite wonderful that Germany hasn't gone much more reactionary, seeing what propaganda plus French policy have done to drive it that way. It is the most hopeful sign, politically, in this country during the last 2 or 3 years. [Kreisau, 7.5.1924]

Helmuth James turns seventeen

Leaving Berlin and its swirl of political events, Dorothy returned home to Kreisau and the children. Of her eldest son, now seventeen, she writes:

The Boy is enjoying his holidays tremendously, & his father & I are enjoying him. He really is a treasure. He seems to be much cleverer than I ever expected him to be, & he has such a trustworthy character. On Sunday last he didn't go with us to Weistritz [a village near Schweidnitz], because, as he said, there was nothing he so much liked as being alone at home with his Father; you may imagine how the Y. T. purred! Then with a smile at me: he loved being alone with me too, but if I stayed, others would stay too, so it couldn't be done! [Kreisau, 24.4.1924]

The Boy was a great pleasure to us at Easter, in many ways still quite a child, but so dependable, so steady, & with a heart of gold. He is a great reader, & has read quite remarkably for his age. His relationship to his Father is quite delightful, & vice versa. The Y. T. is very proud of him, & they are great friends

131

& the Boy admires & understands his Father so well. At the same time he is very modern, & belongs, intellectually, to the youth of today with a European outlook, quite an interesting study. I am longing for Dad to get to know him, for I feel sure he would grow very fond of him & derive much pleasure from his grandson. [Kreisau, 7.5.1924]

In Berlin, Count and Countess von Moltke attended a performance of a new opera, *Boris Godunov* by Modest Mussorgsky ("very tragic but interesting & the music very good" [Berlin, 12.3.1924]). Back at Kreisau, in May, they hosted a concert for 120 guests at which the cellist, Max Baldner,[107] played "almost everthing by heart, with closed eyes, & his cello just sobs, really wonderful" [Kreisau, 2.5.1924].

At night the moon was shining, and Kreisau was in bloom.

Driving home last evening from our Wednesday [church] service[108] in the moonlight was quite dreamlike. [Kreisau, 15.5.1924]

. . . how I wish you were here to enjoy the *masses* of white orchids in the woods, the lilies of the valley too were quite wonderful. [Kreisau, 12.6.1924]

The little white scented orchids have blossomed in thousands in the woods. This evening we are having the first strawberries, & next week we shall be having cherries—delicious. [Kreisau, 19.6.1924]

The Count continued to make strenuous efforts to ensure the success of the estate's large farming operation.

The Y. T. has taken really infinite pains with the Spring Sowing & got everything in wonderfully, in spite of our not having been able to use our oxen. His industry & doggedness are really wonderful. [Kreisau, 15.5.1924]

[He] is doing all he can to make this harvest a success; then, by November, he can more or less see what income & what expenditure we have . . . & then if our income hasn't improved

132

enormously, we must change our way of living entirely & cut down expenses. [Kreisau, 22.5.1924]

A wounded veteran was working on the estate, and the the *Jugendamt* (Youth Department) was doing good work with children.

We also have a "Kriegsbeschädigter", i.e. war cripple, but he is outwardly not a cripple at all, for as you know every concern that employs 50 workpeople *has* to take on one Kriegs Beschädigter, this man . . . is to look after our woods & watch the fields later on, when the harvest time draws near. . . . There is a "Jugend Amt" attached to every Landrats Amt [local state government], & the illegitimate children, especially, are looked after now by the Jugend Amt & enjoy official protection. . . . really good work is being done. [Kreisau, 12.6.1924].

C.B. (Carl Bernd), then eleven, was "just the typical man en miniature, loves horses, shooting etc, . . . has a heart of gold, very sunny & loving with a great sense of justice, very practical, & of all the children he has the most religious feeling" [Kreisau, 3.9.1924].

Plans were now being made for Helmuth James to take three years of agricultural training, although his heart was already in politics.

He would like best to go for politics or to study National Economics, but of course once his 3 years farming are done he must start earning money. He is very keen about politics, & thanks to his English blood, has much more aptitude for them than most Teutons. Need I say that he is *not* Deutsch National?! [Kreisau, 26.6.1924]

Out of concern for her mother's health, Countess von Moltke urged her father to retire from his demanding post as chief justice of Transvaal, so that Lady Rose Innes might lead a quiet life. She gently teases her civic-minded mother, "It is wearisome work being a pillar of Society." [Kreisau, 10.7.1924]

133

About Muttel, her mother-in-law, Dorothy had mixed feelings of love and frustration.

> She is so dear & kind & not a bit of a pagan, with the faith of a little child, it is quite touching. She is in many ways an uncomfortable woman to live with, & there is a great deal of egotism in her make-up, especially on the surface, but she is hewn out of a big & worthy block, she is a personality, with no littleness about her. If she had not lived such a life of self indulgence & ease, she might have been a really wonderful woman. [Kreisau, 11.11.1924]

The League of Nations and War Guilt

The question of whether Germany would—or could—join the League of Nations absorbed Countess von Moltke.

> There is a great deal of talk going on in the papers here about Germany joining the League, & also about War Guilt, a very sore subject in this country. I personally don't see how Germany can join the League just yet—even if the others are ready to admit her on equal terms—seeing that nobody in the Fatherland accepts the Versailles Treaty in their hearts. Alsasce [Alsace] & Lorraine, the Danish bits, & Posen yes, but the Corridor, Memel, Danzig & Upper Silesia, the War Guilt idea & so on, nobody would agree to voluntarily. But there is a marked improvement in the European atmosphere, there is no doubt of that, . . . [Kreisau, 17.9.1924]

Article 231 of the Treaty of Versailles, subsequently called the "War Guilt Clause," required Germany to accept responsibility for World War I, and thus reparations. This was a sensitive issue in Germany.

> The German political situation at present is very interesting, what with League admission, Conservatives perhaps entering the government, trade negociations [negotiations] with England & France & a hundred internal questions as well. As you say the question of War Guilt won't be really solved for another 20 years, & for the other nations it is a question of quite secondary importance, but for the Germans it is a matter

134

which concerns them most tremendously, & they all feel very acutely the stigma it contains. [Kreisau, 3.10.1924]

"Whipped Cream"

In October, Dorothy took her second son, Jowo, to Breslau to hear Richard Strauss[109] conduct a frothy, lighthearted ballet called *Schlagobers* (Whipped Cream), a piece that Strauss wrote in the early twenties to counteract the gloom and destruction of World War I. It was criticized for, among other things, its political subtext.

The acquisition of a new invention—the radio—brought Dorothy and her family closer to England, and even to South Africa.

> Really radio is a wonderful invention. The other evening Jowo heard the band playing at the Savoy Hotel in London & the clapping & remarks that ensued, & then the clock at St Pauls striking 11 p.m.—all this up in Herr Roesners room on the 3rd floor! I tell him, soon he'll be hearing Daddy making a speech somewhere! Jowo is intensely interested in his radio & is building a larger apparatus for himself. [Kreisau, 10.9.1924]

> I am very much looking forward to Daddys address at the unveiling of Schreiners memorial.[110] I have never forgotten Daddy making a tiny speech (just a "few remarks") at the meeting called to consider building a sanat[o]rium for consumptives, & raising the level of everything immediately. It was splendid & just like him. [Kreisau, 17.9.1924]

An event of interest at this time was the successful flight of a German Zeppelin (a type of rigid airship) across the Atlantic. "Everyone here is most excitedly watching for the arrival of the Zepp[e]lin in America," Dorothy wrote on October 15, the day it landed in New Jersery [Kreisau, 15.10.1924].

Ulla

In early October, Ulla wrote a thank-you letter to Lady Rose Innes, in which she expressed her deep affection for the Moltke family.

My dear Lady Innes,

Do[rothy] just gave me as a present the lovely white sweater you knitted for her. Now I cannot withstand the pleasure to thank you very cordially for it.

It is so pretty and *so* becoming; it will be a comfort to wear it on ship-board on my way to Boston and in Boston, in which town I fear to be eaten up by home-sickness and by longing for Do and Helmuth. It seems such a strange plan in this world's [illegible word], that the people who best understand each other are allowed such short times only to be together, is it not?

Creisau with all its inmates are such a joy to have; the children have developed into very lovely beings, I feel each is [a] dear friend in my heart, inhabiting the little room Do leaves for them.

Ever so many respectful greetings to you, dear Lady Innes,

Yours gratefully

Ulla Oldenbourg.

To everyone's delight, Ulla visited Kreisau a month later.

I am enjoying Ulla very much naturally, not having seen so much of her since 1916 when she spent 6 weeks here. The Y. T. is very fond of her too, & the children just adore her, she plays with them as if she were a child herself. She will be leaving us for America in a few days I fear. [Kreisau, 11.11.1924]

On the occasion of his seventieth birthday, Dorothy writes her father:

I feel that my children are greatly blessed in having you for a grandfather, Darling, & I hope they will prove worthy of their inheritance. [Kreisau, 9.12.1924]

1925

A loan in time of need

In early 1925, the economic woes of the Moltkes' estate—high inflation, unavailability of credit, low prices for their crops of rye, sugar beets, and barley, and clover seed ruined by excessive rain—were not uncommon in that area. The Count's predicament forced him to write to Dorothy's mother, Lady Rose Innes, asking for an extension on a loan to the following autumn. This loan, he wrote, had kept him from bankruptcy, a misfortune that had befallen a number of estates in their neighbourhood. In June and July, he continued the struggle to obtain loans inside Germany, but without success. "The truth is," Dorothy writes, "there is no capital in the country" [Kreisau, 28.6.1925].

> . . . the Y. T. *is* rather worried just at present, but things always right themselves more or less in time & none of us mind being poor so *very* much, though it is delightful having money I must admit. [Kreisau, 25.7.1925]

The "Easter Egg"

The Moltkes' spirits were raised by the gift of a motorbike from Sir James. This machine, which they called the "Easter egg," brought hours of delight to the Moltke sons.

> You would rejoice to see how the "Easter egg" is used. . . . the "egg" is used almost all day long. The 3 brothers are all frightfully keen to be "Klemme Äffchen" [literally, "clinging monkeys"—a German exression for bikers] & one has to have the wisdom of Solomon in order to deal justly with them. [Kreisau, 23.5.1925]

Meanwhile, twelve-year-old Carl Bernd (C. B.) had become interested in defending the house from rats, which abounded in the nearby Peile Stream.

> C.B. asks me to tell you that he shot a large rat the other day, quite near the house—most useful. [Kreisau, 1.6.1925]

Dorothy describes for her father her brief visit with her

mother in England.

> I *did* so enjoy my visit to England, Darling, every bit of it, & as I am speaking poor German at present, I imagine my English must have greatly improved. We had no "social engagements" which I hate, but saw just people one liked, which is so much more satisfactory, in fact the only "real thing." [Kreisau, 16.10.1925]

Conference at Locarno

From October 5 to October 16, 1925, an international conference took place in Locarno, Switzerland, the aim of which was to assure that there would never be another world war. Representatives from seven European countries— Germany, France, Belgium, the United Kingdom, Italy, Poland, and Czechoslovakia—met together to work out a series of treaties that would prevent future German aggression by making the boundaries outlined in the Treaty of Versailles inviolable and by requiring that Germany resolve future border disputes through negotiation rather than by force. The Locarno Treaties were signed in London on December 3 and created a feeling of hope for world peace, known as the "spirit of Locarno."

> We are all very excited about Locarno, though very little definite news has as yet leaked out. Still, things seem to be progressing better than one would have thought possible. If some sort of good security pact is created, I may hope that my sons may be spared the horrors of war, an inestimable blessing. I think it was splendid of Germany to offer to renounce all claim to Alsace Lorrain [*sic*.], don't you? [Kreisau, 16.10.1925]

> I feel very happy about Locarno & feel that Europe & sanity have taken a great step forward. Did you see an article in last Sundays Observor [*sic*.] by Garvin [the editor], enumerating all the spiritual & intellectual affinities which exist between Germany & England? A very good sign, but almost tragically funny when one thinks of the press propaganda during the last

138

10 years. [Kreisau, 24.10.1925]

Yet, at the end 1925, the economic obstacles still seemed overwhelming.

> Economically Germany is in a *very* bad way. There is absolutely no money anywhere. The shops are empty, big firms go bankrupt daily, & every factory, farm, business or household is dismissing employees, so that unemployment is rife. America won't give us loans except at 12 % interest which is more than even a successful business can stand. [Kreisau, 11.12.1925]

On the home front, Dorothy was preparing for some elaborate entertaining at the *Schloss*.

> We are very busy at present rehearsing for the theatricals tomorrow. Nineteen of us in the house, & 36 tomorrow evening! A great business. (I see Daddy shake his head.) But as long as it isn't too often it really is very pleasant. We have killed a pig & the Y. T. shot two buck, so we are well off for supplies. [Kreisau, 24.10.1925]

Her father was evidently concerned that "too much burden falls on my shoulders as regards making both ends meet, family calls etc." She assured him:

> Well Darling, nobodys life is a bed of roses, for the very good reason that if it were, we would grow spiritually so fat & flabby that, again symbolically, there would be little difference between a jellyfish & ourselves. And, though of course I am sometimes tired, & nervy, I am a most happy, contented person, . . . [Kreisau, 7.11.1925]

In October, the Moltkes' eldest son moved to Berlin to begin his studies in law, economics, and international stock trading. Helmuth James stayed with Ulla, who gave him a room free of charge. Dorothy felt that it would "do him no harm to have to be very economical. Having too much money is more dangerous than having too little" [Kreisau, 16.10.1925].

Ulla was a help to the second son, too. Because of her

marriage into the Oldenbourg publishing family, she had connections with the world of art history, the field in which Jowo was considering a career. A plan was made in late 1925 for Ulla to take him to Italy with the curator of the Kaiser Friedrich Museum, "to see whether he has the makings of a 'Kunst Historiker' [art historian] in him" [Kreisau, 26.12.1925].[111]

A young stranger

Near the end of the year, a young stranger appeared on the Moltkes' doorstep.

> The other evening we were sitting in the Halle, when a man of about 30 appeared at the front door. He introduced himself as Herr von Kameske (a well known family) saying he was a refugee from the Baltic States, his fathers estates having been confiscated. He wanted to pass his forestry exam & then try & get an appointment in the Finnish Forest Department, as his only living relative, a sister, lives in Helsingfors [Swedish name for Helsinki, Finland]. In order to get enough money to pay for his examination fees he went about selling silhouettes which he made himself. What could I do but buy one? Luckily it really was quite attractive. He said: "Oh, yes, it needs moral courage to go about like this, but it must be done." I thought it rather splendid & very gritty. [Kreisau, 26.11.1925]

1926

On the cold January evenings of 1926, Count von Moltke read Rudyard Kipling aloud to the family.

> The Y. T. is reading the Jungle Book to the children in the evening & the other night after he had read about Mowgli being turned out of the Jungle by the wolves, & Acila [Akela] & some of the others speaking up for him in a really fine way, we found our dear little Furor Teutonicus [German furor], (C.B.) weeping! I must admit my eyes were very moist too, for the Y. T. had read the story really beautifully, & it *is* very

touching. But I love C.B's mixture of courage (& swagger) & softness of heart. He is a most loveable creature. [Kreisau, 28.1.1926]

Helmuth James was having a profitable year in Berlin, where he attended a lecture by Albert Einstein.

The Boy seems very happy here & *very* pleased to see us. He heard Einstein lecture the other day & was tremendously impressed, said he was quite fairly easy to understand. [Berlin, 5.2.1926]

The Boy is indeed a great joy to me. He is much brighter than last summer, & altogether more attractive, Berlin has done him a lot of good. He works hard, 8 hours a day at least, & is very interested in his law studies. . . . The Boy wants . . . to go in for the same career as Dr. Ohle, namely, Civil Service. [Kreisau, 25.3.1926]

Frau *Doktor* Eugenie Schwarzwald

In April, Helmuth James received an invitation from a woman who was to have an important impact on his life— Frau *Doktor* Eugenie Schwarzwald (1872–1940), a Jewish progressive educator and philanthropist.

Born in 1872 in the part of Austro-Hungary that is now Ukraine, Eugenie Schwarzwald went to Switzerland as a young woman to study at the University of Zurich. Obtaining a doctorate, she became one of the first women in Austro-Hungary to receive a university education. In 1900, she married a successful lawyer and financier, Dr. Hermann Schwarzwald of Vienna. Eugenie Schwarzwald, an educational visionary, diminutive in size but with a powerful personality, ran progressive girls' schools. Students studied with prominent artists such as Oskar Kokoschka and Arnold Schönberg, and had the opportunity to prepare for university. During the First World War I, she took on the role of social worker and opened soup kitchens for refugees all over Vienna. After the war, she began a number of recreation homes for children called *Erholungsheime*.

141

In August, at the Frau *Doktor's* invitation, Helmuth James went to her summer villa, "Seeblick" (Lakeview), located on Lake Grundlsee in central Austria. There he made some valuable contacts, both artistic and political.

> Helmuth James writes very happily from Grundl See [*sic*.]; he has a knack of falling on his feet. Has met a lot of interesting people there, [August] Strindbergs[112] daughter-in-law, Hofman[n]sthal,[113] Austria's most renowned poet, etc. His hostess is now trying to get him some position as "Elève" [élève—pupil or student] in the German delegation to the League of Nations. [Kreisau, 8.8.1926]

Another artist young Moltke met through Eugenie Schwarzwald was the great pianist Rudolf Serkin, with whom he and his family enjoyed a lifelong friendship.

Soon Eugenie Schwarzwald took Helmuth James under her wing and introduced him to the literary and political lights of Vienna.

> Helmuth James arrived home on Monday, . . . You will be amused to hear that the English branch of the Int. Law Association asked him to become a member of *their* branch as well as of the German, so that is his first & fitting official connection with England! A Frau Dr. Schwarzfeld [Schwarzwald], a woman of 50 or so, the founder of a famous girls school in Vienna & a great philanthropist, has evidently taken a great fancy to the Boy (she has no children) & she has rather "launched" him in literary & political circles in Vienna. So he is going to study for a term at the University there . . . so as to cement, as it were, all the interesting connections started there. . . . [Kreisau, 17.9.1926]

Dorothy writes prophetically of her eldest son's potential for good in the world.

> Of course all mothers are apt to think their children are swans, but I really think it very probable that the Boy may do big work in the future. Of course it is all very unequal at present, & we must watch carefully against self-conceit (strangers treat

142

him so seriously, as if he were 25 instead of 19) but he certainly has plenty of brains & works hard. [Kreisau, 8.8.1926]

In June, the Moltkes attended a wedding at which Kaiser Friedrich's[114] aide-de-camp was present.

I was taken in to dinner by a dear old man of 80, former A.D.C. to Kaiser Friedrich & the brother of a famous poet, [Ernst von] Wildenbruch. . . .[115] My other neighbour at dinner, by the way, was a Herr von Richthofen, from the Foreign Office. . . . My old gentleman at the wedding said Kaiser Friedrich was completely in "Vickys" [Victoria, Friedrich's wife and eldest daughter of Queen Victoria of the United Kingdom] hands, & she ruled completely. How much might have been different if she had had more tack [sic.] & less head, or at any rate another kind of intelligence. [Kreisau, 10.6.1926]

Grunting pigs

German-Italian relations were becoming strained by Mussolini's attempt to force the cultural assimilation of non-Italian citizens in the Austrian Tyrol. The resulting tension jeopardized Jowo's plans for travel in Italy.

I wonder whether you have seen Mussolinis speech on Germany & the Italianization of Tirol reported anywhere? It is the greatest piece of cheek imaginable. Before the war it would most probably have been the forerunner of an ultimatum. It affects us personally too, for with such strained relations between this country & Italy, Jowos headmaster will never give him his leave in May. All Germans are cancelling their visits to Italy as a protest. Jowo is naturally very agitated, & there is still hope that by May things may have blown over a bit, so we must just wait & see. . . . Ulla is paying all his expenses, so he really is a most lucky infant. [Kreisau, 10.2.1926]

On the way back to Kreisau after a trip to Berlin, the Moltkes' car broke down.

143

. . . after spending an hour pushing & trying devious tricks, we got hitched on to a peasants cart who promised to take us to the nearest town. Very ignominious, with grunting pigs in the cart in front! However after crawling along like this for about 2 minutes, the motor suddenly started again, & we were able to go on by ourselves. [Kreisau, 10.2.1926]

"We live cheapest at Kreisau"

Count von Moltke continued to try to find ways of improving the family's economic situation.

The Y. T. has been racking his brain to think of some way of earning more money, but without capital & in an over-populated country it is really impossible. In spite of the big house—& the many relations—we live cheapest at Creisau. [Berlin, 5.2.1926]

But the war reparations claimed a significant portion of whatever the farm—their main source of income—was able to bring in.

We sell cheaply & the consumer buys dearly, since 13 Pfennigs a lb on flour & 10 Pfennigs a lb on sugar goes for Reparations! And so it is with most things naturally. [Kreisau, 31.3.1926]

Fortunately, another opportunity to earn money presented itself at this time: the Count was asked by a Zurich publisher to translate the memoirs of Colonel House, Woodrow Wilson's most trusted advisor, into German.[116]

The Field Marshal's papers

In April, a huge *Vaterländisches* [Fatherland] Fest took place at the *Schloss*, to which thousands came in honor of the great Field Marshal.

Several thousand people must have been present, they had motor busses to bring & take the crowds. . . . The subject taken was the FeldMarschalls character: simplicity, duty, & religious sense, & these were held up as ideals for all. No touch of party politics, nationalism or chauvanism [*sic*.]. [Kreisau, 30.4.1926]

In September, a contingent of representatives from the Moltke Museum in Berlin came to Kreisau to borrow some artifacts, papers, etc., for the museum.

> They are putting everything in order for us, which is all to the good, & the Boy is working his way through all the papers in our archive & finding many interesting things among them. Among others, one of the first newspapers ever published in Germany, about 1740. [Kreisau, 17.9.1926]

Helmuth James discovered some interesting documents.

> The Boy is sorting all the Archiv[e] papers, & the other day he came across a paper set by the General Staff in 1892 for Vatel [Grandfather] to work out, beginning "on the evening of 31st July, France & Germany mobilize, on 4th August, France declares war; what orders does the G. Staff issue?" Isn't it a curious coincidence that the suppositional dates are those which actually occurred in 1914? [Kreisau, 24.9.1926]

When the Geneva conference proved to be a disappointment, as only the United Kingdom, the United States, and Japan participated—Italy and France having withdrawn from the negotiations—the Countess expressed her own frustration.

> Darling Daddy, I wish I could hear your views on Geneva? Here's a pretty mess, here's a how-d'you do! . . . That Germany & England have been so alienated by events is a real tragedy, for there is no doubt, the Germanic peoples are predestined to pull together. . . . Really the fiasco at Geneva is most serious, & may have very far-reaching results. Helmuth James who knows lots of the younger generation at the Foreign Office & in Government Circles says the old die-hards (who still flourish in the country) are quite at a discount & that a spirit of liberalism & Europeanism is abroad, which is a very good thing. [Kreisau, 17.3.1926]

There were tensions within Germany about foreign policy.

> There is a silent struggle going on in this country as regards its

145

foreign policy, which is very interesting to watch. There is one group who favours a raprochement [*sic*.] with Russia, as the "natural" allay [*sic*.], & "natural" buyer for Germany, then a larger group favour England & what Sir Graham calls the Nordic races. To this group belongs Stresemann [German Foreign Minister], most of the Peoples party, the Democrats & many others. And now a new party has arisen of Pan-Europeans, which favour an understanding with France; to this group the Socialists belong, who see in England, now that the Liberal Party is dead, the exponent of Imperialism, & there is a good deal of talk about the untrustworthiness of English promises etc, as shown in Geneva & so on. . . . There is no doubt, that the only way of saving Europe is to come to some sort of an understanding, both economic & on the question of armaments, but how are we to expect reason & self restraint from Moussolini [*sic*.], the Poles, & Roumainians [*sic*.], or even the French? [Balfanz, 26.5.1926]

An apparent rapprochement between the French and German foreign ministers, Aristide Briand and Gustav Stresemann, in September, raised Dorothy's hopes for world peace.

I think Geneva has been a distinct success this time, don't you? Briand[117] & Stresemann certainly want to come to an understanding, & if they do, we may legitimately feel that Europe has been saved for a generation or two anyway. [Kreisau, 24.9.1926]

A trip to Berlin by "motor" in October afforded an opportunity to meet former Field Marshal and now President of the Weimar Republic, Paul von Hindenburg, aged seventy-nine.[118]

In the afternoon we had tea with Hindenburg. I had never met him before, so was particularly interested. He is a plain man but not at all brutal looking, as his photos so often depict him, with charmng eyes, & a certain bewildered-childlike expression about his eyebrows & forehead which rather touches one. He has natural dignity, & I feel sure finds his position most difficult. He is not half so "conservative" as his die-hard friends would like, & altogether shows tact & comprehension for realities. The "Famiglia Moltke" were alone, only Hindenburgs A.D.C. (i.e. his son) & daughter in law, who is hostess, being present. [Kreisau, 30.10.1926]

Sir James, who had served as chief justice of South Africa since 1914, was about to step down. Dorothy sends him words of comfort.

Growing old *is* a very difficult matter, but it can be turned into a state of blessedness, not only for the person himself but for his surroundings. The world, & especially youth, *needs* the experience, the detachedness, of age. [Kreisau, 4.12.1926]

There are not many public men in the world today to whom power, success or money are side issues, & yet men like you are the leaven of the world, dear Author of My Being. [Kreisau, 17.12.1926]

As the year ended with the usual Christmas festivities, Countess von Molkte reflected:

. . . in the Fatherland everyone loves Christmas, & it has managed to keep its atmosphere of religion & childlikeness even in this modern, American world of ours. [Kreisau, 31.12.1926]

1927

Wehmut

In January 1927, the Rose Inneses once again journeyed north to Germany for an extended visit at Kreisau, also for a cure for Lady Rose Innes at a spa in Dresden, the *Weisser Hirsch* (White Stag).

After a happy summer with the family, Sir James and Lady Rose Innes left Germany for England, en route back to South Africa.

It was a blessed summer . . . Darlings, having you so

exclusively for so long, & I am indeed thankful, & feel I love you more than ever, if that were possible. You were so *sweet* to us all. [Kreisau, 5.9.1927]

Asta & I have just been picking up quantities of Apples which I am taking in this evening for Ete & one or two others. And then she climbed into the hazelnut tree, where we longed for Daddy & his crooked stick to help us. . . . The roses grow more lovely from day to day. . . . I miss you both at every corner. I miss the reading together, our strolls in the garden (snipping off dead flowers)—I emptied the last vase of sweetpeas you arranged, today with what the T[e]utons call "Wehmut" [wistfulness], I don't think there is quite an English equivalent, for it is something much more tender than melancholy. . . . I never cut Wurst in the morning without thinking of you, dear Flen, & today I am going to buy Semmel [a German bread roll] (in the bag) which makes the little flea most active. As to the 3 o'clock & 5:30 trains, I never hear them arriving without thinking of Dad. Nuf sed. [Kreisau, 7.9.1927]

Still looking for ways to raise money and economize, the Count was considering a plan to sell Wierischau—one of three properties bought together in 1867 by the Field Marshal—w]hile "keeping Creisau as *our own* free possession, not making it a 'Stiftung'[foundation], as we had at first thought" [Kreisau, 13.12.1927]. Another plan was to remove from the large *Schloss*, which was expensive to heat, to the smaller, simpler *Berghaus*.

I think we shall probably go to the Berghaus "for good" after all, leaving someone in the *Schloss* to air it, make the butter etc. I will send you a list of our expenses down here, & you will see that we just can't afford it. In spite of my rigid economy it's the heating, the electricity the larger number of servants & [and] the larger number of guests (in spite of everything) that make the *Schloss* impossible for us. Schönchen, wonderful as usual, knows no difficulties for herself, & we are still thinking out ways & means. [Kreisau, 25.12.1927]

148

1928

The *Berghaus*

On New Year's Day, 1928, Dorothy announced to her parents the decision to take up residence in the *Berghaus*.

> . . . towards the end of the month we are going to move to the Berghaus for the winter at least, . . . Maybe we will return to the *Schloss* in May, or else remain at the Berghaus & settle down for good. . . . Both we & the servants must first get used to living on a less "lordly" scale, do more for ourselves etc, & that is much easier in a small house, than in the big one. [Kreisau, 1.1.1928]

The general economic depression was felt all around them.

> Schwengfeld & other estates we have inquired about, all had a deficit this year—. . . [Kreisau, 22.1.1928]

> The papers here are full of the woes of the farmers. . . . It is a certain melancholy consolation to feel that others are in the same boat too. [Kreisau, 28.1.1928]

> This sort of painful readjustment is going on on every side, & one is thankful if it is only that, & not a break down completely. . . . Two bad harvests, much too high interest on loans, & grinding taxes are the cause. Luckily our live stock is good & very plentiful. [Kreisau, 4.2.1928]

The cows, however, were "doing splendidly—several producing 28 liters a day! Poor things" [Kreisau, 2.3.1928].

Soon the family moved to the *Berghaus*.

> . . . we are getting on well, & settling down into the little house wonderfully well. We still have workmen in the house, which is a great bother, but they will be finished by Saturday, & then we shall celebrate the first baths solomanly [solemnly]! [Kreisau, 9.2.1928]

Although a little sad about leaving the grand *Schloss*, by June, Dorothy was thoroughly enjoying her new home.

149

> You wouldn't recognize the drawing room at the Berghaus, it is simply charming, I feel quite enthusiastic about it! . . . One wonders what will become of the *Schloss*, & the Lembachs [*sic.*] [paintings by Franz von Lenbach][119] & imposing vases & other signs of past greatness, & whether we or our children will ever again live there. I hardly think so, but it makes one a little sad, for I have been very happy there & am very attached to the old house with its spacious rooms & dignified staircase. Still, the Berghaus is much more in keeping with our income, & that makes for peace & lessens worry. One thing I enjoy up here immensely & that is, we are so much more in the country. The birds are delightful, & we have the most exquisite views from every window. I've neglected the garden so far, haven't had time, but next year it will come into its own. [Kreisau, 8.6.1928]

The children pitched in.

> The boys have been *so* helpful about the Spring cleaning & moving in, C.B. even put in a pane of glass for me, & the others have been varnishing floors, moving furniture & being handy men in every sense of the word. [Kreisau, 8.6.1928]

She enjoyed the wildlife outside the house and took on the job of making the garden profitable.

> There are quantities of birds at the Berghaus, & they even keep Aunt Nell,[120] poor dear, awake in the early morning. Yet they are fascinating, & pheasants stalk about as if the garden was only there for them. Did I tell you that I have taken over the financial side of the *Schloss* garden as well, & am trying to make it pay for itself? Which it hasn't done for a good long time? That is, pay its way *and* provide us with vegetables & fruit at the same time. [Kreisau, 19.5.1928]

Given the instability of the German economy in the twenties, the family thought it wise to transfer ownership of the *Berghaus* to Dorothy, since, "according to German law . . . the wifes property can *never* be touched by the husband or his creditors" [Kreisau, 20.4.1928]. This arrangement gave her a greater sense of security and reassured her parents of her economic safety.

> . . . should we ever go insolvent, say, as a result of several bad seasons, then we should always have this home. [Kreisau, 2.9.1928]

> Darlings, you can't think how pretty & attractive this little house is. When I come down to breakfast, with the sun streaming into the three front rooms, it is a truly warm welcome. [Kreisau, 17.11.1928]

For Helmuth, selling off the Wierischau property was emotionally painful.

> We think it a very good arrangement, especially as it is very unusual to have the whole thing paid for in cash down & no mortgages. Poor old Y. T. this is the first "Lichtblick"[ray of hope] in financial affairs for several years. . . . It is a great wrench, parting with part of ones property, . . .[121] [Kreisau, 13.7.1928]

Peeling carrots at the Löwenberg *Lager* [camp]

In March, Dorothy and her husband paid a visit to the camp in Löwenberg where Helmuth James was working. The Moltkes' gifted and idealistic eldest son, now twenty-one, had become acquainted with Eugen Rosenstock-Huessey, a professor and philosopher who ran an experimental *Arbeitslager* (work camp). There, fifty young men of different backgrounds—students, professionals, trade union people, workmen, et al.—did manual labor in the morning, then attended lectures, discussions, theatricals, and other events in the afternoon and evening. The visit to the camp proved to be a new and interesting experience for Count and Countess von Moltke.

> Our Löwenberg expedition was a great success. . . . All shades of opinion were represented, from Agrarian to Kommunist, & all were to state their opinions freely, which they did, creating so to speak a friendly opposition. The Y. T. sat at dinner next

151

to an enthusiastic trades union Socialist from the Zeiss works at Jena, a workman, & they got on so well, that the workman ended by presenting the Y. T. with a book about the founder of the Zeiss works with a nice little dedication! Everybody there were equals (no titels [*sic*.] like Herr Professor, or Bischop [*sic*.] etc which T[e]utons so love used) all opinions were there to be aired, all equal; you should have seen your grandson scraping carrots for dinner in the kitchen! 180 people were present, old, young, middleaged, we payed [*sic*.] 3 M[arks] a day & were given 5 meals for that, rough & ready meals of course, but wholesome & appetizing. You would both have been intensely interested. [Kreisau, 30.3.1928]

On another topic, Dorothy was able to inform her father about the relationship of the great Field Marshal to Bismarck.

Daddy, you write about the antagonism between Moltke & Bismarck. Yes it was very strong. B. couldn't stand having equals near him, & M's popularity was very galling to him. In the Moltke Zimmer in Berlin is a letter written by M. to the old Kaiser complaining that B. was constantly thwarting his orders, & saying he would retire if that continued. . . . B. was a great tyrant & very intolerant. . . . I am looking forward to the Suffrage Congress next year in Berlin & hope to see some old friends there, but oh, Mother dear, it won't be the same without you leading your gallant South African brigade. [Kreisau, 24.5.1928]

Cosima Wagner's daughter, Furtwängler, and a public bath

In May, the Moltkes hosted a dinner at which one of the guests was Gräfin Gravina, Cosima Wagner's daughter [Kreisau, 10.5.1928]. In June, they attended a concert in Görlitz, where they twice heard J.S. Bach's High Mass in B minor, and Anton Bruckner's Symphony No. 7 conducted by Wilhelm Furtwängler[122] ("It was like being in a wonderful gothic church") [Kreisau, 3.6.1928]. And in August, they heard the great Wagnerian tenor Lauritz Melchior.[123]

Dorothy was deeply sympathetic with the lot of less successful musicians, as in the case of a relative who was experiencing career difficulties.

> We are much disturbed by the news that Madi[124] has given up her singing altogether, partly because she has no new engagement for the autumn, & mostly because her health (read in part "nerves") can't stand the strain. But its *so* tragic. She's almost starved for her music, T. Katze has sold all her good jewellry [*sic*.] to pay for her lessons & keep, she sings beautifully I believe—& the result is this. Its too sad. And they've no money. [Kreisau, 15.6.1928]

One June afternoon, Dorothy ventured out for a new experience—going to a local public bath.

> Yesterday afternoon I went to the swimming baths in [Schweidnitz]. For the first time, Darlings, I wish we had been there together, it was *too* funny. A very nicely arranged business, crowded with humanity of every age, sex & waist measurement. . . . It is too public & too populated for my taste, but then I am past forty, & that makes a difference. [Kreisau, 29.6.1928]

August 1928 provided an excellent harvest, and the weather was absolutely glorious.

> From my bed I can see 2 golden wheat fields & the mauve of the clover in flower. Today the Boy & I went for a walk there & found the wheat fields alive with young pheasants, & a pair of deer within 5 feet of us, standing quite still. [Kreisau, 15.8.1928]

Sadly, though, it was a very bad season for fruit.

Church appointment

Good news came when Count von Moltke received a new appointment: Christian Science Committee on Publication for Germany, a one-man committee responsible for correcting misinformation about Christian Science in the public media for the whole of Germany. This important position meant that

Helmuth would be spending much more time in Berlin and away from Kreisau, which he had entrusted to the hands of the estate's inspector, Herr Mann.

> . . . on the other hand [Helmuth] draws 7,000 Marks a year (he can be re-elected) & I know the work will interest him & make him very happy. With our competant [*sic.*] inspector & occasional visits here he can still look after things in Creisau, so we are really very pleased about it. . . . I shall miss him of course very much, but next year anyway I'd be away several months visiting you, (if you'll have me!) & I'll have a good excuse now for going to Berlin now & again! [Kreisau, 15.8.1928]

After retiring from the bench as chief justice, Sir James, too, took on a new job: volunteer head of the Child Welfare Services of South Africa.

> Daddy dear your child welfare activities seem growing larger every month. Having Social Workers Diplomas is a very good plan, & ought to induce quite a number of young women with a "social conscience" to go in for the work. [Kreisau, 8.11.1928]

Meanwhile, "the native question" was looming in South Africa.

> Even the Schles. Zeitung [Silesian Newspaper] had a paragraph on the government crisis in S. Africa. . . . The native question looms larger & larger in all South African problems. We, here, are up against a pretty serious dispute too; (though nothing compared to the question of colour) there is a huge lock-out in the iron industry in West Germany & the owners haven't accepted the States arbitration verdict, which since the Revolution has always been final. So it is, among other things, a question of flouting the State authority which is pretty serious. [Kreisau, 8.11.1928]

Germany was still suffering from the aftereffects of World War I.

The political situation here is very precarious at present, & there is a good deal of talk about "putches" [*sic*.] & so on, though I hardly think that such things are likely to occur. But no headway is made politically about Rheinland Occupation, Reparations etc, & at home there are strikes, no money anywhere, & general dissatisfaction. [Kreisau, 24.11.1928]

Christmas again!

But Christmas was here again.

It is very cold out of doors . . . but perfectly calm & sunny, really ideal weather, especially Christmas weather. . . . We have a charming tree in the Wohn-Zimmer [*sic*.] [living room] which dominates all three rooms, &, in these small rooms, really looks like a bit of the forest in captivity. . . . Such wonderful moonshine, that Asta & C.B. went out after supper tobogganing till 9 p.m.—the delightful enthusiasms of youth! [Kreisau, 23.12.1928]

Somewhat wistfully, Dorothy savored the company of her eldest son.

. . . the Boy is always busy, mostly writing & studying. Just between ourselves I must tell you that he is the greatest joy to me, so unselfish, so thoughtful towards his parents, always cheerful & helpful & very forthcoming. I enjoy these weeks with him quite consciously, realizing that I'll probably never have him so completely again. [Kreisau, 29.12.1928]

And the Count sold off some more land.

1929

It was fourteen below zero in Silesia in January 1929, and the Moltkes were dressed for skiing.

Asta does look such a funny little figure in her grey knickers, like a plump little partridge, . . . [Kreisau, 7.1.1929]

Dorothy, too, took up the sport, practicing two to three hours daily, and joined in the fun with horses and toboggans.

> The Carl Viggos came over immediately after lunch & we had their horse & ours with toboggans hung on behind & then one or two ski-ers [*sic.*] at the tail end; it was a sort of combined tailing & ski-joring [*sic.*], & was *great* fun. We drove all about, there was much laughter & a good deal of tumbling about, which kept us nice & warm. [Kreisau, 31.1.1929]

> During the severe frost the hares & deer came into the garden in search of food, & the pheasants look upon it as quite a part of their hunting ground. [Kreisau, 24.2.1929]

In February, Dorothy turned forty-five. Among her most treasured gifts was her parents' "'understanding love,' which is so rare a quality" [Keisau, 24.1.1929].

> So much love in the world tends to grow irksome since it doesn't leave the object loved free enough to work out her or his own salvation on her particular lines. [Kreisau, 24.2.1929]

Progress in her native land was never far from Dorothy's thoughts. More news on the issue of the rights of South African "natives" centered on the National European-Bantu Congress of 1929.

> I was very interested in the account of the European-Bantu Congress, it must have been a revelation to some & an encouragement to all friends of the natives. It is a problem of world wide importance, & our questions of reparations, etc, though important to many millions is small compared to the native question, which may ultimately influence all Africa. [Kreisau, 8.3.1929]

The Count's new work for the Christian Science Church was going well, despite the incovenience of having to be so far from Kreisau.

> The Y. T. is very interested in his work, has a lot to do & is doing it well, but its an uncomfortable sort of life for him without a home. Still that is inevitable—I'm very glad he has this new work and interest nor do I really think that Creisau

suffers much anyway. Herr Mann is an excellent & dependable man & he, the Boy & I really run things, the Y. T. just trying to steer the finances through the storms & eddies. [Berlin, 11.1.1929]

The two eldest Moltke sons were studying for important examinations that winter. Happily, "Jowo passed his *Abitur* [final high-school examinations] with flying colours!"[125] [Kreisau, 17.3.1929]. Helmuth James, too, passed his examinations and immediately set about finding employment. Dorothy experienced a mild case of separation angst mixed with pride in their accomplishments.

Giving Jowo up made me feel rather like a hen watching her ducklings swim across the pond. He's such a child still, dear infant, & so full of high expectations. [Kreisau, 26.4.1929]

Of course I purred over General Smuts' letter, though personally I don't consider the Boy's article anything very special, but it's nice to hear other people, especially such people as he & Daddy, think it good. There's no doubt the Boy has ideas & I feel sure has a great future before him. [Kreisau, 21.4.29]

For a while it seemed that Helmuth James would be going to America to work as a journalist for an American newspaper. He was, however, later advised "not to go to America just at present, when the developments in this country are likely to be of a very important nature (Reparations Bank etc) so he has decided to stay here, & go into one of the big banks in the statistical department" [Kreisau, 23.6.1929].

Dorothy was happy that her husband was able to make occasional visits to Kreisau.

The Y. T. was here for a day & two nights—couldn't get away for longer—this week. He is looking very well & is evidently in his right place, doing good work & enjoying it. [Kreisau, 4.5.1929]

Soon she would temporarily exchange her role of "hen" for

157

"fledgling," as she prepared to make another trip in late July to South Africa, where he would remain for the next four months.

> Goodbye my dear old Birds. I'll soon be in the old nest now, chirping, in spite of my 44 years, as if I were a fledgling. [Kreisau, 21.7.1929]

Crisis at Kreisau

When Dorothy returned to Kreisau at the end of November, it was not the same Kreisau that she had left: the Moltke estate was in deep economic crisis. Up until this time it had seemed that, in spite of difficulties, Kreisau was being managed reasonably well—as well as could be expected during this period of economic hardship for virtually all Germans. News came in late 1929, however, that, in fact, Herr Mann had become seriously ill and Kreisau was in chaos.

> The financial position is much worse than I imagined.... Herr Mann by the way died.... He had evidently been mentally unhinged for some time ... for he had paid some bills twice, sold more potatoes & wheat than we possessed, had received the money for them & now we can't present the goods & so on. Terrible confusion. And yet we have a revisor [auditor] in Schw. [Schweidnitz] & a "Guts Sekretär"[estate secretary] in Creisau, but neither said a word.... We are all quite bright & cheerful in spite of everything, the children quite splendid. [Kreisau, 23.12.1929]

At this point, Helmuth James came up with a plan to rescue the property from catastrophe.

> You'll be wanting to hear news of us I know. The situation is as follows. The Boy presented the creditors . . . with a plan for putting things on a healthy basis. . . . It is quite impossible for some one not on the spot to realize how things are. . . . it's a great help that the Moltkes, including my children, all have the faculty of being quite calm & even cheerful in the most harassing situations. It's worst of all for the Y. T. & though he's very sweet to every one, he is very upset, naturally. Even

158

if we do go into liquidation we don't expect it to mean losing Creisau, since it is most difficult, well nigh impossible, to find buyers just now. . . . The Boy is appointed by the creditors to look after everything here. . . . [Kreisau, 28.12.1929]

In the midst of this family crisis, Dorothy was touched by the kindness of her Moltke relatives.

All the relations here have been so charming, & I've had lots of letters of welcome etc, which is all very comforting at a time like this. [Kreisau, 28.12.1929]

1930

Solving Kreisau

After many years of trying to cope with Kreisau's difficulties from two hundred miles away, Count von Moltke finally turned its management over to his eldest son and returned to his work in Berlin.

Helmuth James formed a limited company out of the estate's creditors, "their shares, so to speak being the money we owe them."

They have chosen a very able & agreable [*sic*.] Dr. Jüngst as their representative, . . . if the creditors finally approve of this scheme, we shall continue to get our "Deputat" from the estate (eadibles [*sic*.] which the farm produces) but that is all. . . . This means very strict economy, which is never pleasant, but one small comfort is, that it is happening equally to quite half our neighbours. . . . The Boy is as busy as ever. . . . Four days in Breslau running conferring with creditors,—not an enviable job at all. If only things come to a head on Wednesday, we'll be so glad.

Goodbye Darling. Don't let this letter worry you more than you can help. We are well & strong & ready to cope with the difficulties which arise, so there's no need to despair. [Kreisau, 13.1.1930]

Finally, in late February, an agreement with the creditors was signed, and the family became more hopeful about Kreisau's future.

> Of course, as you say, it is still quite probable that the scheme in the end won't work, the debts will prove too heavy but . . . its worth the trial, for we don't want to lose Kreisau if we can help it. [Kreisau, 28.2.1930]

> Herr von Berlin, who was here yesterday, said it was astonishing that the Boy had been able to get all the creditors to agree . . . at all. In spite of everything, there had been an element of good luck (& efficient work) in it all. [Kreisau, 23.3.1930]

Soon, Dorothy's mother arrived for another visit, gracefully adjusting to the family's new circumstances.

> You will be able to guess, I know, *how* lovely it is having Mother here. . . . the way she adapts herself to a large & young family with straight[en]ed means in a small house is simply astonishing. She is so wonderfully young & elastic. Every one is charmed! [Kreisau, 23.3.1930]

Later, Sir James came, too, and the Rose Inneses remained abroad—at Kreisau and in England—for several months.

In October Dorothy went to England to see her parents off before they journeyed back to South Africa. Returning to Berlin, she "found the Y. T. very well, but with a great deal of work on his hands" [Berlin, 5.10.1930].

As her wedding anniversary approached, Dorothy reaffirmed her choices in life.

> Darlings, although I've gone so far away, I want you to know that, from my point of view, I have never regretted it. (For your sakes I sometimes think, oh dear I'd never have the courage (?or egoism?) to do it again) And that my heart is very full of gratitude & love for all your sweetness & unselfishness in all these years. Also, I should like to confide in you that I have the most splendid children in the world, . . . [Cadinen, East

160

Prussia, 17.10.1930]

Freya Deichmann

Through the good auspices of Frau *Doktor* Eugenie Schwarzwald, Helmuth James met and befriended a bright young woman who would later become his wife: Freya Deichmann of Cologne. They had become acquainted the previous year during Helmuth James's stay at Eugenie Schwarzwald's summer villa at Grundlsee. Dorothy took an immediate liking to the attractive nineteen-year-old student and, after a visit by Freya the following year, wrote from Berlin:

> Freya left us on Friday. She was very loathe to go I think. She is studying history; short hand & typewriting this winter in Cologne, the former at the University there. She is a dear child, & suits us well I think. What Helmuth's feelings towards her are, I can't tell. Anyway they are very good friends. [Berlin, 10.11.1930]

Dorothy was also pleased with Jowo's prospects for a career in art history.

> Jowo is back in Munich now, having had a really wonderful 5 weeks, first in Vienna & then in Florence, . . . Frau Doctor . . . thinks he will make a great success of his profession!! [Berlin, 10.11.1930]

And Dorothy was enjoying life with her family in the smaller but commodious, *Berghaus*.

> "My very dearest Pelicans," she writes:

> You can't think what an improvement having another sitting room is, & we use the piano a lot too, Asta is very keen on playing duets, & we play together. Indeed she is very sweet just now, & very nice to me,—I thought I'd just mention the fact, as I know you think the children don't appreciate me enough—fond parents!! . . . You can't think how happy I am in my dear little house & the still dearer children around me. I consider I am a very fortunate young woman. [Kreisau,

161

20.11.1930]

"We live in troubled times"

"The government is now making an herculean effort to bring down the cost of living," Countess von Moltke noted in November, "it is almost the key to their remaining in office, for all salaries from Hindenburgs to the smallest civil servants are to be reduced from 1st Jan.—& most of them are very inadequate even without this curtailment" [Berlin, 10.11.1930]. The freezing temperatures in November did not help.

> It looks as if we are in for a very cold winter, which is horribly unfortunate for the political situation, & that tragic army of unemployed. There have already been several small disturbances in Berlin, nothing very serious, no one killed, but it is symptomatic. *What* a state the world is in, . . . [Berlin, 14.11.1930]

Helmuth James returned from a trip to Vienna, Munich, and Berlin, where he had attempted to persuade the *Stiftung* (foundation) to buy the Field Marshal's historic home at Kreisau. But the economic times were not favorable, and the young man found it difficult to struggle against "the prevailing pessimism," which was "very strong" [20.11.1930]. In Vienna, he tried to auction off some valuable family paintings by Franz von Lenbach (1836-1904), a German painter of the Realist style who painted many famous people of his time, including Field Marshal Helmuth von Moltke.

> The Lenbachs are to be put up for auction on 4th Dec. I only hope they'll fetch a decent price, though the times are not auspicious. Hel. James says that Vienna is "trostlos" [miserable], everyone who has anything worth selling in art or furniture or books or jewellry [*sic*.] is doing so, . . . In fact, dear Flens, we live in troubled times, which makes us all the happier & more thankful for the love & affection which exists between us. [Kreisau, 28.11.1930]

162

One of these pictures was a portrait of Bismarck, which he did manage to sell.

> The Bismarck picture by Lenbach was sold on Christmas Eve for 5000 M, of which we get a little less than 4500. It is not much, but in these times of depression one is pleased, & astonished, when pictures sell at all. [Kreisau, 29.12.1930]

And he received an offer from Hindenburg to buy all the Field Marshal's mementos.

> The Boy is responsible for this coup; . . . The Boy will strain every nerve in the coming year to sell Creisau if he can to the Stiftung, failing that, to anyone else he can, for he thinks that is the only satisfactory solution. [Kreisau, 19.12.1930]

Heinrich Brüning

Dorothy was to some degree heartened by Chancellor Heinrich Brüning's[126] attempts in late 1930 to improve the economic situation through financial reforms.

> In the mean time the Reichsrat ["upper house," whose members were appointed by the German states] has passed the Governments reform measures—all financial—& on 4th the Reichstag meets & it is still very uncertain what the Governments fate will be. I personally expect he, Brüning, will manage to pass his bills, but if he can't, he will probably use dictatorial rights, since there is no opposition willing to take office, & one can't have a general election every three months. Personally I think Brüning is doing wonderfully well, but of course the Nazis & Kommunists who go in for wild talk are more popular in hard times than the man who cuts down salaries. [Kreisau, 20.11.1930]

> Politically things are very exciting & precarious here. Personally I think Brüning is rather wonderful, & he certainly has courage & is doing a most disagreable [*sic*.] job not for his own power or popularity, but simply because he conceives it to be his duty. But the opposition, especially on the right, make me boil with rage. They have no sense of responsibility at all,

they refuse to support him, & then when at last the Socialists support him, the Right say: how can we vote for a Government that is hand in glove with the Socialists? . . . It is hopeless. We are lucky, in spite of such childish irresponsibility to find men like Hindenburg, Brüning & Dietrich[127] (the finance minister) willing to take the burden on their shoulders. [Kreisau, 6.12.1930]

"With what anxious hearts thousands all the world over will enter 1931," Countess von Moltke reflected somewhat apprehensively. "It is a good thing that we cannot look into the future" [Kreisau, 6.12.1930].

1931

Unemployment and Nazi promises

In early 1931, Dorothy Thompson,[128] head of the Berlin bureau of the *New York Evening Post*, visited Kreisau for the second time. She and her husband, Sinclair Lewis, who had recently won the Nobel Prize, had visited previously in 1926, when Helmuth James took them around Silesia to show them the mining conditions there. The two Dorothy's had "lots of interesting talk," presumably on the politics of the day [Kreisau, 14.2.1931].

Brüning was making valiant efforts to bring order to the *Reichstag* ("lower house" of elected representatives) and to revive the economy.

Here things are fairly quiet, as quiet as they can be with 3½ million unemployed & the Nazis making the most extravagant & wild promises. Everything possible is being done to help the unemployed, continuation schools, trade schools etc started, & new roads, dams, canals etc started to give work. Brüning is a very fine man, an aesthetic, filled with the idea that it is his mission in life (& a very hard one it is) to see Germany through these years of crisis & depression. [Kreisau, 3.1.1931]

The Nazis & [*and*] Conservatives walked out of the House

164

[*Reichstag*] as a protest because the Chancellor [Brüning], . . . has tried to make the working & debating of the House run more smoothly, & be less subject to the obstruction tactics of the radicals. It was a ridiculous step to take, pardonable perhaps for the inexperienced & very youthful Nazis, absurd for the Conservatives who are practically all over 50, & belong to the governing caste. [Kreisau,14.2.1931]

In connection with increased tensions between Germany and Poland, Dorothy mentions that one of her husband's cousins, Hans Adolf von Moltke, [129] had just been appointed ambassador to Poland—"a difficult task, & vitally important" [Kreisau, 9.1.1931].

The atmosphere between Germany & Poland is full of explosive possibilities & is a real danger to the world. . . . there is not an atom of good will on either side. Really, I suppose there has never been a more unstatesman[-]like treaty, than the treaty of Versailles, & the many faults in it will be paid for by the blood & misery of countless thousands,—its a depressing thought. A war against Poland could easily become popular in Germany; luckily, in a way, France's sure intervention, makes people see the madness of it, for the moment, but it doesn't cure the evil. [Kreisau, 9.1.1931]

In late January, Countess von Moltke took steps to raise some money and decided to part with some valuable jewelry.

It was sweet of you to be so sympathetic about the sale of the tiara, but as a matter of fact, it never really seemed to belong to me. I wore it when I was presented [at court], 21 years ago, & was never likely to wear it again, except perhaps at one of the childrens weddings, but even that is hardly likely. Any way, we had always planned selling it. [Kreisau, 29.1.1931]

She also sold to "different village people superfluous cupboards & tables etc," reduced the household staff to one maid, and took on some of the cleaning herself [Kreisau, 7.2.1931].

I turn out the four rooms downstairs, on Saturdays with Frau

165

Kiskes [Kiske's] help, the other days alone. It takes me 1½ hours on Wednesdays & Saturdays, & hardly half an hour on the other days, & I don't mind it a bit. [Kreisau, 7.2.1931]

A young man named Skornia, an unemployed miner from the Löwenberger camp and a socialist, was helping the Moltkes get rid of some beds, probably left over from the post-WWI quartering.

This young Skornia is . . . such a nice fellow, though only a work man, & one on the dole too. He isn't trying to be a "gentleman", he is just what fate has ordained him to be, but a charming example of his class. Idealistic, simple, clever; it makes one feel there is hope for the future when one meets proletariat of this type. He spent the night here too, as he has to see about the 100 beds, which are being removed at last from the Schloss. [Kreisau, 29.1.1931]

In his letter to his children in January 1944, Helmuth James would recall with gratitude his mother's self-sacrificing efforts to economize.

Mami lived at that time in Freya's room and I next door in my present room, and we had to have frequent discussions about money matters, in which I had to tell her she had to save still more, or do without something that she would have liked to have. In the year 1930, in which I had promised to reimburse our creditors, we also sold furniture and silver, also some things to which Mami was very attached. None of that was of any importance. We could have been much, much poorer, and thanks to Mami it would not have changed the free, peaceful, happy atmosphere of the house at all. This certainty, that Mami was prepared to make any sacrifices that were necessary to bring Kreisau out of debt, this was one of the fundamental reasons that especially made it possible to come out of this chaos.[130]

Good news at last

Thanks to the hard work and expertise of Helmuth James and the new estate manager, Herr Zeumer, as well as the cooperation of Dorothy, the fortunes of Kreisau were gradually improving.

> Herr Zaümer [Zeumer] is away taking a course on pig-feeding, so as to be able to do still better in that line. Money of course is very scarce, but everything is better regulated than last year, things run more smoothly, & the Boy has practically no nervous strain now, I'm thankful to say. [Kreisau, 29.1.1931]

More good news was the progress the other children were making. "Asta is developing charmingly, & is very attractive, & very much more thoughtful towards me," her mother wrote in January [Kreisau, 23.1.1931]. Willo had passed his *Abitur* (high-school graduation examination) and begun looking for a position as apprentice to a builder and contractor in Schweidnitz. And Jowo was flourishing in his chosen field of art history.

> He is *very* interested in his work, & reads practically nothing else, but concentrates on ancient art up to Baroque. . . . There is no doubt that he is very happy in his work, & it is hardly too optimistic to hope that he will get a job in 2 years time, more or less, for he works hard, is very reliable & seems to be very attractive. [Kreisau, 20.3.1931]

Nazi bigwigs

Dorothy Thompson, who was writing a series of articles on Germany for her American newspaper, the *New York Evening Post*, invited Helmuth James "to meet & discuss economic questions with 3 of the Nazi big wigs [*sic*.], [Gregor] Strasser,[131] who leans towards the socialistic side, [Gottfried] Feder, the intellectual[132] [whose byzantine Nazi reasoning mystified the young man] & another whose name I have forgotten" [Kriesau, 7.2.1931].

> They discussed things for about an hour, but the Boy says he simply can't understand them. It's like discussing astronomy with some one who believes that the sun is not the centre of our system, but, say, Saturn. He didn't find them foolish or wild, but simply starting from some hypothesis which he didn't

167

grasp. [Kreisau, 7.2.1931]

When fighting between Communists and Nazis broke out in the streets, Dorothy reassured her parents.

She blamed the conservatives for the country's political problems.

> The stupidity, in things political, among German Conservatives, the late "ruling classes", is enough to make one weep. No wonder the country came a cropper. On the other hand, ... Germany ... has brought forth some excellent men since the war, so one need not dispair [sic.]. [Kreisau, 14.3.1931]

Dorothy saw France's arrogance as a threat to the Geneva peace talks (the Conference for the Reduction and Limitation of Armaments, or the World Disarmament Conference, beginning in 1932 in Geneva, Switzerland).

> I'm very concerned about Geneva & . . . Briand & the high handedway France rules the roost. It will mean disaster to Europe in the end. [Berlin, 16.5.1931]

> A good deal depends on who takes Briands place I should think. There is no doubt that reason has very little to say in international politics. [Kreisau, 23.5.1931]

But she finds some hope in Brüning's governance, although he was given little credit.

> I think the Government, & Brüning especially, are doing fine work, considering the difficulties, & it is heartrending to see how *no* one belonging to the Nazi or Hugenberg parties (i.e. almost half the nation) will give him an ounze [sic.] of credit for anything, but defame him & airily talk nonsense till one sometimes feels quite sick about it. Such lack of judgement, such a want of responsibility, such a being gulled by cheap tournure de phrase [turn of phrase], is really alarming, for it is practised [sic.] by people who are otherwise quite sane, often clever, & good & reliable otherwise. Of course there are probably more sane people than one realizes, only they make

168

less noise than the others. [Kreisau, 8.6.1931]

Reading Adolf Hitler's autobiographical manifesto, *Mein Kampf*, revealed to Dorothy the irrationality of his thinking.

> Hitlers Life, called "Mein Kampf" was recommended to me as being very interesting, & as I know very little about him I got Monika to lend it to me. It is packed full of the most ridiculous nonsense about Jews & "Marxismus" [Marxism] & so on, & yet all through it one feels that Hitler isn't a rascal or a fool, but a man of deep emotions who does not allow his reason or his judgment to do any work—& this is a leader of 7 million voters! [Kreisau, 8.6.1931]

She breathed uneasily as Germany narrowly escaped disaster.

> You'll have read how near the edge of the precipice Germany was last week, it really seems like a miricle [*sic*.] that nothing catastrophic happened. Brüning made a very statesmanlike speech last Tuesday (23rd) which was broadcasted, throwing out a "feeler" towards France, . . . We have still 4 millions unemployed, & this at the height of the season, & with no reserves & only short term foreign credits which always constitute a danger. [Kreisau, 28.6.1931]

Everything, Dorothy wrote, depended now on Brüning's success in securing a deal with the French and the British, as he attempted to stave off the Nazis and the Communists, who were nipping at his heels.

> The quiet is most striking, superficially, one notices nothing of the crisis, but they say that if Brüning has no success either in Paris or London then the Nazis or the Kommunists will make a bid for power. Who can tell? There has never been a similar situation, so who dares prophesy? You will be following everything with painful interest I know, & by the time you read these lines, the German situation will probably have greatly changed. [Kreisau, 20.7.1931]

Regarding their personal economic situation, Dorothy took heart that "thanks to a good season & Zaümers [Zeumer's] touchingly rigid economy, the ship is still afloat." Her mother buoyed the family's spirits with her unending stream of hand-knit clothing ("everyone is amazed at the amount of knitting Mother gets through") [Kreisau, 17.9.1931]. But the outlook was still dark.

> . . . no one knows what changes & upheavals the winter will bring, & it seems to me that Englands future looks very somber too. I wonder what we are all heading for—communism? autarky? (Do you know the word, it is much in vogue here, meaning national states which are practically selfsupporting [*sic*.] & have more or less a Chinese wall round their frontiers.) . . . It is astounding, how little reason, as opposed to passion & stunts, rules the world. However, people always seem to muddle through in the end, & I feel sure we all shall do likewise, but its a painful process, & one understands how in the middle ages people retired into monasteries & wanted to have nothing more to do with the madness of mankind. The people of midieval [*sic*.] times had however one big advantage over us, viz. they all believed in God & a future life, whereas so many doubt in our day, & that makes life seem so much more useless & unreasonable. On the other hand, we of course are much more humane & that means much. [Kreisau, 17.9.1931]

Finally, Dorothy's spirits rose to gratitude for their "Island of Peace."

> We are all well & cheerful & call our dear little Berghaus an "Island of Peace" in the ocean of unrest & difficulties around us. All the children are well & very dear, . . . Jowo is enjoying England enormously, & the dear Parents are well & prosperous (as one counts prosperity nowadays), so haven't I got a lot to be glad about? And I am. And Freya & Helmuths future fills me with content too, though my heart bleeds for all young people. Ever so much love[,] The Child [Kreisau, 17.9.1931]

The wedding

In October, Dorothy felt encouraged that "Brüning got a

majority in the Reichstag," and she expected that "in time a way out of the impasse will be found internationally" [Köln (Cologne), 17.10.1931]. She was also looking forward to another trip to South Africa. And she was anticipating with joy the wedding of Freya Deichmann and Helmuth James on October 18—the very same date of her own wedding and that of her parents—although her joy was tinged with sadness at the future the world held for the young couple.

> So the wedding really is to be on 18th—nice, isn't it? . . . Dear Boy, I feel very tender towards him, & wish I could lighten things for him. Not only the general depression & the Creisau difficulties, but, more than these, the trend of politics in this country depresses him, we are getting further & further away from moderation & reason, & there are de facto even now only 3 real parties left—Nazis, Kommunists & Centre i.e. catholics, & one doesn't like any of them. . . . One wonders how it will all end, not only here, but everywhere in the world. [Kreisau, 10.10.1931]

For about a century the Deichmann family had been prominent bankers in Cologne, with a grand mansion in the city and another house in the country.[133] Just before the wedding, however, the Depression wiped out the Deichmann fortune overnight, leaving the family almost penniless. The result was that the wedding of Freya and Helmuth James was necessarily a very simple affair. But these circumstances in no way dampened the young couple's spirits.

> . . . here I am in Köln [Cologne], lovely sunny weather & a *very* happy young couple. Helmuth was in Berlin on Monday & Tuesday on business & was able to settle several matters so satisfactorily that he is feeling quite lighthearted, & they are, after all, going to have a short honeymoon (a hateful word) before returning to Kreisau & work. So thats very reassuring. If this Berlin arrangement hadn't succeeded, he wouldn't have been able to spare the time.

> Monday [October 19]. Our young couple left yesterday afternoon by car for Coblenz, & then they want to make their

way leisurely down the Rhein to Zurich where Frau Dr. [Schwarzwald] is lecturing on 22nd. She is quite unaware of the plan, so imagine her joy. By the end of the week they expect to leave again for Kreisau. [Köln, 17.10.1931]

Unfortunately, the young bride's father, Herr Deichmann, had taken ill and was unable to join in the festivities.

After an informal dinner for fourteen on Saturday night, Helmuth James von Moltke and Freya Deichmann were married in the Deichmann home the following day, October 18, 1931.

On Sunday at 1:30 p.m. a much curtailed & simplified service in the house, & after that an excellent dinner, but only for 14 people, & then an hour or two later the two dears went off, taking Hans [Freya's younger brother] with them in the car as far as Koblenz, en route for Frankfurt & his work!! It was all so natural, happy & simple, you would have been delighted I know. Carl Deichmann, Freyas elder brother, "said a few words", about the three wedding couples[134] & I enclose our menu with signatures, to show you that you were thought of by all, & that, with me, the little flea was very busy. . . . The Deichmann house is beautiful. Like one of those old "hôtels" in Paris. More like a spacious country house than a town dwelling. Much taste & money has been expended on it, & now, next month, it is to be closed. Freya had no bridesmaids, no music, & we had no hats or gloves on, the men in dark lounge suits, everything as simple as possible, which was so right. [Köln, 17.10.1931]

Sadly, a few days later, Freya's father suddenly died.

After a brief wedding trip, Freya and Helmuth James returned to Kreisau, where they received a warm Silesian welcome in the middle of the night.

Last night at about 8 p.m. I got a telephone message to say that Helmuth & Freya would be here at 1:38 in the middle of the night, instead of the early morning. So Julian, Asta & I got up from our chaise longues at 1 a.m., lit chinese lanterns & went

172

to the station to meet them. Hirsch (the old Förster [forester]) & Mamsel had of course constructed a triumphal arch for the young couple, & we decorated that too with lanterns, so everything really looked very festive in spite of the unholy hour. . . . I quite agree with Daddy that the future looks dark indeed. I feel so much for the young people, who have such very meagre prospects of success & happiness, however hard they may work. . . . I can't tell you how thankful I am that I have the Berghaus & how I love it. One great asset my children have,—they like simple pleasures, they all know how to work, & none of them expect a life of ease, so they are well prepared for the battle of life. [Kreisau, 25.10.1931]

My young couple are such dears & so happy together, it really is a pleasure to see them. Freya is so natural & impulsive, very unspoilt & fresh. Helmuth is very reserved, but one can see, in a hundred little ways, how happy he is. [Kreisau, 30.10.1931]

He and Freya are so charming together. I keep wishing you were here to see their delightful companionship. [Kreisau, 15.11.1931]

Back at Kreisau, Helmuth James returned to the problem of salvaging the estate. In November, he was advised not to make any decisions about Kreisau for the moment.

Things are so unsettled, we may have the "Dritte Reich" [Third Reich] (the Nazi ideal) in three weeks time, . . . Everyone tells us Berlin is terrible, most nerveracking [sic.], no one knows what may happen the following day, & of course such uncertainty is fatal to business of any kind. [Kreisau, 8.11.1931]

Fortunately, Helmuth James's meeting with the creditors in Berlin was successful.

This is a Christmas letter, & it seems almost incredible that about 5 weeks after you have read it, I shall be in your arms,— a very solid & compact "Christmas present," none the less loving for being a month late. . . . The meeting with the creditors passed off exceedingly well. Nobody was annoyed, in

173

fact they said that Kreisau couldn't be better administered than it is now, they were quite satisfied with the way Zaümer [Zeumer] & the Boy run things, & they asked the Boy to suggest the best steps for them to take—which was a great compliment to my first born. We are going to take advantage of this new Osthilfe Emergency Decree. . . . [Kreisau, 29.11.1931]

Osthilfe (Eastern Aid) was a policy of the German Government to give financial support to bankrupt estates in East Prussia. Dorothy explains that it gave "a certain body of men, called the 'Osthilfe', the power to suspend or reduce the payments of debts owed by Eastern (i.e. "Ost") agriculturalists to their creditors" [Kreisau, 22.11.1931].

For us personally this may prove extremely useful, but it isn't right, & undermines all right feeling about obligations, & of course destroys confidence. Your legal mind will be horrified, so is the Boy[']s. [Kreisau, 22.11.1931]

Nevertheless, she saw it as "a gleam of hope, & very agreeable outlook for the year 1932" [Kreisau, 29.11.1931]. Dorothy conveys her son's impressions of Berlin in December 1931.

He found the atmosphere in Berlin a spot quieter than it had been, & it seems almost possible that the Government could keep the ship of state a float. Hitler of course is a dark horse, no one knows what he means to do. He has his 700,000 enrolled members completely under control so far, & has sent a sort of "ambassador" to London & one to Rome! Where is this going to lead to? . . . I've not got much faith in the National Government, its made up of too many ingredients. [Kreisau, 7.12.1931]

Foreboding turns to near despair in her next letter.

. . . the world is terribly upset & I can't see how its ever going to straighten out again. [Kreisau, 11.12.1931]

On a happier note, Dorothy attended a celebration of

Schwester Ida's fiftieth birthday.

> . . . there was a charming little ceremony at the Spielschule. Children & Jungfrauen [young women] sang, the Pastor "spoke a few words", the different societies & the "Gemeinde" [congregation] gave her presents & it was all very touching & "echt deutsch" [truly German] as Daddy would say. [Kreisau, 30.10.1931]

C.B., who was an excellent athlete, "had taken the first prize for 100 meters in his division (those born in 1913 & 1914) for the whole of Schlesien [Silesia]!" [Kreisau, 25.10.1931]. Jowo was happily pursuing his study of art history in Frankfurt, where Freya's aunt, Frau von Schnitzler, "rich, mondaine [worldly], & rather high browed, [had] taken him under her wing" [Kreisau, 22.11.1931]. And while Mamsell, the cook, was away, Countess von Moltke gave her daughter a cooking lesson [Kreisau, 11.12.1931].

On December 30, 1931, Dorothy prepared to board ship in Rotterdam, bound once again for the shores of South Africa.

1932

Herzlich willkommen [Warm welcome]

"My Darlings," Dorothy wrote from the ship that was carrying her back to Germany after a four-month visit with her parents. "Do the egrets still fly over your heads, & is Mother still so thrilled about them?" [Nearing Lobits, 13.5.1932].

Helmuth, Ulla, and three of the Moltke sons met her in Hamburg and brought her back to Kreisau.

> Helmuth & Freya, Asta, Leno, Ete & Peter[135] (with a pink paper rose on his collar) were all at the station to meet me, also Schwester with dozens of small waxen [flaxen] haired children. I had an arch of firs with a "herzlich willkommen" placard in the middle, & lo I was at home! We had tea on the stoep [porch] on a charming tea cloth that Asta had made for

175

me as a surprise. [Kreisau, 12.6.1932]

Back in "the Fatherland," Dorothy was once again faced with the grim reality of Nazism's gathering influence and power. Although there are moments of light and hope, the subject of Nazism and Hitler's rise to power dominates her letters for the next three years, until her death in 1935. For her parents, in South Africa, she was the "woman on the spot," reporting on German politics as the German Government, like a man with a stick trying to save himself from a pack of encircling wolves, attempted to stave off the aggressive encroachments of the Nazis. In a desperate move, Hindenburg dismissed Heinrich Brüning on May 29.

> Hindenburg's action came as a complete surprise to everyone, Brüning included. . . . The question is: will they make room for a Nazi government or take the latter into the government, & if so what will the Republican part of the nation do? We are indeed skating on very thin ice. In the mean while, Clausi[136] tells us most of the Reichswehr [the German military] sympathize with the Nazis, so it looks as if nothing can keep the Hitlerites from coming into power, except their own lack of a practical programe [*sic*]. [Kreisau, 16.6.1932]

Dorothy expressed concern about the unrest in Poland, near the eastern part of Germany, where Helmuth James and Freya had recently been for a visit with Hans Adolf and his family, and where they had seen Polish men and women performing military exercises.

> In Danzig the Poles are disgracefully cock a hoop, so everything is in readiness for a conflagration. [Kreisau, 23.6.1932]

Of great concern were the growing ranks of the Nazi Storm Troopers, or Brownshirts— the *Sturmabteilung* (S.A.).[137]

> Added to this . . . the Republican guard called Reichsbanner[138] & above all the Nazis (the S.A. troops) are all armed (for home use, not for shooting "enemies" only for ones compatriots) so there is bound to be a flare up & some bloodshed, though I

don't think it will be more than local & spasmodic. Brüning committed a grave error in not suppressing these illegitimate squadrons (I suppose he wasn't strong enough) & von Papen favors them. Lamentable. [Kreisau, 23.6.1932]

I haven't made much mention of politics in my letters, because I simply don't know what to say about things. It really seems like a disease in Germany, & it is chilly weather for people with liberal standpoints. Personally, I don't think the new government is doing so badly, except for the fact that the Nazis (under whose influence they seem to stand) insist on von Papen doing some incredible things, such as allowing the Storm Troops to parade again, & the Nazis to wear uniforms, which has resulted in a reign of terror in the streets & a very serious situation between the Southern States & the Reich (for the former have refused to allow the wearing of uniform) & the Nazis have become more swollen headed than ever. Nearly every day there are uproars at one or other of the Universities, & as a result of the Nazi epedemic [*sic*.] people think the best way of answering an argument is by sticking the opposing party on the head. [Kreisau, 29.6.1932]

Nazi girls

Even schoolchildren like their own daughter, Asta, were feeling the effects of the "Nazi epidemic."

It is deplorable, & I do feel so terribly sorry for those young people (like mine) who are simply out of place in the noisy & brutal world of people without ideas. Even Asta has had horrid experiences at school where nearly all the school girls are Nazis, & who as a matter of course try to bully the whole school. The older people are afraid (many of them) to take a stand against this senselessness, as they think they will lose their positions when the Nazis come into power, & no one can afford to lose his job nowadays. So there you have a sad state of affairs. Liberal thought & ideals, humanism in fact, seems dead. I wonder whether it will revive later on? In the meanwhile a young man like Helmuth, or Hans [Deichmann,

Freya's brother], Jowo or Willo feels disgusted, depressed & entirely out of place. It is indeed deplorable.

We however in our dear little Berghaus, try to forget all the noise & intolerance outside & are happy & cheerful, & oh so sorry that this happy time with the children is fast coming to an end. But life never stands still does it? [Kreisau, 29.6.1932]

Careful management of the estate by Helmuth James and Zeumer was at last paying off: the farm was again flourishing.

Farm affairs are as satisfactory as is possible. Zaümer [Zeumer] & the Boy between them have brought down the expenditure enormously. The cow herd is excellent, we have twice as many pigs as last year, the harvest promises well. [Kreisau, 9.7.1932]

The Count and his sons were getting on with their lives. Willo found work in Schweidnitz ; Jowo was becoming an expert on a pupil of Rembrandt[139]; C.B., who was excelling at sports but not, unfortunately, in academics, struggled to prepare for school examinations; and the Count, now a teacher of Christian Science in Berlin, was preparing to teach his first class of students.

Living in a mad house

By July, the crisis in Germany had deepened.

We . . . are living more or less in a mad house. . . . the result of again allowing the S.A. troops (there are said, on good authority, to be 400,000 of them, 4 times the size of the Reichswehr!) is that we are now really living in a state of latent civil war. Every week end there are clashes between Nazis & Reichsbanner or, more usually, Communists, resulting in dozens of wounded & one or two deaths. The poor Schupos [Schutzpolizei—uniformed police] have 15, sometimes 18, hours duty on Saturdays & Sundays & the situation is really getting beyond their control. The great question is: what is going to happen after 31st July? There are some very able men in the von Papen ministry, able that is, at their business, not necessarily as statesmen, but nobody seems to be supporting them. The masses are so worked up by all this propaganda & senseless criticism & hate of one another, that one despairs of any sane judgement being passed on 31st. It is all very lamentable. [Kreisau, 14.7.1932]

July 31 was the date set for the national election.

Well, my Darlings, since last I wrote, the political weathercock has taken a complete turn, in Prussia especially. I cannot say that we are pleased at the turn events have taken, but one must wait & see what the results are. The new ministry for the Reich is not so bad, if only they were not bound hand & foot to those impossible Nazis, who really rule the roost without incurring an onze [ounce] of responsibility. We will see what happens after next Sunday. I don't think the left can possibly attempt an armed opposition against the Reichswehr plus all the Nazi troops, but of course a general strike is within the bounds of possibility. But the Iron Front[140] has no money, (who is ready to pay for anything so old fashioned as liberty & liberalism these days?). . . . At present everything is quiet, but of course the situation is fraught with danger. [Kreisau, 25.7.1932]

July 31, Election Sunday, was a lovely, warm summer's day.

. . . the streets in Schweidnitz full of Nazi flags (& a good many Iron Front ones too) Nazis in uniform conspicuous everywhere, but everything quiet & no [elections] as far as one could see—that is the picture in these parts on this fateful day. [Kreisau, 31.7.1932]

Dorothy voted for the *Deutsche Staatspartei* (the German Democratic Party), although, with such uninspiring choices, she found it difficult to know what to do.

The next day, she learned that the "partial election results which have been published seem to show a huge increase for the Nazis" [Kreisau, 31.7.1932]. A week later, however, it appeared that the Communists had prevailed, with "a setback for the Nazis, especially considering the fact that they [the

179

Nazis] spent much more lavishly on propaganda & electioneering than did any other party. The Communists are the real victors, & the situation is in no way clearer than it was before the election" [Kreisau, 6.8.1932].

Despite these momentous events, the Moltkes' lives went on as before.

> You are probably anxious to hear some news about the political situation, but that is just the most difficult thing to give you, because neither I nor most other people understand what is happening, & by the time you read this, events will probably have spoken for themselves. Suffice to say, that, although these outrages have up till now been very frequent & a disgrace to the nation, we are quite unaffected by it all, & can go our several ways as if the last 18 years had never been. . . . *Our* life goes on just as usual, . . . We went for a heavenly drive on Saturday, in the late afternoon, to the Henscheur [Henscheuer Mountains] . . . . We arrived there at 8 p.m. walked about in the fir woods there for about an hour (the scent of the needles was delicious) then partook of coffee or chocolate, & returned by moonlight to a cold supper at 11 p. m. Kreisau, 19.8.1932]

A few weeks later, the family received a generous gift of money from the Rose Inneses for Asta's education, enabling the seventeen-year-old girl to go off to boarding school, complete with a new wardrobe.

> I told Mamsell that it was for Astas school, mostly, & she said "Die Muttel und der Vatel werden ein ganz besonderen Platz im Himmel haben" [Grandmother and Grandfather will have a very special place in Heaven], they were so good to us! And I quite agree with the old lady, though with a somewhat different interpretation. [Kreisau, 9.9.1932]

"Hitler put himself outside the pale"

In August, events took a turn for the worse when the Government sentenced five Nazis to death at Beuthen, Silesia. Hitler's callous reaction shocked and alienated many

Germans.

> Politically the excitement at the beginning of the week was intense, about the death sentence passed on 5 Nazis at Beuthen. To my mind, Hitler put himself outside the pale, by not even deploring the very brutal murder, but issuing menacing dispatches about the "bloody action of the Government" etc. It has really been a good thing for it has shocked many people, like Leno & others, who were inclined to sympathize with the Nazis, & it means that the Government won't be able to cooperate with these people, who have lost all sense of proportion, of reason & of right.

> We are all now waiting breathlessly to see what Papen will do with the Reichstag; probably dissolve it, rule autocratically & prepare a new franchise law, which everyone agrees is a crying need, since with P.R. [proportional representation] we can never get a working majority. Of course, if the Government & the Nazis are antagonistic, the question is: won't the latter try to organize a Putsch (they are said to be fully armed), or will the Government suppress them? The strange thing is, that while all these really vital struggles are going on, our ordinary civil life goes on as usual, & one notices little of the undercurrents. [Kreisau, 29.8.1932]

Franz von Papen

Although Dorothy felt "quite inadequate to explain things" to her parents about politics "because they are so muddled & incomprehensible," she did her best to summarize the events of the day [Kriesau, 3.9.1932]. One thing was clear: she abhorred Hitler and the Nazis. But she had no confidence in Franz von Papen[141] and his government, either, whose policies, in her opinion, spelled the end of democracy in Germany.

> The general opinion is that Hitler has missed his opportunity & passed the zenith of his power. But of course to be governed as we are at present is very ignominious. Papen has no large body behind him (to say nothing of a majority) & is simply held by

181

Hindenburg—an old man of 85. What a situation! Papen is a well-mannered, pleasant man of the world, known to his friends as "Fränzchen," a man of no outstanding ability or force. . . . The Papen cabinet are very competent & will possibly bring in a number of excellent improvements, but, what we liberals all feel, its good bye to democracy, to the republik & to a number of other things which we consider essential to mans progress & humanization. *What* a chance has been thrown away of making Central Europe one of the bulwarks of freedom & progress. [Kreisau, 3.9.1932]

Equally dismayed was her son, Helmuth James, who "feels it acutely, as do all liberal minded people" [Kreisau, 3.9.1932].

Yet Dorothy expresses a measure of optimism about the ability of the Papen government to prevent a takeover by Hitler.

There is no doubt that the Papen government is very competant [*sic*], & there is less of an atmosphere of hopelessness about than there has been for years. People are beginning to reckon with the possibility of better times, & that as the winter season is approaching. Whether it will be possible to keep Hitler from power no one knows, & at present an unholy alliance is being contracted between the Catholics & the Nazis. Should they succeed in forming a working majority, their next concern will be to try & oust each other, & in my opinion the Catholics will win, for they have a cohesive party, a programe [*sic*.], astute leaders, & a spiritual foundation, i.e. the Catholic faith. [Kreisau, 9.9.1932]

Translating a biography of Mary Baker Eddy

In September, Dorothy suddenly moved to Berlin, where she would remain for several months in order to assist her husband with his translation work. The Count had been commissioned to translate into German an important new biography of Mary Baker Eddy by Lyman P. Powell.[142]

You will be surprised at the heading, & so am I. On Thursday morning the Y. T. telephoned to tell me that the translation work which we are to do together had arrived, & that I had better come as soon as possible, as the book is to be published before Christmas. [Berlin, 19.9.1932]

The work of translating the biography was intense, requiring a great deal of time and effort from September to December. Yet it was an assignment that Helmuth and Dorothy enjoyed, and for the next several weeks, they worked tirelessly to finish it in time for Christmas. In addition to the translation work and his Christian Science practice, the Count was busily engaged in teaching Christian Science to his first class of students.

While assisting her husband in Berlin, Countess von Moltke also helped her recently married son and his bride get settled in their small, but cozy, flat. Dorothy was struck by her eldest son's resemblance to her father.

I so often find very strong traces of you in the Boy, which touch me deeply. He is less balanced in judgement than you, got more of his father's impetuosity, but it is often as if you were speaking when it is a question of ethics or in a matter of right versus opportunism. [Berlin, 16.10.1932]

Last days of the Weimar Republic

In September, Papen was muzzled by the Nazis at the *Reichstag*.

We were all *very* excited, as you may imagine, at the "goings on" in the Reichstag last Monday, when Papen wasn't given permission to speak. The Nazis are really impossible people,— fancy their posing now as the guardians of the parliamentary system! [Friedenau (Berlin), 19.9.1932]

She still held out for the democratic majority that opposed autocratic rule.

At the same time I *was* pleased, & a good deal surprised, to find that the Reichstag was practically (95%) unanimously opposed to dictatorial rule. . . . It gives one an uneasy feeling to realize that it is General Schleicher with the Reichswehr who

183

are really the masters of our fate, & these notes on re-armament are very unwise & unsettling for the whole world. On the other hand there is undoubtedly a large mass of opinion—a majority still—which is genuinely democratic, & doesn't hold with the present system of autocratic government. I don't myself, & yet, I ask myself, what have we to put in its place? [Friedenau (Berlin), 19.9.1932]

Opposed as she was to the autocratic style of the Papen government, it seemed preferable to the Nazis, "who are such partisans that they can no longer judge between right & wrong, their formula being: Nazis = right, those of other opinions = wrong" [Friedenau (Berlin), 19.9.1932]. At the end of September, "all Germany was celebrating wonderful old Hindenburgs 85th birthday" [Friedenau (Berlin), 30.9.1932].

In spite of their aggressive tactics, it still did not look to Dorothy as if the Nazis would succeed in gaining power.

Here we have nothing to say as to how we want to be governed. A pure autocracy, but not, I gather, merciless or intolerant as most autocracies are. . . . We are all very interested to see what the elections (the 5th in this year!) will bring forth. No one expects the Nazis to gain any more, au contraire [on the contrary]. At present they can find nothing better to do than to break up all *Conservative* (Hagenberg) [Alfred Hugenberg] meetings! [Berlin, 7.10.1932]

However, she was "very distressed at the way things are going here, politically I mean" [Friedenau (Berlin), 16.10.1932].

. . . we are drifting back into pre-war conditions, militarism, with all that it implies in stupidity, isolation, tactlessness, & crude nationalism, & we all feel that the advance made during the last 18 years has been entirely thrown away & destroyed. It is very tragic, & of course the end of a régime like the present (if it lasts long enough) is war. [Friedenau (Berlin), 16.10.1932]

Dorothy's account of a dinner with Helmuth's cousin, Hans Carl von Hülsen,[143] who was "in touch with those around Papen," gives a vignette of the inner struggles between Hindenburg and Hitler [Berlin, 23.10.1932].

> [Hans Carl] told me that when Hitler was called to Berlin in order to be offered a post (or posts) in the cabinet, Papen & his colleagues were quite prepared to give him the Chancellorship, but Hindenburg stubbornly refused, & only saw Hitler for a few minutes, asking him very coldly if he would accept some minor post. As Hitler had been led to expect much more, he refused, whereupon Hindenburg—relieved—ended the interview. An extraordinary man, isn't he? I for my part, can't understand the workings of his mind. But he is extraordinarily popular, as much so I should say, as old Kaiser Wilhelm I was. If pictures of him are shown in the cinema, there is always clapping & applause. [Berlin, 23.10.1932]

By early November, the Moltkes and the rest of Germany were "awaiting with breathless interest the election results, & wondering what will happen next" [Berlin, 6.11.1932].

> One thing is pretty certain, the Communists are sure to have great gains; . . . Unless we get better times & recover economically a bit, I don't see what is to prevent the Communists from seizing power in the long run. . . . On the other hand, I very much dislike the present powers that be. It is the mentality of 1914—glorification of war, love of military display, self glorification which is called "nationalism" i.e. patriotism & so on. . . . Tuesday. The elections passed off very quietly, & we are all greatly rejoicing at the losses the Nazis have suffered. Everyone is guessing what Hindenburg & Papen will do, & whether the Nazis will be forced to take office & accept responsibility. [Berlin, 6.11.1932]

Meanwhile, all trams, buses, and underground railways went on strike—strikes organized by Nazis and Communists—causing further inconvenience and instability.

185

Even the page boys aren't a bit impressed by Hitler

"We are of course all rather breathless & excited at Hitlers attempt to form a majority Cabinet," Dorothy wrote two weeks later [Berlin, 20.11.1932].

> Personally I don't think Hitler will be able to form a cabinet, he isn't capable of working with other men, except those who obey his every whim & speak to him in the 3rd person, as one does to a king in this country! . . . I'm sure Hitlers going to be a huge frost, & after that his disappointed followers will all go communist. [Berlin, 20.11.1932]

Despite his royal pretensions, those who got an up-close view of the *Führer* were not overawed by him in the least, as Dorothy discovered when she visited Frau *Doktor* Eugenie Schwarzwald at the hotel, the Kaiserhof in Berlin, where Hitler was staying.

> He is staying at the Kaiser Hof Hotel, where Frau Doctor always stays, & there are always crowds round the hotel, but to my surprise I find that the Hotel employées—even the page boys—aren't a bit impressed by him. The lift man said to me yesterday when I went to see Frau Dr.: "Ja, es ist komisch, wir Deutschen müssen immer etwas haben zum anhimmeln; (offer incense to) erst war es Wilhelm, jetzt Hitler—fürchterlich." [Yes, it's funny, we Germans must always have someone to worship (literally, "offer incense to"); first it was [Kaiser] William, now Hitler—frightful.] [Berlin, 20.11.1932]

As Hindenburg struggled to respond to the crisis, Countess von Moltke was dismayed at the Conservatives' disillusionment with democracy and their desire to revert to autocratic rule.

> No one can forsee [*sic*.] the immediate future. Up till now, in this crisis, Hindenburg has acted very wisely, more like his "old self" than during the Papen regime. All the parties & papers of the Right were loud in their abuse of the "Parliamentary System". We must have an "authoritative Government", the party system is open to grave abuse, the talk

186

about "Government by the People" is the exploded jargon of the 19th century etc. Well, we tried an authoritative government, not responsible to the Reichstag, which was simply ignored, & the result is a complete fiasco. So now Hindenburg is asking again for a government with a Reichstag majority behind it! [Berlin, 20.11.1932]

Our "crisis" is still flourishing, & Hitler, as usual, has chosen to avoid all responsibility. Many people say communism is bound to take over the Government sooner or later, but who can prophecy [sic.]? Hindenburg has behaved very wisely & it is the parties of the Right who are to blame, for they simply *won't* unite & work with one another. [Berlin, 28.11.1932]

The government was now searching for a new chancellor to take the place of Papen, who had left office on November 17. At the end of his mother's letter is a postscript in Willo's hand giving the latest news.

Meanwhile Papen has gone, but nobody knows who is going to take his place . . . . Today at 12 all newspapers told that Papen was coming back but in the evening Hindenburg is trying again to find somebody to take over Papen's place. [Berlin, 28.11.1932]

Nazis lose ground

Finally, a replacement was found—General Kurt von Schleicher.[144]

Well, we have a government at last, & everyone except the Nazis & Communists are willing to give Schleicher a chance. He must be a very able man,—there has never been so young a general in German history—whether he is a politician remains to be seen. He has the reputation of being ambitious & none too particular as to what devious paths he treads towards his goal—the very antithesis of Brüning—, but though this is a great pity, it is a fault which most big & successful statesmen have. Meanwhile the Nazis have lost a large number of seats in the elections in Thuringia, although the great Adolf & all his henchmen were canvassing. [Berlin, 5.12.1932]

187

Schleicher seemed to have made a good start as chancellor.

> Schleicher is doing very well, & trying to undo the prodigious mistakes made by Papen; . . . The situation is much improved & people are buying freely for Christmas, which is a good sign. [Berlin, 12.12.1932]

> Schleichers manifesto . . . was the speech of a sensible, un-dogmatic soldier, &, in spite of his reputation, bore the impress of honesty. It has met with a very good reception everywhere, excepting the Nazis & Communists, whom no one can please. [Berlin, 17.12.1932]

Dorothy took note of the blatantly anti-Semitic policies of the Nazis.

> Did you see in the papers that a large number of patriotic womens societies in the States have protested against Einstein being allowed to enter America on the ground that "no one can understand his theories, & they are therefore useless"! Not much advance since the middle ages, is there? Of course the *real* reason is that he is a Jew & what is here termed an "Edel Kommunist" ["salon communist"]. By the way, while we are on the subject of patriotism run mad, the Nazis who form the government in Thuringia (until the last election on Sunday) have taken away all pictures from the Gallery in Weimar that have been painted by "foreigners", & all pictures painted since 1900 (designed to get rid of Libermanns [Max Liebermann's] works, Germanys most distinguished modern painter & a Jew.) It is almost inconceivable, but of course defeats its own purpose in the end, for people won't stand that sort of thing long. [Berlin, 5.12.1932]

An event of note in December was a lecture by Lord David Cecil, British biographer, literary historian, and educator.

> Did I tell you of Lord David Cecils lecture last week? It was excellent. So typically English, with delightful streaks of humour, quite inconsequential, as it were, yet full of meat. *Such* a weird looking young man, very able, with a forehead so large that it seemed almost a caricature, & yet such a slight,

188

delicate & degenerate body. [Berlin, 5.12.1932]

As the year 1932 drew to a close, C.B. was doing better in his studies; Asta had new dresses for school; and Dorothy was eagerly awaiting her mother's arrival in Germany.

1933
"It is like a hideous nightmare"

"There is a huge Nazi demonstration (about what? No one knows) planned for this afternoon on the Bülow Platz," Dorothy wrote from Berlin in late January.

> Now you must know that the Communist Headquarters, the Karl Liebknecht Haus, is on the Bülow Platz, so you may judge what may happen. Of course it is pure provocation on the part of the Nazis but the government didn't want to give them a grievance by forbidding the mass meeting. So that part of Berlin, the centre of the city—looked like an armed camp, police with machine guns "protecting" these miserable Nazis, & the roof tops round the Bülow Platz bristling with arms & men. The result is that on Wednesday the communists are clamouring to have a demonstration too.
>
> Monday. Yesterday passed without bloodshed, thanks to the police, but really, pacifist though I am, I'd like to get rid of all the Nazi leaders, no matter how. The last fortnight there have been unceasing efforts made to persuade Hitler or one of his chief men to enter the cabinet, or at any rate to "tolerate" the government, but all to no avail, they just say no, arrange demonstrations like the one yesterday, strike poses & roar out platitudes. In the meanwhile they are a dreadful obstruction, considering the number of seats they occupy in the Reichstag. [Berlin, 22.1.1933]

Finally, on January 30, Hitler became chancellor of Germany.

> So Hitler is Reichskanzler [Chancellor of the Reich] after all. The situation is very serious, because practically all the

members of the new cabinet are bent on breaking the Constitution. They are a terrible lot. Of course, it may in the end prove beneficial that these incompetant [*sic*.] reaktionaries [*sic*.] make such a mess of things that their halos disappear. But what will the cost be? And I rather fear that the Conservatives & a large number of Nazis (though they perhaps less so) will learn nothing, however glaring the incompetence & irresponsibility may be, but will look for the faults some where else. It is very sad. And this is where we are 14 years after the Revolution. [Berlin, 30.1.1933]

In the next letters, she gives more details, together with sober reflections.

I'm very worried about our political developments, & see much trouble & bloodshed (internal) ahead of us. Every pretense of justice or constitutionalism is being thrown aside, & the Government & Hindenburg are behaving in a really shameful way, repressing their opponents, the Left (who voted solid for Hindenburg), & suppressing the liberty of the press. The latest coup has been to completely eliminate the Prussian Government (by decree it has been deposed) for the inadequate reason that the Government want a general election on 5th March (hoping for a majority, though why bother, since they rule entirely by decree) & the Prussian Landtag [state parliament] refused to dissolve as there was no reason for it to do so. And all my worthy friends of the Right neither see the danger nor the hipocrasy [*sic*.] of the whole proceeding. It is a country which has become unbalanced & lost all judgement. It is really frightfully depressing. [Berlin, 6.2.1933]

We are really living in an atmosphere where "might" has altogether succeeded "right." Of course that is inevitable with a dictatorship but we haven't even the bright side of a dictatorship, i.e, a strong man with *ideas*, a constructive plan, an affirmed policy. Instead, we have a cabinet of men who distrust one another, who have no ideas, except to suppress the "Marxsists" [*sic*.], & who are hurrying to put their party men into all the responsible positions in the civil service. It will be

190

interesting to see what 5th March brings us. The tragedy is, that there is no middle party left; (it is much the same in England, where, practically, you have only the Conservative & the Socialist parties, only of course everything here is in a 100% more aggravated mood, more unbalanced, fanatical[)]. The centre party is a middle party, but only the catholics vote for it. So that there is no middle-class party to help the trades unions & proletariat. It is considered very probable that a few days before the elections the Communist Party will be forbidden altogether. [Berlin, 12.2.1933]

I *do* wonder what the results of the election will be. Hel. James who was at Kreisau this week end, says the whole village is for the Nazis, for the price of pigs has risen! Alas democracy. And on such issues, parties get pushed into power or fall into oblivion. The irony of that, is that Hugenberg,[145] the Deutsch National Leader, clapped on the high tarifs [*sic*.] which have resulted in higher prices, not the Nazis at all! In the mean while, the Nazis are not governing, they are simply looking after their party interests, turning out good officials who are not of their political opinion & putting in their own men,—a disgraceful exhibition, especially glaring in the case of the head police officials. . . . I am sending you the Home Ministers decree to the Prussian police. Needless to say Hermann Göring is a Nazi.[146] It is a shameful document. [Berlin, 20.2.1933]

Dorothy tries to reassure her anxious father.

There are stormy times ahead of us I fear, & there will be much bloodshed. What blindness, it is like a hideous nightmare. You needn't worry about us, Dear. We are quite out of the limelight. What madness. [Berlin, 28.2.1933]

Meanwhile, Lady Rose Innes had journeyed once again from South Africa and, after taking another three-week cure at the *Weisser Hirsch* in Dresden, arrived in Kreisau for a two-month visit.

In early March, prior to her mother's return to South Africa, Dorothy accompanied her to London, where the two ladies renewed contact with their English friends at several teas, luncheons, and dinners. Writing from her ship en route to England, she reports to her father about the fire that broke out in the *Reichstag* on February 27.

> . . . not only the Communists but the Social Democrats, who are moderate, level headed & very well disciplined, are being ruthlessly persecuted. Of course this can't go on indefinitely & the counter revolution will, necessarily, be just as ruthless, so that the future looks black indeed.
>
> No one believes that the Communists set the Reichstag alight, but the few opposition papers which still exist are so gagged that they do no more than record facts, & even these judiciously, as otherwise they will be suppressed immediately.[147]   [Deutsche Ost-Afrika-Linie, 5.3.1933]

From London, she continues:

> I am really ashamed of what is happening [in Germany], & of course the economic consequences are sure to be disastrous. What you read in the papers is in no way exaggerated. Göhring [*sic*.] is a morphinist (the result of a severe wound during the war) & has been with Moussolini [*sic*.] for 3 years learning "methods", & the results are quite in keeping with these facts. . . . I can't think that strange coalition will last long, do you? It is too unnatural. [London, 14.3.1933]

Nazi censorship had made it dangerous to send abroad letters containing any criticism of the Government, requiring careful self-censorship, "so please don't be too outspoken in your letters," Dorothy advised her father [London, 22.3.1933].

In late March, mother and daughter bade each other a tender farewell as Lady Rose Innes set off on her 8,000-mile voyage back to South Africa. After dinner at The Ladies' Empire Club, Dorothy "drove away to Liverpool Station leaving her waving on the Club Steps" [Berlin, 26.3.1933].

Mysterious dismissals

Back in Berlin, Countess von Moltke describes the

192

deceptively peaceful atmosphere in the city.

> On the surface everything looks perfectly calm & orderly, the Shops are open, . . . & to me the most striking superficial difference is the absence of so many social-democratic & communist papers, & the want of news, opinions or views in those papers which used to belong to the opposition & are still tolerated. There is no opposition discernable in them any more, & so they are not worth reading. But there is probably much more going on behind the scenes. . . . Even conservative high officials are being dismissed & Nazi followers replacing them. [Berlin, 26.3.1933]

She notes with dismay the dismissal of Jews from their positions in hospitals and theaters.

> And doctors in communal hospitals, & actors & actresses in state theatres are being given their congé [leave] wholesale on the ground that they are Jews. On the other hand, the stories of "brutalities" seem to have been exaggerated, & have anyway quite stopped now, as far as one knows, though of course without a free press one really knows very little. It is a most humiliating position, & so unworthy of a self-respecting people. [Berlin, 26.3.1933]

She notes also the dismissal of competent, experienced Conservatives in favor of inexperienced, untrained young Nazis.

> In Reichenbach the Government got rid of a most excellent & experienced Landrat (a Conservative, Graf Degenfeld by name) & have appointed a youth of 26 who has studied for 4 terms—Kunst Geschichte [art history]! Not even law. It is said that not more that 8% of the Nazis belong to the Intelligentsia, so of course they have difficulty in filling all these vacancies. We are very much wondering whether all these officials who have been sacked are to be given pensions & where the money is to come from; I'm afraid the answer is simple: from our pockets. [Kreisau, 10.4.1933]

Hitler's birthday was marked by elaborate festivities—

festivities in which the Moltkes refused to participate.

> The 20th was Hitlers birthday. There were torchlight processions (in Kreisau even) & the houses were illuminated, & the flags flying. (Needless to say, I did neither.) Never did Kaiser or Bismarck have such festivities. I take it, a third joined in from conviction, 1/3 because the others did & 1/3 for fear. Kreisau is quite Nazi, although the price of pigs (& of all other agricultural products) has fallen again. [Kreisau, 23.4.1933]

"Between the devil & the deep sea"

Germans faced the dilemma of having to choose between two evils—Communism and Nazism.

> The Deutsch-National (conservative) neighbours I have spoken to (also) are extremely disturbed & perturbed, but say: if we don't support them, things will be worse, & a revolution from the left would be a hundred times worse, which is true. We are indeed between the devil & the deep sea. But of course the conservatives are to blame for the mess, for they helped Hitler into the saddle. At the last election but one (in November) the Nazis lost 2 million votes & were hopelessly in debt. I must say Hitler behaves modestly & quietly & it looks as if his men are out of hand. Anyway they are presenting their bills & they get in return the good positions in every walk of life. [Kreisau, 23.4.1933]

> Life on the surface however goes on exactly as before, but the newspapers bring practically no news of a political character except "Verboten, verboten" & then lists of people who have been fired or arrested or superseded. Anyway it is very thorough revolutionary work & they certainly don't mean to give their opponents a chance, & for that one cannot blame them I suppose. Anyway we have nothing to take their place, no leaders & no party that is strong enough, for the communists are radicals & all for illegality, while the socialists are for legal action. The burgeois [*sic.*] parties are no more, nor do the Conservatives (Hugenberg & Papen) really exist any

more. What a state of affairs. [Friedenau (Berlin), 25.6.1933]

The Moltke children were no less affected by the oppressive new regime.

I feel very sorry for my boys too especially Helmuth & Willo who just hate this new & illiberal spirit which is now rampant [in Germany]. [London, 22.3.1933]

Nazi domination was already threatening Helmuth James's legal career.

Yesterday our papers said that all successful candidates will be examined a second time by the Minister of Justice as to their suitability from a "national point of view" i.e. whether they are Nazis or not. That of course looks bad for the Boy, & it is quite possible that things may develop in such a way, that, after all, he & Freya may accept Mothers invitation & come out on a visit to you next Christmas. Of course one cannot see ahead & must just sit still & await the course of events. One can make no plans. [Friedenau (Berlin), 30.4.1933]

For the young lawyer and his wife, justice in Germany had begun to lose all meaning.

The Boy has lost all relish for his work at the Supreme Court, since even there "righteous judgement" as the Bible says, is no longer judged. And he & Freya together with hundreds of other law students say: whats the good of studying something that becomes more obsolete each month? We all live a sort of hand to mouth existence—not materially but intellectually—& wonder what will come next. [Friedenau (Berlin), 15.5.1933]

Political conditions were also destabilizing the career of the Moltkes' third son, Willo, who had recently found work with a builder named Block.

The business part of Willos work is still unsettled, for the reason that this "Siedlung" [estate], Friedenstal, belongs to a Jew, a Herr Solomon, & for that reason everything is uncertain, people are not building either, everyone is anxious & over cautious. . . . A nemesis which we all foresaw, but which is

195

very hard on the innocent victims like Block & Willo. [Friedenau (Berlin), 22.5.1933]

The Lawyers' Camp

In July, Helmuth James decided to go to an "Assessor Camp" for young lawyers, a necessary part of his legal training.[148] Dorothy describes the brainwashing by the Nazis in these camps.

Now that [Helmuth James's] exam is drawing near . . . the question of the "Assessor Camps" is becoming rather acute. Of course it is all very distasteful to him, but I hope, if possible, that he will go through with it, so as to get his Assessor title so to speak. In these camps they are, for six weeks, to hear nothing except lectures on: 1. what the national-socialist revolution implies 2. the position of the S.A. within the Nazi movement & a third theme on similar lines. They are to take no law books with them into camp, & I suppose when they are not listening (for 6 long weeks) to these eulogies they will be made to drill or something of the sort. [Kreisau, 8.7.1933]

The idea is to make good Nazis of these future functionaries during the 6 weeks, drumming into them the virtues & ideals of Hitlerism, & that of course to many will be very distasteful (singing of Nazi songs etc.) The head of the camp is a S.A. man who has, for this purpose been made a Public Prosecutor! Nuf sed! [Kreisau, 17.7.1933]

This development, however, afforded Dorothy an opportunity to get to know her new daughter-in-law.

I have had Freya for three days all to myself. She is a delightful creature, & just the right wife for Helmuth, being full of strength & optimism. She, indeed they both do, love the Berghaus so, & it would have been perfect if Helmuth could have been appointed to the court at Schweidnitz. . . . But alas all these happy plans are wiped away, & they must start again with something else, &, in all probability, somewhere else. . . . It is really touching to see how devoted Helmuth & Freya are to Kreisau. . . . Freya is a delightful child & Daddy will be

196

charmed with her. She is so spontaneous & warmhearted, clever & attractive. [Kreisau, 8.7.1933]

The tense political situation took its toll on the Count's younger brother Peter von Moltke.

Poor Peter has had a bad nervous breakdown (heart) caused by the very painful political occurnces [*sic.*] in his parts. He has been ordered to Altheide (near Landeck) & he & Lotti arrive there on 15th. [Kreisau, 12.8.1933]

"Atrocity lies from abroad"

The Nazi government systematically suppressed information about the atrocities being committed against the Jews.

The ordinary citizen who doesn't happen to have Jewish acquaintances has no idea of what is happening to these unfortunates. If he does hear some story, he has been taught by his newspapers to put it down to "atrocity lies from abroad" & as there are special lay courts for dealing with atrocity reports & the accused get 1 to 3 years imprisonment for spreading atrocity reports, you may imagine that people are rather careful about talking of such things. It is altogether an eye opener to see how a nation can be hypnotized into believing certain things. It is all done by means of slogans & suggestion, & only the more enlightened can free themselves of this miasma, & they with difficulty.   [Berlin, 30.4.1933]

A women's suffrage organization that included Jews was dissolved.

Some days ago I went to a meeting of the former "Staatsbürgerinnen Verein" which is the German branch of the World Alliance for W[oman] Suffrage.[149] It is being dissolved (having been founded in 1865) as the Government won't let any organisation remain which does not accept the "Aryian [*sic.*] paragraph" (i.e. no Jews on the board or committee & no new Jewish members to be admitted) & which has any aims not countenanced by the Nazis. So there we are. [Kreisau, 2.7.1933]

197

Christian Scientists, too, were highly suspect in Nazi Germany. In July, the Count went to Boston on church business, presumably to discuss this problem with headquarters.

> The sensational piece of news for this mail, is that the Y. T. leaves tomorrow for America! Boston of course & an official visit, for there is so much that needs talking over, & discussing. It is lovely for him to have this change. He will be back on 4th August, & will find so much work here, that the chances of his coming to Kreisau grow less & less. [Friedenau (Berlin), 2.7.1933]

Lord Astor

One of the Christian Science luminaries sent to Germany to aid the Count in his work was Waldorf Astor.[150]

> Whom do you think I was with last evening? You'll never guess—Lord Astor! The Directors in Boston have sent him & two other prominent C.S. [Christian Scientists] from London to help the Y. T. straighten things out a bit, & we met them last night to talk things over. Quite a pleasant man. [Berlin, 28.9.1933]

By now, Dorothy has discovered that her mail is being censored by the Nazis.

> I was *most* interested at Dad reporting that my previous letter to you had been obviously opened. Well, well, we live in strange times. [Berlin, 28.9.1933]

Hitler on the silver screen

During a visit with her husband to the cinema, where they viewed footage of Hindenburg and Hitler, even the usually perceptive Dorothy was momentarily deceived by the onscreen appearance of the *Führer*.

> This afternoon the Y. T. took me to a cinema as a rest after the strenuous week. Among the "pictures of the week" were Hindenbourg [*sic.*] replying to his 86th birthday

198

congratulations. This was received in dead silence. After that about 15 or 20 pictures of the "Fest der Bauern" [Farmers' Festival] (last Sunday) with Hitler & flags, "Trachten" [traditional costumes] & all the excellent apparatus the Nazis have at their disposal for celebrating festivities. There was no cheering until the last, when a certain amount of applause was forthcoming. It was rather significant & there was no real enthusiasm. There is no doubt that it is easier to make promises than to keep them. There is no doubt Hitler is quite sincere, not at all self seeking, & touchingly modest for his own person for a man with such power, but of course he too is finding that its easier to destroy than to construct. [Friedenau (Berlin), 8.10.1933]

Some of the Moltkes' friends were deceived by Nazi propaganda. And from this point on, Dorothy's letters include complimentary remarks about Hitler (for the benefit of the censors).

Yesterday two of the Y. T.'s friends were here to lunch. He is Bank manager in Königsberg & she is one of the Y. T.'s last years students. They are both very nice indeed and— enthusiastic Nazis. It is quite instructive to see how everyone (it is the same with religion) takes that part which appeals to him & ignores the rest. The Kübarts wax eloquent about the wonderful spirit of self-sacrifice, & idealism in the creed, & ignore everything else. There is undeniably much idealism in the movement, especially among the youth, that's the strength of its appeal,—self-sacrifice, comradeship, self discipline— that is its idealistic side. The renvers de la medaille [opposite side of the coin] I need not dwell upon, you are aware of it, & besides, it might have unpleasant consequences! It will be interesting to read historys judgement of Hitler. I must say he has much that is admirable, though I doubt whether he is a strong man. You know of course that he neither drinks or smokes or eats meat, never wears a hat. I have never seen him, but on paper he looks anything but inspiring, though he must have a very winning personality, for some types at any rate.

199

The Moltkes were distressed by news that the new regime had left the League of Nations.

> It's all horribly serious, & the worst is, one has no confidence in the men at the helm. I feel sure it was done much more for inner political reasons than for forcing the hands of the other nations, &, from that former point of view it is probably, for the moment, a very clever move. But of course its playing with fire, if there is a blaze, it's we who have to pay, that [*sic*.] the awful part. Personally I don't think there is imminent danger at the moment, but of course, with dictators, there is always a danger that they may throw caution to the winds & stake everything on one idée fixe. [Berlin, 16.10.1933]

They were shocked by some unexpected news of a more personal nature: on October 17, the Count received a telephone call informing him that his position as Christian Science Committee on Publication for Germany had been terminated. This development, Dorothy wrote, was "quite incomprehensible, for he has been most successful in his office" [Berlin, 30.10.1933]. They learned that the primary reason for this decision was that some Nazi-leaning church members considered him too aloof from the Nazi Regime and recommended that he be replaced by someone more neutral. Needless to say, this not only was a deeply humiliating experience for the Count but also involved the loss of much needed income. (See Chapter Eight of Part II for more details about this episode.)

A letter from November reveals how differently members of the same family dealt with life under the Nazi dictatorship. The Moltkes' second son, Jowo, abandoned the family's stand against Nazism and joined the Storm Troopers. Dorothy was deeply troubled by this decision.

> I was rather boulversé [*bouleversé*: shaken] to get a letter from Jowo yesterday saying he had just joined the S.A. (Nazi storm troops.) It seems to me quite unnecessary, but he is 24 years of

age & must know what he is doing. If C.B. were to join I should consider it quite natural & right, since he has always had Nazi sympathies. Jowo thinks it's good for his future, & has deliberately silenced his judgement & reason & is determined to "make the best of it." The Schnitzlers [Freya's aunt and uncle] are Nazis (their huge chemical works I.G.B. of which he is director make huge profits out of the incredibly large demand for brown shirts & Nazi flags) & that has no doubt soothed his misgivings, especially as he meets lots of Nazis there [in Frankfurt], & never hears or reads any criticisms. We, on the contrary, hear & read hardly anything else. I must admit that its bad, unprofitable & unfruitful to be in such whole-hearted opposition to the powers that be, & I wish, especially for Helmuth James & Willo, that it were otherwise; but thats where Daddy comes in, we all can't compromise with our consciences, & thats what I don't like about Jowos action, though it will probably prove most useful in obtaining a job. . . . In talking over the matter of Jowo's joining in S.A. with the Bendlerstrasse, I was a bit more reconciled, since they say, that if you want a State appointment (& Jowo does) you *must* join.[151] Thats why Helmuth James won't enter the civil service. Willo of course is lucky in having chosen a "free" career. [Berlin, 5.11.1933]

Christmas at Kreisau

"I'm *so* glad we came to Kreisau for Christmas," Dorothy wrote. "I don't remember our ever having spent a happier Christmas" [Kreisau, 31.12.1933]. The family enjoyed a moment of hilarity when C.B. tried out a new shaver.

Christmas Day. . . . We have all had a very happy and completely harmonious Christmas, & there has been much laughter. Willo was given an electric shaving apparatus, & C.B. asked if he could use it this morning. He did; & the result was that he came down to breakfast with 3 large plasters on his face where he had cut him self! We were almost hysterical with laughter, & as one of his plasters was on his upper lip he had to hold it together everytime he laughed as other wise the

201

wound (not really serious) opened. This made him doubly funny, for he was constantly holding his little plaster moustache, & this made us laugh all the more. He is altogether very good company just now. [Kreisau, 22.12.1933]

On the last day of 1933, Countess von Moltke pondered the events of the past year.

What a year this has been! Of course the year 1914, though one didn't realize it, perhaps brought more in its train than any other I have lived through, but 1933 has been a greater intellectual upheaval to us in the Fatherland. The points of view, the values, the ideals have changed more radically than ever before. A *horrid* year. And what has 1934 in store for us all? What a mystery it all is. [Kreisau, 31.12.1933]

She also enjoyed the winter beauty of Kriesau.

Tuesday. Such a lovely day, with the trees heavy with snow; yesterday there was a hoar frost which was beautiful too, though the sun was wanting to make it perfect. The big Birch is quite fairy-like today. The deer have been in the garden & nibble off all my carnation leaves! Dear things, luckily it won't really damage the plants. [Kreisau, 31.12.1933]

1934

"It's a mad world"

On the occasion of her father's seventy-ninth birthday, Dorothy sent her congratulations.

The dear Dads birthday, . . .What a wonderful stretch of history to look back upon, what changes you have seen in public life & general outlook,—the position of women, & many other great social changes & upheavals. [Kreisau, 8.1.1934]

Her second son, Jowo, was beginning to experience some success as a promising art historian.

202

While in Berlin (about 10 days ago) he met Prof. [W.R.] Valentiner, one of the leading Kunst Historiker [art historians], with a world wide reputation & director of the Art Gallery in Detroit [Detroit Institute of Arts]. He was very kind to Jowo & talked shop with him for two hours & gave & lent him lots of photos. One photo of a picture was puzzling Prof. V., who thought it might be an early Rembrandt, &, lo & behold, Jowo identified it as an unknown [Jan] de Bray![152] Now that was not only very exciting but very encouraging & did Jowo a lot of good, making him more confident. [Berlin, 14.1.1934]

Yet a great uneasiness pervades Dorothy's writing about her family's prospects.

It is impossible to make plans even 6 months ahead, everything is in a state of fluctuation, & nobody can foresee developments. That is anything but pleasant, but one gets used to it, only, as the Y. T. truly says, it takes away all ones initiative to do anything constructive, this feeling that nothing is stable, & in three months time the whole structure of our life may have changed completely. [Friedenau (Berlin), 20.1.1934]

The news of Germany's nonaggression pact with Poland did little to comfort her.

Well, well, its a mad world my masters, & I can only hope that it is sincerely meant on both sides. [Friedenau (Berlin), 27.1.1934]

The family tried to carry on as normally as possible, mixing somewhat awkwardly with their Nazi acquaintances.

Esther Arnim is giving a dance here in Berlin this evening, that is, her parents are giving it for her. Herr von Arnim has a very important position, as "Landeshauptman[n] von Brandenburg" [head of provincial government of Brandenburg], is a Nazi, & they have a beautiful official residence, so it ought to be very nice. Asta & C.B. are there. Asta refused "for reasons of economy", but I thought parties like that are none too common these days, & have a certain value as teaching one deportment etc, so, when I heard that she had refused, I wrote at once to tell her I was quite willing to pay for her fare. [Friedenau (Berlin), 27.1.1934]

A Schnitzler cousin became engaged to a high-ranking young Nazi.

> Freya will be interested by the way to hear that Lilo Schnitzler is engaged to a Herr Schultz [Herbert Scholz], Röhm[']s[153] right hand man. The engagement is to be made public at Easter. Jowo met Herr Schultz [Scholz]. . . at Lilos dance in Berlin & thought him very nice. Of course he's a great Nazi, but then so is Lilo, he is good-looking & well educated & attractive in every way. The only drawback indeed is the extremely ordinary name. Lilo I believe, is blissfully happy, & doesn't let her Mother boss her any more, which everyone is so pleased about. [Nürnberg, 25.3.1934] [154]

Against the backdrop of Hitler's manic performances on the radio, Dorothy and her husband continued to do translation work for the Christian Science Church.

> We both have a great deal to do. I am doing some translating at the moment—just a short pamphlet—but its work I like & its quite well paid. Then too its been washing day & I've been in charge of the kitchen. . . . Today is the anniversary of Hitlers assumption of power, & the wireless is bellowing forth speeches of the great man. [Friedenau (Berlin), 27.1.1934]

Dorothy also helped her son and daughter-in-law prepare for a trip to South Africa.

> On Thursday I went to Frau Nier's & assisted at the last trying on of Freyas really lovely outfit. In one of the dresses she looked at herself critically in the mirror & said "Ob dies Kleid mein Grossvater gefallen wird?" [Do you think my (husband's) grandfather [Sir James] will like this dress?] So you see, dear Flen, how important your opinion is, even to extremely attractive young women who don't know you!! [Berlin, 5.2.1934]

She kept the Chief Justice informed about the trial of those accused of setting the *Reichstag* on fire the previous year, on February 27, 1933—a situation that Chancellor Adolf Hitler exploited in order to nullify civil liberties in the "*Reichstag Fire Decree*," or Decree of the Reich President for the Protection of People and State, issued the day after the fire by President Paul von Hindenburg.

> I quite agree with what Dad says about the Reichstag fire trial. Of course they didn't give the trial to the strongest & most courageous judge, but to one of a much smaller mould. However he did try, in the end, to assert the independence of the law, under terribly trying conditions, conditions quite inconceivable to you & those outside. Another & still more independant [*sic.*] judgement has been passed since on a bunch of communists charged with murdering an SA man. [Berlin, 5.2.1934]

On the lighter side, Dorothy reported that her music-loving husband, who was fascinated by gadgets and new inventions, had bought a gramophone.

> The children all shake their heads at "Papi's Leichtsinn" [frivolity], but we all enjoy it very much indeed. [Berlin, 13.2.1934]

In March 1934, the Moltkes' athletic fourth son, C.B., who had struggled in school, finally decided to join the *Reichswehr*—the German military, not to be confused with the Nazi *Sturmabteilung* (S.A.). This career move filled Dorothy with misgivings as well as hopes for her son.

> As far as my feelings go, I don't like him going into the Reichswehr, it is so contrary to our outlook, & I fear they are so "discipline mad" that the individuality of a soldier is rather apt to be warped or broken during the process of training. On the other hand, it is a first rate corps, they say the finest in the world, there are chances of advancement, especially with C.B's nature & name, & there is scope in it for both intellectual & sportly (to coin a new word) achievements. [Friedenau

A month later, however, C.B. gave up the idea of soldiering and took a job as an apprentice in a large paper mill in `Stettin, much to Dorothy's relief.

In late March, the Moltkes' daughter, Asta, was bound for a school run by a Frau Wirsching, an art historian in Dachau, in southern Germany near Munich. It seems the youngest Moltke was a bit forlorn at the prospect of going so far from home. But she soon settled into this unusual school.

> It is an old square, peasant house, roomy & attractive, simply but tastefully furnished (Bauern Styl [peasant style] mostly) with a good sized garden & a meadow for the poultry. Frau W. herself . . . is a "Kunsthistorikerin" [art historian] & gives the girls lessons in art history & takes them to Munich to see what they have learned about. She has only a charwoman & the four girls & she do all the work, so Asta will learn a lot, I hope. [Berlin, 2.4.1934]

> She had to kill a cock when last she wrote, for Sundays dinner & wasn't looking forward to the job! She writes very cheerfully, but whether she is making the best of things or whether she is genuinely happy I am not prepared to say, but incline to the former thesis. [Friedenau (Berlin), 7.5.1934]

Young German pilots in the area enjoyed buzzing the school.

> There is a flying school near Dachau, & the girls got to know some of the young pilots, who embarras [sic.] them considerably by constantly flying low over the Pollnhof, looping the loop, waving frantically etc & causing quite a sensation in the little town! [Friedenau (Berlin), 7.5.1934]

As it turned out, Asta was not happy at Frau Wirsching's and was sent to another school.

During a visit to Seeshaupt, in Bavaria, Dorothy observed that the political climate there was altogether different from that of Berlin.

They tell me every one, including the peasants in that part of the world thinks politically as we do. Indeed I seldom meet people who think otherwise, that is so astonishing. . . . Dachau was full of Austrian Nazis in SS[155] uniform kicking their heels, with nothing to do, for they can't go back to Austria, since they have put their money on the wrong horse. [Berlin, 2.4.1934]

The Count engaged as church soloist in Berlin

In mid-March, Count von Moltke appeared in a court case in East Prussia, "as an expert on C.S. (Christian Science)." He was also hired as soloist at the Christian Science church in Berlin.

. . . he has an ideal voice for lyrical & religious music, but on the other hand it is irksome, for it means that he has to be here every Sunday, except when he takes a summer holiday. [Friendenau (Berlin), 14.4.1934]

Respite at Kreisau

By early June, Dorothy was back at Kreisau, where she anticipated the arrival of a few P.G.s (paying guests) and looked forward to enjoying once again the peace and quiet of the countryside, and the companionship of the people on the estate and in the village. "But," she adds, "I confess that I am looking forward to the Y.Ts quiet presence very much all the same" [Kreisau, 10.6.34].

Soon the Count arrived, and the couple enjoyed a pleasant respite of two weeks together at Kreisau before he returned to his work in Berlin.

We have been practising sacred songs every day here, and that has been very nice. Indeed we are having a very restful fortnight together—seeing no one, no telephon [sic.], hardly any newspapers. . . . The Y. T. and I go for long walks over the fields, and that is very interesting too. [Kreisau, 16.6.1934]

Jowo completed his thesis at the university and was very busy "mugging up for his exam next month, with a great deal of S.A. [Storm Troopers] practise thrown in" [Kreisau,

25.6.34].

Dorothy rejoiced that "the Kinder"—the children, Helmuth James and Freya, who were visiting her parents in South Africa—"get on so well with the relations" [Kriesau, 25.6.1934].

> Both of them have a very fine feeling for genuineness, so that they can appreciate someone who is diametrically opposed to them in outlook, education, religion, taste or anything else, as long as that person is genuine. I hope the Innes relations find the Kinder as pleasing as they find them, but I don't really doubt it; though younger people are often rather overawed by Helmuth James. [Kreisau, 25.6.1934]

In the meantime, she was expecting another P.G. named Gertrude Lehmann, a teacher who "needs much quiet poor thing. It is no joke teaching in this Nazi world, with their 'Weltanschauung' [world view], which has to be drummed into the heads of all the children" [Kreisau, 10.6.1934].

Of great concern at this time was a severe drought, which Dorothy connected with the political turmoil in Germany.

> If only we could get a few days of steady rain it would be splendid, but the weather seems upset everywhere, & can one be surprised, seeing how upset the world in general is? The insanity of the world makes one despair. [Friedenau (Berlin), 20.5.1934]

The one source of sanity and comfort for Dorothy, the Count, and Ulla was their religion.

> . . . people like Muthy [the Y.T.] Ulla and me can always find some consolation in religion, and we are older too and haven't to begin our lives in these abnormal times. [Kreisau, 25.6.1934]

View from across the border

In late June, Dorothy went to Potštejn, Czechoslovakia, not far from Kreisau—"3 to 4 hours from Kreisau in a

Bummelzug [slow train]"—where she and Frau *Doktor* Schwarzwald stayed at the home of Countess Dobrzensky, a friend of the Frau *Doktor*'s [Berlin, 26.5.1934]. From there she was able to express her thoughts more freely about the future of Germany.

It seems so strange yesterday to suddenly—without any outward sign, except that passports were examined & all German newspapers confiscated—be in a country where one can write & say what one pleases—more or less. The houses look the same, the scenery is the same, but what a difference really! No one knows what is going to happen in Germany, but grumbling is rife. Nothing has improved except that there is very little blood-shedding & street fighting as there used to be between Nazis & Communists, & that very large numbers of youthful unemployed are usefully working in Labour Camps &, less usefully, in the S.A. Then too I really believe class distinctions have been a good deal obliterated. But otherwise, everything else has changed for the worse, appallingly so. The more decent Nazis (& there are many such) are so depressed & disgusted at the intrigues & corruption, that many won't have anything to do with the party any more. But without a free press nobody can air his views or organize any resistance or improvement. *That* is the Nazis strongest card,—we have nothing to put in their place. People talk of a military dictatorship, (the Reichswehr isn't at all Nazi) but who knows if there is a personality capable of taking command. Hitler is still much admired, though no one now—as at first—calls him a Statesman or even a great man—but his simple personal life appeals to them & the majority believe in his sincerity, which I don't. You have no idea how the Nazis have confused the peoples minds, by never giving words their proper meaning, & yet deluging us so with phrases that no one has time to think. It is simply emotional. But everybody is sick of it. Even Dr Alexander told Muthy [the Y.T.] the other day in Breslau how dissatisfied he was.

What I am really afraid of is war. Whether it is possible or not

209

for Germany to wage war during the next 5 years I don't know—we are too ignorant of what goes on to really form an opinion. Most people think it out of the question, & I incline to that view myself, but one never can tell, & it is a nightmare to think of what that would mean personally to us. However it is a great comfort that the Reichs Wehr are more or less normal people, less infected by this ghastly Nazi doctrine than most others.

Muthy [the Y.T.] suffers acutely from the whole business. He says he feels sick when he reads a German paper, so we always read the Basler Nachrichten [Swiss German-language newspaper] which is excellent. If he could, he would emigrate tomorrow, & so would Willo & Jowo too. Hans Heini Portatius [a neighbor] the other day said: "how I envy Helmuth being out of Germany." Thats what the Nazis have made of the country—that everyone would like to emigrate. I do wish Helmuth [James] could find work for a few years out side of Germany, for he & Freya will feel things more acutely even than we do after their months in a normal world. Daddy thinks of resistance etc. Revolutionary methods have changed, & now with the radio & the press, with airplanes & bombs & machine guns, organised mental & physical resistance are almost out of the question. Besides, by far the best is to let the Nazis have their day, & eventually the house of cards will fall to pieces. Of course we have to pay for the music, but you'll never kill this pernicious doctrine, until it has proven itself a failure. So one must let it have its day, till the people won't listen to it any more. You mustn't think from all this that we are desperately unhappy. We aren't. We find much that gives us pleasure, & as practically all our friends & relatives are Antis, we always have plenty to talk about. Kreisau Nazism has paled very much, & everyone there (though not in Gräditz) would welcome a change. Everything goes very well with us personally, & now that the Registered Mark plan works & the drought has broken, everything goes well with us personally. And I am intensely grateful for that. We try to talk about politics as little as possible & are in all other respects happy

210

people. Genia [Schwartzwald] . . . is unspeakably sad at all this hate & turmoil & madness in the world, & also very anxious about Herr Doktor [Genia's husband], who though quite fairly well, is without any "Lebens Mut" [courage to face life] whatsoever. . . . She thinks that Nazism will ultimately come in Austria too, though not necessarily with the Anschluss [annexation of Austria] as well." [Potštejn, 28.6.1934] [156]

The Night of the Long Knives

The weekend of June 30 through July 2, at least sixty-five people—possibly as many as four hundred—were brutally murdered in an event known as "The Night of the Long Knives." This purge was ordered by Hitler himself, who wished to rid himself of potential rivals in the S.A. (Storm Troopers), including Ernst Röhm, its leader and a former Hitler supporter.

Reeling from the shock of this news, Dorothy put pen to paper five days later.

> I know that you have been thinking a great deal of us these last days. I am only just beginning to recover from the effect of the last five or six days. In such revolutionary times as we are living in, one often feels quite unable to put one's mind to anything else, the air is full of rumours. Luckily the temptation to read innumerable newspapers is small, since the papers are so stereotype, and it is very difficult to get hold of foreign papers. . . . I arrived home on Tuesday afternoon [and] . . . found . . . a telegram from Jowo . . . to say that "everything was alright". Dear boy, to telegraph so that I should not be anxious about him, seeing he was in the S.A. . . . Dear Genia . . . . was very much upset at the news we got on Sunday morning, and left us with a heavy heart, not for us, but for the world, where there is so much tragedy. And, what is saddest of all, so much avoidable tragedy. [Kreisau, 6.7.1934]

Wishing with all her heart that her son Helmuth James, still in South Africa, could stay out of Germany for a while longer, Dorothy, too, considered the idea of emigration.

211

I *do* wish Helmuth James could keep out of it for another year or two, but it doesn't look as if it is possible. It has been the greatest "Herzens-beruhigung" [ease of mind] to me to have him out of things all these months—Daddy won't understand that, no one can, who hasn't had some experience of Continental present-day conditions. It isn't a question of courage, its a question of waste. I am all for courage and sacrifice under certain conditions, but under present circumstances it isn't, spiritually, worth it. Honesty, however, makes me admit, that Herr Dr. [Schwarzwald] for instance, thinks the good people ought to remain in Germany. But I think the price too high. After all, the Pilgrim Fathers left their country, and nobody thinks they were cowards or unworthy. And nobody thinks worse of the men who emigrated to America from Germany in 1840. The Voortrek[k]ers did likewise too. The fact is, since March 1933 I can't bear the state, any state, and consider the wellfare [*sic*.] of the individual as infinitely more important than the wellfare [*sic*.] of the state. . . . The Y. T. sends me all the foreign newspapers he can lay hands on every day; many are banned and there is a great run on those that are allowed in. Our papers bring practically no news whatsoever. [Kreisau, 6.7.1934]

In late July, the Moltkes attended an event in honor of *Schwester*.

Yesterday was a tremendous success. First we had a "Feier" [celebration] at Schwesters in the open. Our new Schoolmaster had coached the children beautifully & they sang & recited a number of things, Herr Pastor and the Franken Steiner Pastor spoke, Schwester received congratulations, presents & flowers galore. Then the "Auswärtigen Guste [*sic*.]" [out-of-town guests] came to tea at the Berghaus, we were 20 in all. Julian [Frisby][157] helped with everything, & increased British sympathies all over Silesia, . . . [Kreisau, 28.7.1934]

By the end of July, Jowo had successfully completed his doctorate in art history. A month later, he joined up with the *Reichswehr* (the German military), which was not yet under

Nazi control.

It isn't particularly pleasant to "do ones year" when one is 25 years of age, but it really seems the wisest thing to do, for they promise him special consideration in getting a state job later on. . . . His attitude is one of cheerful resignation. [Kreisau, 9.9.1934]

Dorothy took a philosophical view of his joining the regiment in Döberitz.

Dear Child, the first 6 weeks will be trying, but when once they can salute properly & are a bit trained & are given occasional leave etc it will be better, & Jowo is determined to make the best of it. [Berlin, 30.10.1934]

The Moltkes' third son, Willo, was busy with architectural plans.

Willo is working very hard, partly because his exam starts in November, but also partly because he is so interested in the plans he is drawing for a "Winter Sport Baude" [winter sports hut]. He works about ten+ hours a day and sometimes more. [Kreisau, 2.9.1934]

Having her children at home with her during the summer months was a source of great satisfaction to Countess von Moltke.

I hate to think that these are the last really long holidays at home Jowo will have, . . . But I am quite aware how unusually lucky I have been up till now, in having my children so much with me, especially Helmuth James, and I am indeed gratefull [*sic*]. [Kreisau, 2.9.1934]

The last day the family spent together that summer at Kreisau proved to be a particularly peaceful one.

Oh, la tristesse des fins des fêtes [the sadness of holidays' end, . . . This morning the two boys & I went to church in Gräditz, just to cheer our Pastor up in these bleak days for the Evangelical Church. Then we lunched at the Schloss, a good

213

bye party, & the rest of the day was spent out of doors, supper & breakfast partaken of on the stoep of course. One was quite loth to have the day pass, so beautiful & peaceful was it. The views & colouring lovely beyond words, the garden & the lawn so bright & cared-for & the little house looking so reassuring in the midst of all this "Lieblichkeit" [loveliness], which isn't quite such an ambitious word as "beauty." And now its over, & while I write Willo is playing the "Heroica" [Eroica Symphony] from Beethoven on the grammaphone [*sic*.]. Such a happy, contented & grateful family—grateful for their many blessings—if *only* the world outside was different! [Kreisau, 9.9.1934]

At the end of her letter, Dorothy expresses her concern for the young couple returning from South Africa to the "mad world" of Europe in 1934.

And now goodbye dearest old Pelicans. The Kinder will be leaving you in 2 days time. My heart is heavy for them, for it is a mad world they are coming back to, & one that will distress them profoundly.

However there is in spite of all this a great deal to be thankful for, one of the chief blessings being the old birds at Kolara.[158] [Kreisau, 9.9.1934]

Church work

In mid-September, Dorothy and her husband returned to Berlin so he could teach his next class of Christian Science students. There she helped him with the class and did some translating work of her own.

The Y. T. started his class this morning. That is always a very important occasion, the most important for him of the whole year. It lasts a fortnight, every morning from 9 till 12.30 or 1 p.m. I attend too, to help in various ways. That of course means crowding everything else into the afternoon & evening. And today I was asked to do a difficult piece of legal translation into English, which will keep me more than busy for the rest of the week. But it means earning some money & that is always stimulating! [Berlin, 17.9.1934]

When the class was over, the Count went to Boston to meet with church officials there. "There is so much that needs a 'face to face' talk, & matters to be arranged over there, that he feels it necessary for his work, as indeed it is, to go over" [Berlin, 2.10.1934]. Dorothy wrote on October 8, "The Y.T. left on Friday morning. I miss him very much, . . ."

> I have a great deal to do, because apart from my own quite voluminous correspondence, I have to see about the Y.T's really large one. And you can't imagine the number of difficulties that arise in a country where there are so many "Verbots" [bans] as regards industry & frontiers especially. [Berlin, 8.10.1934]

Countess von Moltke took time out from her work in Berlin to go to Kreisau for some "rather important church elections" and to present "Mamsell the faithful tyrant" (the von Moltkes' cook and housekeeper) with a brooch for faithful service [Berlin, 20.10.1934]—a celebration that was "echt Deutsch" (typically German) [Berlin, 30.10.34].

Back in Berlin, she wrote her parents again, apologizing for the delay.

> I have never, I think, begun my letter to you so late, but when one has several children in the house one doesn't seem to have a free minute. There is always somebody arriving or leaving or wanting a little talk or a little attention—& how gladly one gives it! [Berlin 30.10.1934]

By early November, the Count was back from America, and the family was reunited also with the young couple returning from South Africa.

> We thought them both looking very well, even Helmuth, who though thin has more colour & looks healthier than of old. It did my heart good to see them. . . . [Helmuth James] has had a charming letter from Smuts in reply to one he wrote him. They both (he & Freya) love Africa & love you both still more. The

way the Boy talks of Daddy is really quite touching. [Berlin, 4.11.1934]

Dorothy's last letter, dated November 18, 1934, was written from Berlin, before she sailed once again to South Africa.

It isn't easy of course leaving the family here, especially leaving the Y. T. & I wish I could bring him with me. But there it is, one can't have everything. Freya the dear child arrived from Kreisau at 6 p.m. & spent the evening here & has just left. And now I'll say good night too. It *will* be lovely to see you both. [Berlin, 18.11.1934]

After a five-month stay with her parents, Dorothy returned to Kreisau in the spring of 1935. In June, the Moltkes took a trip to Balfanz, Pomerania, to see Helmuth's younger sister Monika and her husband—the Nazi-leaning Rittbachs—with whom the Moltkes found themselves in sharp disagreement over politics. During the visit, Countess Dorothy von Moltke died suddenly, on June 11. Her daughter-in-law Freya wrote in her memoir, *Memories of Kreisau*:

Her death was completely unexpected; she was only fifty-one years old. The domination of Germany by the National Socialists had struck to the core of her being. She had not easily acquired her loyalty to Germany, but she stood the test in the First World War. Now she had lost the Germany that she was ready to trust, and she knew that her children were in danger.[159]

The family was grief-stricken. On a visit to Kreisau a few weeks after her death, the Count said, with tears in his eyes, "*Kreisau ohne Mami ist zu triste!*" [Life without Mami is too sad!][160]

Dorothy's parents, too, were devastated. "The bottom dropped out of our little world," her father wrote sadly at the end of his autobiography. "I cannot even now do more than record the fact."[161] The bereaved Chief Justice was unable to add another word to his memoir.

An Anglican service for Countess von Moltke was held the evening of June 14, 1935, at Christ Church, Kenilworth, a suburb of Cape Town, South Africa. That same evening, at Kreisau, a burial service was conducted in German, including readings and prayers from the Christian Science textbook, which Dorothy and her husband had helped translate twenty-three years earlier.

The Count continued his work as a Christian Science practitioner and teacher in Berlin for four more years. In 1937, he married Anne Marie Altenberg, a German Christian Scientist who was one of his students.

In 1939, Count Helmuth von Moltke died. Countess Anne Marie von Moltke died in 1951.

The story of the children is told in the Epilogue of Part II.

Schloss Kreisau, 1870. This original drawing by Richard Püttner shows the large manor house that Field Marshal Helmuth Carl Bernhard von Moltke bought with money given him by the Kaiser as a reward for winning the Battle of Königgrätz against Austria in 1866.

Field Marshal Helmuth Carl Bernhard von Moltke (1800-1891) in uniform, circa 1871. This was the year Field Marshal von Moltke led the Prussian forces in the final victory over the French, which resulted in the establishment of the German Empire.

Visit by Kaiser Wilhelm II to *Schloss* Kreisau, September 22, 1890. The Kaiser is second from left. To his right is Dorothy von Moltke's future mother-in-law, Ella von Moltke. Barely visible through the ivy at far right (in the white circle) is Helmuth von Moltke, Dorothy's future husband. Arriving by train at four o'clock in the afternoon, the Kaiser was personally welcomed by the almost ninety-year-old Field Marshal. The Field Marshal died seven months later.

Moltke-Schloss Kreisau Kr. Schweidnitz i./Schl.

Schloss Kreisau in 1900. The pair of cannons on either side of the staircase was captured from the French in 1870 during the Franco-Prussian War and given to Field Marshal Helmuth von Moltke by Kaiser Wilhelm I.

Sir James Rose Innes (1855–1942), father of Dorothy von Moltke, circa 1914. Sir James was Attorney General under Cecil Rhodes and Chief Justice of South Africa from 1914 to 1927. He was an early advocate of the rights of blacks in South Africa. Almost all of the letters in this book were written by Dorothy to him and her mother, Jessie Rose Innes.

223

Jessie Rose Innes (1860-1943), mother of Dorothy von Moltke, 1902. Active in advancing the rights of women, Lady Rose Innes occasionally travelled abroad to give speeches at conferences on woman suffrage and served as President of the National Council of Women.

The Moltke family (Dorothy's future in-laws), circa 1902. Seated: Helmuth's parents, Count Wilhelm von Moltke (Vattel) and Countess Ella von Moltke (Muttel). Standing, from left to right: Margarethe, Peter, Monika, Leonore, and Helmuth. In front: Carl Viggo (Helmuth's youngest brother).

Arrival of Helmuth and Dorothy von Moltke at Kreisau shortly after their wedding in Pretoria, South Africa, 1905. Now married to the new Count von Moltke, Dorothy became Countess von Moltke and the *Gutsherrin*—Lady of the Manor—a role she played with exceptional grace.

The Moltkes' eldest son, Helmuth James, about age four, circa 1911. Helmuth James would grow up to become the leader of the anti-Nazi Kreisau Circle, dedicated to planning the reconstruction of Germany on a democratic, non-militaristic basis. After a trial at the notorious *Volksgerichtshof* (People's Court), he was hanged on January 23, 1945.

Kaiser Maneuvers, Third Army Corps, near Kreisau, September 1912. Kaiser Wilhelm II is second from the left. Third from left is Chief of General Staff Helmuth von Moltke, nephew of the great Field Marshal and uncle of Dorothy's husband. In 1913, Dorothy's father, Sir James Rose Innes, who was visiting the family in Silesia, watched these military exercises with fascination and described them in his *Autobiography*.

228

The committee that translated *Science and Health with Key to the Scriptures* by Mary Baker Eddy into German in 1911-1912. From left: Helmuth von Moltke, Ulla Schultz (later Oldenbourg), Adam Dickey, Renate Hermes (later King), Dorothy von Moltke, and Theodor Stanger. For this work, Count and Countess von Moltke travelled to Boston, where they remained for the next seven months before reuniting with their young family.

The Moltke family, 1913—one year before the outbreak of World War I. From left to right: Dorothy, Willo, Jowo, Helmuth James, and Helmuth. They would later add to the family another son, Carl Bernd, and a daughter, Asta Maria.

Dorothy von Moltke (center) enjoying a moment of levity with her father, Sir James Rose Innes (left), and her mother-in-law, Ella Bethusy-Huc von Moltke, 1914. In this year, Dorothy would see her homeland of South Africa go to war with Germany in the First World War.

Dorothy von Moltke with her parents and all five of her children in the Netherlands after World War I, in 1919. Second row, from left: Sir James Rose Innes, Dorothy, and Lady Rose Innes. First row, from left: Helmuth James, Jowo, Willo, Carl Bernd, and Asta.

Entrance to the *Hof* at Kreisau, 1920. The *Hof* was a huge rectangular farmyard surrounded by stables and cowsheds, housing horses, cows, pigs, oxen, sheep, chickens, and other farm animals. In addition to their riding horses, the Moltkes had eight teams of horses for working the fields. Beyond the *Hof*, stretching for miles, lay meadows and fields where barley, corn, flax, peas, rapeseed, potatoes, and sugar beets were raised. About sixty workers were employed by the estate year-round, with additional laborers hired at peak times.

Helmuth von Moltke (1876-1939), circa 1920. By this time, Count von Moltke had become a Christian Science practitioner. The book he is holding is likely *Science and Health with Key to the Scriptures* by Mary Baker Eddy or the Bible.

The Moltke family, 1929. From left: Jowo, Dorothy, Carl Bernd, Asta, and Willo. Skiing was a favorite sport of the Moltke children, and there was plenty of opportunity for it in Silesia, where temperatures sometimes dropped to five degrees below zero (Fahrenheit). The family also enjoyed tobogganing and skijoring (being pulled on skis by a horse or horses).

Helmuth James von Moltke (center) with Frau *Doktor* Eugenie Schwarzwald (left) and Freya Deichmann (later von Moltke), 1930. This photograph was taken at Gründlsee, Austria, where Helmuth James met Freya, in 1929. They were married two years later, in 1931.

Freya von Moltke, wife of Helmuth James von Moltke, 1937. Freya would play an essential role in her husband's work as leader of the Kreisau Circle and during his ordeal in 1944-1945, when he was imprisoned and then hanged.

The *Berghaus* (House on the Hill), not far from the *Schloss*. The Moltkes lived here from 1928 to 1945, often congregating on this porch from which they could enjoy the beautiful views of the surrounding countryside. This photograph was taken in 1940, five years after Dorothy's death. The child on the steps is her grandson, Helmuth Caspar von Moltke.

PART II

THE RELIGION

Chapter One

Trip to Hannover: A young man is healed

Like his famous great-uncle the Field Marshal, who, in spite of having many diseases in his childhood, lived to be ninety-one, Helmuth von Moltke had been a sickly child, plagued with a number of illnesses. When he was being treated for diphtheria, his father, "whip in hand," forced him to swallow his medicine [Kreisau, 4.6.1907]. Later in life, he suffered for an extended period from *einem schweren Nervenleiden*— translated variously as severe nervous trouble, nervous prostration, or depression.[162]

Helmuth's mother, Ella Bethusy-Huc von Moltke, of Huguenot descent, took an interest in unconventional thought systems. In this very conservative society, dominated by the state religion of Lutheranism and alternatively by Catholicism, she was nevertheless able to think outside the box. Hearing of the marvelous healings that had been making news in Germany ever since Christian Science was introduced to that country in the late 1880s, the intrepid Countess von Moltke took her son to see Bertha Günther-Peterson, a Christian Science practitioner in Hannover, Germany, in 1899. Within two months, the young Helmuth was entirely healed through the prayers of Günther-Peterson.

A number of high-ranking Germans were impressed by this healing, including the sister of the Emperor. An article in the *Chicago Tribune* titled "Christian Science in Germany," by D. B. MacGowan, tells the story.

> Berlin, February 6. —Christian Science has gained a substantial foothold in three cities of Germany. . . . Both Mrs. Seal [163] and the Hannover representatives of the metaphysical healing system, assert that among their patients are the wives of many high military officers. The conquest which has made the greatest furor was naturally that of the young Count Hellmuth [*sic*.] von Moltke, the nephew of the Feldmarschall and the son

of the present commanding General at Breslau, Major-General von Moltke. The young Count von Moltke lives on the Moltke estates at Kreisau, near Breslau. He is not now in the public service. He manages the estates.

His health became somewhat impaired and he was persuaded by General and Frau von Garnier, who had, it is said, become convinced of the merits of Christian Science, to place himself in the hands of Frau Gunther [Bertha Günther-Peterson]. He went to Hannover last fall with his mother and spent eight or ten weeks there. After a few conversations, it is said, he became thoroughly converted to the theology and physical and metaphysical views of Mrs. Eddy, and within a short time his splendid tenor[164] was to be heard in every Christian Science service at Hannover. He left for home cured of his nervous prostration.

"I received a letter from him a few days ago," Frau Gunther said last Sunday. "He told me his sister was reading Science and Health diligently and was begging her father to allow her to become a Christian Science healer."[165]

Not satisfied with this triumph, the Christian Scientists have been whispering it about that Science and Health numbers among its readers a member of the royal family. . . . The story is that the hereditary Princess of Sachsen-Meiningen, the oldest sister of the Emperor, whose husband is stationed at Breslau, heard of the case of the young Count von Moltke . . . and through this enthusiastic propagandist secured the famous book.—*Chicago Tribune*.[166]

After his healing, Moltke became committed to the Christian Science Church and remained so for the rest of his life.

Dorothy's conversion

Through her husband, Dorothy, too, became a devoted student of Christian Science, as evidenced by many of her letters to her parents. A letter written in 1909, replying to her father's questions about her faith, reveals the depth of her commitment to Christian Science, to which she was drawn, not out of a need for healing, for she was in excellent health, but out of a love for its inherent idealism.

> Let me say dear Daddy how *very* greatly I appreciate your interest in a subject in which your little girl is so intensely interested, and I think it sweet of you to trouble about it at all, even if it is for her sake. . . . In C. S. the healing of sickness is really a secondary consideration, and its chief value (apart from the help and comfort one is thereby able to give) is that it is a proof that we are gaining a small understanding of the truth. . . . in Christian Science I have found a rational answer to all my questionings and . . . I have found the most wonderful peace, the panacea for all fear, and the greatest incentive not only to pure and right living, but to pure and right thinking too. . . . let me only add that it is *not* a new sect or religion, but simply the teachings of Jesus Christ. [Kreisau, 4.5.1909]

Writing to her father many years later, Dorothy avowed her faith in an afterlife.

> . . . has that which has departed been annihilated or has it only passed beyond our ken? Personally I feel sure it has only gone some where else, but of course no one can prove either the one supposition or the other. It is a divine gift if one *can* honestly believe the second supposition. I wish you could, darling old Dad, it would mean so much to you. But, like love & many other wonderful transcendental things, we can't *make* ourselves do either the one or the other. [Kreisau, 16.7.1926]

These and other letters of Countess von Moltke's emphasize how deeply she and Count von Moltke cherished their religion and proved their love for it in the many sacrifices they made for the Christian Science Church. Their common interest in and commitment to its teachings are apparent in the literally hundreds of references to Christian Science: to Christian Science teaching and services; to the church activities in which they were engaged, including the work of translating *Science and Health with Key to the Scriptures* by Mary Baker Eddy into German; to other Christian Scientists they knew and to whom they gave hospitality; and to the influence Christian

Science had on their lives and the lives of those around them. Count and Countess von Moltke became members of The Mother Church in 1923.[167]

Chapter Two

Class instruction: Learning to heal

On October 14, 1907, the Moltkes packed their seven-month-old son Helmuth James in a hamper and set off for Hannover to learn the art and science of Christian healing. At five o'clock in the morning, they boarded the train at Kreisau, which carried them to their destination 350 miles (563 kilometers) northwest of Silesia, arriving at three-thirty in the afternoon. Traveling with them were the Count's ten-year-old younger brother, Carl Viggo; the nanny, Fräulein Horn; a Mademoiselle Mets; and Schönchen, who was also studying Christian Science. They would all be staying at the home of the Count's mother, called Muttel, in Hannover.

"Here we are, as you see, really in Hannover!" Dorothy exclaimed the day after their arrival. "Today we go to our first class at 5 o'clock, and I am wondering very much what it will be like. We are all three [Helmuth, Dorothy, and Schönchen] looking forward to the work immensely" [Hannover, 15.10.1907]. Although Muttel generously afforded them hospitality and had everything comfortably arranged, it took some creativity on the part of the elder Countess to fit the Moltke family and their entourage into her various bedrooms and sitting rooms.

The "first class" mentioned in Dorothy's letter was the beginning of their course in Christian Science known as Primary class instruction. Their teacher was Bertha Günther-Peterson, the practitioner whose prayers had healed the Count in 1899 and who had just become a Christian Science teacher the year before, in 1906.

Although the *Manual of The Mother Church* does not specify

the duration of Primary class instruction, typically it lasts two weeks. Yet Günther-Peterson's course lasted six or seven weeks, from October 15 until the end of November. According to a report to Mary Baker Eddy from Theodor Stanger, editor of the German-language church periodical, *Der Herold der Christian Science*, Günther-Peterson's explanation for the unusually long duration of the course was that "this length of time was necessary under the conditions in Germany, and that she could not conscientiously dismiss her students after two weeks." At that time, there was no official German translation of the Christian Science textbook, and as Günther-Peterson explains, "much of the time, it seems, is occupied in translating." Günther-Peterson was also considered "very severe," requiring her students to "memorize page after page from 'Recapitulation'" and to write an essay on a section of it.[168]

The demanding nature of the course in Hannover surprised the Moltkes, who had expected that they would have plenty of free time. Instead, they found that they had to study most of the day, then take their class with Günther-Peterson in the evening from five until eight o'clock.[169] In addition, they took music lessons—he voice, she piano—making their schedule a very full one [Hannover, 15.10.1907].

Yet it was a very happy and rewarding time for the Moltkes. "We have heaps to do here for the Coursus [*sic*.][course], read, translate and write papers," Dorothy wrote [Hannover, 15.10.1907]. "Our classes generally last three hours, but they are full of interest, and, what is more, full of satisfaction and joy. Then we have a great deal of home work and our music besides to keep us busy all day long. But it is delightful, and we are all very happy" [Hannover, 30.10.1907].

A lecture in Berlin

During their stay in Hannover, the Moltkes took time out to travel two hundred miles (322 kilometers) to Berlin, to hear a lecture on Christian Science by Clarence Buskirk, formerly an American judge. The evening before the lecture, they attended

245

two evening Christian Science services, one in English, followed by another in German, both of which were well-attended, especially the German one.

> It was beautiful. At the first service the hall was three quarters full and people stood at the back, finding no seats, during the second. The enthusiasm, happiness and striving after an ideal made the meeting just [illegible] (so it seemed to me) and we were very happy there. [Hannover, 17.11.1907]

On the following afternoon, the Moltkes heard Buskirk lecture at the largest hall in Berlin. Although given in English to a large German audience, the lecture was a great success:

> The lecturer spoke in English, but very clearly, and Helmuth was able to follow well. There were between 500 and 700 people there, which, considering that it was in a foreign language, was an excellent attendance. [Hannover, 17.11.1907]

The next day, Dorothy and Helmuth left for Hannover at noon in order to be back in time for their evening class with Günther-Peterson.

When the course was over, Count and Countess von Moltke went to Berlin, while the rest of the group returned with the baby to Kreisau.[170] In the years that followed, the Moltkes would return to Hannover for the annual student meetings with their teacher as often as their responsibilities at home permitted.

Chapter Three

In the practice: Many remarkable healings

Soon after class instruction, the Count plunged into the work of Christian Science healing. In the spring of 1908, he rented an apartment in Berlin,[171] to which his patients came for Christian Science treatment.

While in Berlin, the Moltkes engaged in other church-related activities as well, such as attending a lecture by Edward A.

Kimball, a prominent American lecturer and teacher of Christian Science. They were also involved in some translation work, most likely for *Der Herold der Christian Science*. (A few years later, both Moltkes would contribute articles to the church periodicals.[172]) In August, Count von Moltke planned a trip to England "to study English really thoroughly, and also to see something of the Christian Science work there" [Kreisau, 2.8.1908].

Healings of paralysis, skin disease, and asthma

By the following year, the Count was healing with excellent results. "Helmuth has plenty of work and is doing very well," Dorothy wrote her mother from Berlin. One of his patients, a crippled boy, who suffered from atrophy of the muscles and had not been able to stand for several years, "can stand now for a short time and move his legs, which up till now has been impossible. Some cases are entirely cured already, so that Helmuth is very happy, feeling that he is being able to help people" [Berlin, 10.3.1909].

A letter written two weeks later includes an account of two other healings of conditions that had persisted for long periods of time.

> . . . several of [the Count's patients] are already completely cured; one of an awful skin disease and irritation for which she had tried everything for 5 years, the other of asthma which was so bad that for 7 years the woman never went outside except in very warm weather. From the first treatment on she went everywhere she wanted, even to the Wednesday evening meetings[173] [at the Christian Science church] during the icy weather and now the asthma has completely left her. [Berlin, 24.3.1909]

The success of her husband's healing work was a source of great joy to the Count and Countess, who proudly told her mother, "You may imagine how happy the patients are and Helmuth too!" [Berlin, 24.3.1909].

Diana saved from drowning

The previous year, another wonderful healing had taken place—of the Count's horse, Diana, who had fallen off a bridge.

> On Friday we had rather a nasty accident, nasty at least for our horse, Diana, Helmuths big brown riding horse. We were driving her alone in the Jagd wagen [hunting wagon] and as waggons [*sic*.] with wood had been driving across the little bridge between Creisau and Schwengfeld during the last few days we thought we would do likewise and so drove from Schwengfeld all along the meadow, which Mother will remember. When we came to the bridge we found that the extra planks, which had been laid there for the better convenience of the waggons [*sic*.], had been taken away, but nevertheless we decided to risk crossing as it is just wide enough and Helmuth had done so before as a boy. Of course we all got out of the cart and it was led across; but alas in the middle Diana slipped and fell into the stream. It was a terrible moment for her head was under water and we could not free her from the traces and spikes so that she hung more or less suspended. Only the little "Staller" [stable boy] was with us and while he by hold[ing] the reins high in the air kept the horses head at least partly out of the water, Helmuth tried with a small pocket knife to cut the traces and I started to run home for help. Eventually the poor creature was released and led home and is now slowly, but I hope surely, recovering. [Kreisau, 7.4.1908]

The Count was almost certainly praying for his beloved mare, for the healing was so quick and complete that it astonished even the district veterinarian. "Helmuths horse Diana is, I am glad to say, quite in order once more," Dorothy wrote less than two weeks after the mishap.

> We rode together for the first time since the accident yesterday. It is a great piece of good fortune for us that she has recovered, since the District Vet, who saw her by chance, said that in all his experience he has only known one other horse recover whose head has once been under water. [Kreisau, 19.4.1908]

248

The likelihood that Diana was healed through the Count's prayers is corroborated by a report in 1941 by the head of the Reich Main Security Office, Reinhard Heydrich, who wrote, "In the family of Count Moltke it is generally known that even the horses were healed through prayer."[174]

The Count's relatives healed

Toward the end of 1909, Helmuth's youngest brother, Carl Viggo, then twelve years old, was healed through Christian Science prayer. Another brother, Peter von Moltke, who had been suffering from a boil, turned to the Count and was instantaneously healed. "[Peter] is really quite alright once more," Dorothy wrote, "but feels he would like one or two more treatments before going back to Hannover. When he arrived he was in very great pain, had been for days, but after the first treatment all pain was gone and the boil opened and discharged naturally" [Berlin, 6.12.1909].

This was a condition for which Peter had previously received medical treatment—treatment that had been painful and had required much more time to bring healing. "In the summer he had the same thing," Dorothy explained, "was laid up four weeks and had to have it lanced, so you may imagine how glad he is to have been able to overcome this so easily" [Berlin, 6.12.1909].

A particularly dramatic healing brought about through the Count's prayers was the healing of the master wheelwright, Herr Herford. This beautiful healing of severe kidney pains— possibly kidney stones—must have been an impressive demonstration of the healing power of Christian Science for all who lived or worked at Kreisau or in the nearby town of Schweidnitz.

The cases of Lotte Witzleben and Adolf Zeumer

In addition to these healings through Christian Science prayer, Dorothy's letters contain a few instances in which healings took place without medical help or Christian Science prayer. Precisely because of these circumstances, they were not only of interest to Countess von Moltke but also served as a means of conveying the relationship between thought and health to her parents, who—especially her father—were skeptical about Christian Science and nonmedical means of healing in general.

One of these was the healing of a cousin of the Moltkes, Lotte Witzleben. "I forgot to tell you that Lotte Witzleben has been placed under the care of a woman doctor at Tutzing," Dorothy wrote her parents in November 1924, "with the result that she is quite cured—in 3 months—& has taken an apprenticeship in a bookshop in Munich & is living a normal, happy life,—isn't that splendid?" She described the circumstances.

> The interesting point to me is that all this is the result merely of removing mental obsessions, beliefs, thoughts etc, some conscious, some unconscious. No medicine, diet, or anything else to do with the body, simply the order to live a normal, healthy life, take exercise & *work*. And then of course the psychological side of the case. It is very interesting. [Kreisau, 6.11.1924]

The fact that the illness had been under the treatment of a medical doctor would have appealed to her father, and the fact that the doctor had dealt with the illness without medication gave her father clear evidence, outside of Christian Science, of how thought could affect one's health.

Another such instance was the healing of the Moltkes' estate manager, Adolf Zeumer, whose body was covered with a painful skin condition that the local doctor had been unable to cure. "I've just been down to ask after Zeumer," Dorothy wrote in 1934, "who has a horrid rash all over his body, and has really been very poorly, not sleeping at night for nearly a week, because of the irritation, and really looking very rundown." The loving care given him by the good *Schwester* Ida, however, brought a quick healing—more effectively than the doctor's ministrations. "I'm glad to say Schwester has taken him in hand now," Dorothy continued, "and he is rapidly improving, after being treated for at least a week by the doctor and growing worse all the time." She gaily commended the kindergarten teacher, *"Hoch unsere Schwester!"* [Three cheers for our *Schwester!*] [Kreisau, 18.8.1934].

As in the Witzleben case, this healing, though not accomplished through Christian Science treatment, showed her parents the power of love to bring health and harmony to the human condition.

Chapter Four

"The presence of the all-loving Father": Birth of Jowo

"No, I am not having Schwester [Nurse] Marie to look after me for several reasons," Dorothy wrote her mother in June 1909. Dorothy went on to explain that "she is uncomfortable in the house, she is not a midwife, and so on. Instead I am having a C. S. [Christian Science] nurse over from England, a Miss Flower and I am sending you a list of her medical qualifications, so that you may not feel that I am in the hands of someone who knows nothing about her work" [Kreisau, 15.6.1909].

Countess von Moltke was about to give birth to her second son, Jowo, and was preparing her parents for a change in childbirth methods. The birth of her eldest son, Helmuth James, which occurred several months before the Moltkes were to take Christian Science class instruction, was under standard medical care. By 1909, however, the Moltkes were experienced Christian Scientists and felt ready to have their second child delivered under Christian Science care. They dispensed with the services of *Schwester* Marie and instead hired a highly trained Christian Science nurse from England, Catherine M. Flower. In addition, Helmuth James's nanny, Miss Chalmers—also a Christian Scientist from England—would assist with the birth.

Miss Flower's qualifications were impressive indeed. She held certificates from the British Lying-In Hospital, Endell Street,

251

W.C., where she had received her training; from The London Obstetrical Society "by Examination"; and from The Central Midwives Board, which annually authorized her practicing.[175] Dorothy reassured her jittery mother.

> I wrote asking her for qualifications and saying I wanted to send them to you and she wrote and asked me to tell you that she will take every care of me "that is right from a medical point of view." So I hope you won't feel anxious. She looked after my little South African acquaintance in Berlin when her baby was born this January, and also Mrs. Somers-Cocks and she is highly recommended. I have met her several times in Berlin and liked her and moreover she is a lady. [Kreisau, 15.6.1909]

Schultzchen

The obvious choice for a Christian Science practioner to pray for a harmonious delivery was the Moltkes' family practitioner and friend, Ulla Schultz.

Ulla had first learned of Christian Science in 1899, the same year that Count von Moltke was healed of nervous prostration. During a stay in the country, a friend who had been healed through Christian Science prayer gave her a copy of Mary Baker Eddy's *No and Yes,* which Ulla, being fluent in English, was able to read and understand. "In reading the very first pages," Ulla wrote, "God opened my eyes to the fact, that Christian Science is His Science. The next morning I went to some sick people in the village and brought them of what I had seen of the healing Truth; and they were healed. Right away I had to tell them in German what I had read."[176]

After receiving class instruction with a Christian Science teacher (most likely, the Moltkes' teacher, Bertha Günther-Peterson), Ulla went into the practice and was first listed as a Christian Science practitioner in *The Christian Science Journal* in 1908. Two years after Jowo's birth, she would serve with the Moltkes on the committee that translated *Science and Health* into German, and in 1914, she would become a Christian Science teacher. With the exception of a few years in the early 1920s, and during the two World Wars, when German listings were omitted from the *Journal,* Ulla Schultz (later Oldenbourg) remained a *Journal*-listed practitioner and teacher until 1952.

"No pain or discomfort of any kind"

The experience of giving birth under Christian Science care proved to be a happy and harmonious one for Dorothy, who describes the scene:

> Schultzchen read the 91st Psalm to me, then I walked up and down the room saying the "Scientific statement of being" aloud and then after two pains which though they hurt were not strong enough to interrupt me, I suddenly felt the pressure. . . . There was no pain or discomfort of any kind (except that I was not properly undressed!) and I had hardly got into the bed before the baby was there. [Kreisau, 27.9.1909]

Catherine Flower turned out to be the expert nurse her qualifications had promised. "Miss Flower was excellent," Dorothy said of her. "The afterbirth was rather long in coming, but it was quite in order and came without any pressure or difficulty when it did come" [Kreisau, 27.9.1909]. She reassured her mother that all was well and that she felt "wonderfully blessed" by the experience of giving birth under Christian Science care.

> I only did just what was pleasant and harmonious for me and did not "force" anything at all. . . . Miss Flower, after feeling me, says everything is splendidly normal and in its right place. I tell you all this because I know your first thought will be that although doing all this will not hurt me for the moment, in the future I will feel the effects. This may be so in ordinary cases of mothers getting up so early, but in Christian Science this is changed, and I only can assure you that I am well and strong, that every thing from a medical standpoint is normal, and moreover that I feel so wonderfully blessed and helped by this experience. [Kreisau, 12.10.1909]

Indeed, to those involved, the whole episode seemed to be a

holy experience, "for we all felt the presence of the all-loving Father who 'healeth all thy diseases' during this time very consciously, instead of the Jehovah who cursed Eve and her seed." Dorothy expressed the wish that her parents "could have experienced it with us, not the physical part I mean (for that was but a portion of the outward expression) but the spiritual part, which is the kernel of it all" [Kreisau, 12.10.1909].

Her parents, however, having no great faith in or knowledge of spiritual healing, were understandably anxious when they learned that their daughter was relying on Christian Science for the birth of her second son. As they apparently perceived Christian Science treatment more as the absence of drugs and medicine than as the presence of something substantial and effective, Dorothy felt compelled to give them an explanation of the spiritual basis of Christian Science healing.

> . . . Christian Science treatment does not mean simply letting things go and not taking medicine and medical care. It is just as much a "medicine" in its own way as materia medica, more care is needed, the difference being that in the one the care is material, in the other mental. Just not taking medicine and calling that C. S. is as little the real thing as to stop eating and call that vegetarianism; in the one case one must supplant meat eating by eating vegetables, in the other medicine and medical theories by an understanding of Gods power. [Kreisau, 25.10.1909]

In a final effort to quell their apprehension, Dorothy assured her parents, "I had not been neglecting myself, but simply using other methods, methods of which I know you do not approve, but which I hope you will realize were carefully used. And anyhow, whatever the methods, the result is that I am rosy, well and strong, and that will please you I know" [Kreisau, 25.10.1909].

Chapter Five

The German translation: Preparing the way

The Discoverer and Founder of Christian Science had a great regard for the German people, in whom she saw a readiness for her teachings.

> Germany will be the first European nation to accept Christian Science. Their love of God, their profound religious character, their deep faith, and strong intellectual qualities make them particularly receptive to Christian Science.[177]

Christian Science first became known in Germany in the late 1880s, when Hans Eckert of Cannstatt, near Stuttgart, took up its study. He came to the United States two or three years later to be taught by an authorized teacher. Returning to Germany in 1894, he proceeded to spread the word in the Cannstatt-Stuttgart area.

In 1896, the Moltkes' teacher, Bertha Günther-Peterson, came to the United States for Primary class instruction with Laura Lathrop in New York City. One year later, she began giving Christian Science treatments in Hannover, Germany, with results that astonished people who had not previously known about Christian Science and the healings being accomplished by its adherents.

Meanwhile, an American lady wintering in the city of Dresden was spending many hours reading *Science and Health,* which had been given to her as a farewell present before she set sail from the United States. Mary Beecher Longyear[178] became deeply interested in Christian Science and talked about it with many people in the town. Before returning to the United States, she promised to send someone to Dresden who, she felt, would further the work there better than she could.[179]

When Longyear returned to New York in the spring of 1897, she spoke to Lathrop about sending a worker to Dresden "to carry the Truth to these people." The following day, Lathrop sent for one of her students, Frances Thurber Seal, and told her that she "was the one to answer it and go forth to do this work." Seal immediately accepted.[180]

In December 1897, without knowing the language and with relatively little experience in Christian Science, the intrepid Frances Thurber Seal sailed to Germany, where she practiced healing in Dresden and later in Berlin with remarkable success.

Soon there were many marvelous healings in Germany through the prayers not only of Seal but of other practitioners as well. As Eddy had predicted, Christian Science was flourishing in the land of Martin Luther.[181]

Calls for a German translation

By 1902, Mary Baker Eddy had authorized the publication of the German-language *Der Herold der Christian Science,* the first issue of which appeared in 1903, and now requests for translations of *Science and Health* were pouring into Boston "from all over this planet." She was reluctant, however, to grant permission for a German translation or *any* translation of *Science and Health* at this time, although she also wrote yearningly on this subject, "How deeply I wish that my students would help me."[182]

There were several reasons for Eddy's hesitation about authorizing a translation of the textbook. Her main concern was that translations of her writings convey the exact meaning of the original. "I have seen from experience of translations," she wrote Laura Lathrop in 1897, ". . .the *danger* of letting anyone but a thorough student in languages translate this God-given book."[183]

In 1902, Eddy wrote to Alfred Farlow, "The German question is a most important one. I have said I would be willing they should translate my S.& H. into their language if only I were sure of its being done *correctly*."[184]

Above all, Eddy was emphatic in her insistence on the necessary spiritual qualifications of the translators.[185] In a letter to one of the Germans wishing to translate *Science and*

Health, Eddy's secretary, Lewis Strang, wrote on her behalf, "Our Leader has invariably refused the permission, for the reason that in order to translate the work one would have to be not only thoroughly conversant with both English and the language into which the translation was to be made, but he would also have to possess an understanding of Christian Science at least approximately as great as that of Mrs. Eddy herself"[186]—a high standard indeed! Another obstacle was the possibility of legal complications, which had been pointed out to her back in 1897 by the editor of her church periodicals, Septimus J. Hanna.[187]

Finally, Eddy's desire was that students, of whatever nationality, read the textbook in the original English, as she expected that the English tongue would "ere long become the universal language."[188] When the German translation was eventually published in 1912, the preface explained:

> It was her [Mary Baker Eddy's] thought that it would be better for the student to read SCIENCE AND HEALTH in its original text [i.e., in English], and thereby gain a clearer sense of its teaching than was possible through study of a translation, which could not adequately express her revelation of Truth in its primitive strength and purity.[189]

Fanny von Moltke

In the decade before a German translation was authorized, however, a number of non-English-speaking Christian Scientists—especially in France and Germany—were eager to see the textbook translated into their native tongues, and continued to press for translations.

One of these was the Count's distant cousin, Countess Fanny von Moltke, who, coincidentally, had also taken up the study of Christian Science.[190] This Countess von Moltke had become a devout follower of Mary Baker Eddy, with whom she enjoyed a correspondence lasting from 1904 until 1910, the last year of Eddy's life—a correspondence that concerned, among other subjects, a German translation of *Science and*

Health. The Countess even had the rare privilege of an interview with Eddy at her home in Chestnut Hill, in 1908.[191] Although Fanny lived in Frankfurt-am-Main, she was also listed in the *Journal* as a practitioner in Berlin from 1910 to 1915,[192] and so it is very likely that she and her Moltke cousin were acquainted and may even have discussed the matter of a translation.

In January 1904, Fanny, bursting with enthusiasm, sent Eddy a letter urgently requesting "that 'Science & Health' might be translated into German & now, knowing this book better & seeing almost every day a new light shining forth from its pages, I cannot retain this request any longer."[193] Eddy, however, was concerned that "a retranslation of my book would be filled with errors." She was particularly aware of the challenge posed by translating the words "mortal mind" into German. In a long letter to the Countess, she explained her reasons for declining her request.

> Your desire to have my book "Science And Health with Key to the Scriptures" translated into the German language expresses one of the warmest wishes of my heart but I fail to know how this can be done properly and conscientiously.

> In the English language the term mortal mind means error, illusion and nothing else. But in German your term for mortal mind is "mortal spirit" and Spirit used thus contradicts the meaning and rules of Christian Science. In our language the word Spirit means God and as a proper noun is never used in any other sense or significance.[194]

Restrained though she was by the limitations of German, and of French as well, the author of *Science and Health* acknowledged her desire to give those nationalities a translation.

> In a true translation for you of Science And Health I would joy to be a German to the Germans in language as I now am in spirit. When first I wrote "Science And Health" I deeply desired to have that book translated properly and sent to Germany. The

idealism of the Germans seemed to me quite in accord with the realism of Christian Science in other words it seemed to be more spiritual than that of most languages.

Yet the problems remained, and Mrs. Eddy would wait on God to see her way through this seeming dilemma.

But I have learned at length that neither the German nor French language is capable of expressing the absolute Science of Christian Science.

However much I may yearn to have the people understand Christian Science I fully realize that only God in His wisdom and love can point the way thereto, and I wait on Him in hope and faith.

Another letter from Eddy to Fanny at this time (the one above being undated, it is not clear which letter was sent first) indicates that she did not feel that the Countess was fully qualified to do the translation. On April 29, 1904, Eddy urged William P. McKenzie, a Trustee of The Christian Science Publishing Society, to politely decline the Countess's offer on the basis of linguistic limitations.[195]

Enclosed is the last letter to me from Countess Von [sic.] Moltke. I am not the one to settle this question. Will you please reply to her officially, as you understand it and have the Publishing Society settle this question. In her letter to me she has a sentence in English that contradicts what I know from other portions of her letter she meant to convey in her meaning. Assure her that Mrs. Eddy would have had her book translated into the German language years ago were it not for the difficulty of conveying her exact meaning in the German language.[196]

In the fall of 1905, Fanny wrote Eddy another letter, in which she humbly accepted Eddy's decision to postpone a translation, fully acknowledging the wisdom of her Leader's decision. "About a year ago[197] I asked you to allow 'Science and Health with Key to the Scriptures' to be translated into German," Fanny wrote on November 24, "and though my wish is, and ever will be, the same, I have seen since then how

259

wise it was of you not yet to give that permission. I admire your wisdom, and I am waiting silently and patiently, knowing that the right time will be revealed to you." Two weeks later, on December 11, 1905, Eddy sent the following reply:

> "The meek will he guide in judgment: and the meek will he teach his way. All the paths of the Lord are mercy and truth unto such as keep his covenant." "Endeavoring to keep the unity of the Spirit in the bond of peace." "Unto the upright there ariseth light in the darkness." "For as a prince hast thou power with God and with men, and hast prevailed."

Eddy must have felt she needed to explain to the field why a translation of the textbook was not forthcoming, for she had both the Countess's letter and her own response printed in the *Christian Science Sentinel* and *The Christian Science Journal*, and reprinted in *Der Herold der Christian Science*.[198]

In a letter to another follower, Eddy expressed her sense that the time for a German translation had not yet come, writing, "The dear Countess Von [*sic*.] Moltke has come to see that your text-book, Science and Health, cannot be translated at present, not even in Germany."[199]

Geist versus *Gemüt*

One of the biggest stumbling blocks to translating *Science and Health* into German was the problem touched upon in one of Eddy's letters to Fanny in 1904: how to translate Mind, one of Eddy's synonyms for God. When *Der Christian Science Herold* (later renamed *Der Herold der Christian Science*) was first authorized by Eddy and published in 1903, Mind as a synonym for God was translated *Geist*, and the human mind was translated *Gemüt*, as in *sterbliches Gemüt* (mortal mind). But *Geist* was also used to translate another synonym for God, Spirit. The opportunities for confusion are obvious.

The April 1903 *Herold* contains an example of this in the lead article, which was a partial translation of the chapter "Science, Theology, Medicine" from *Science and Health*. In 1903, the phrase at the end of the first paragraph on page 108—"the only sufferer is mortal mind, for the divine Mind cannot suffer"—was translated *das sterbliche Gemüt* [mortal mind] *das einzig Leidende ist, denn der göttliche Geist* [divine Mind] *kann nicht leiden.* In the third paragraph, the phrase "shuts out the true sense of Spirit" was translated *den wahren Sinn des Geistes* [Spirit] *ausschliesst.*

Clearly, this was not an ideal solution, and in 1907, the editors of the *Herold* considered using *Gemüt* instead of *Geist* to translate Mind meaning God. But they rejected it on the basis that the use of *Gemüt* "would prevent our showing the clear distinction between Christian Science and pantheism, because *Gemüt* means to the average German 'much in many minds.'"[200]

Many Germans, however, felt that using *Geist* for both synonyms was incorrect and blurred the distinction between the two. One of these was Fanny von Moltke, who found that *Gemüt* brought her inspiration and was far closer to the English Mind. "When I am reading Science & Health translating Mind with 'Gemuet,'" she wrote Eddy in July 1908, "it is wonderful how the light is growing clearer and brighter, in wondrous radiance it shines chasing away the darkness of mortal 'gemuet' (mind,) for it maketh God All-in-all."[201]

Meanwhile, without an official translation available, Germans who could not read English were reading the passages from *Science and Health* that had been translated in the *Herold,* as well as unofficial translations of other bits and pieces of the textbook that were floating around Germany and causing confusion.

The Count gets involved

By 1907, Fanny's cousin, Helmuth von Moltke, had also become involved in the translation issue. Quite possibly, because of the prestige and influence he wielded as a prominent male member of the German aristocracy, Count von Moltke may have been called upon by the German Christian

261

Scientists to spearhead the movement to obtain a German translation of the textbook.

Apparently unaware of Fanny's letter of November 1905 to Mary Baker Eddy, published in the *Herold* of May 1906, and probably unaware that Fanny had had any correspondence at all with Eddy, the Count, on May 23, 1907, made an impassioned plea to Eddy for permission to translate the Christian Science textbook. Although his English was good enough that he was able to read *Science and Health* with a dictionary, he wrote to her in German, perhaps because his wife, who could have corrected any mistakes in his English, was away visiting her parents in South Africa.

"How many in Germany are actually able to read this book," he argued, "one out of a thousand perhaps." With only three churches and two societies in all of Germany at that time,[202] he added, "Is it therefore surprizing that the movement here in Germany spreads so slowly?"

Then he came to the point.

> Has no one yet been found who has offered to translate Science and Health? . . . How shall a *people* be taught when they have no textbook in their mother tongue? . . . It is as if God were showing them a beautiful Paradise from afar, but only into which some chosen ones, whom *outward* circumstances have permitted to speak the language spoken there, may enter. . . . You have done so much for us; would you kindly complete the full measure of your benevolence, and give us what we all need here, a translation of your book in our mother tongue.[203]

The Count concluded by offering to translate the textbook himself and to send her a sample of his work—a translation of the chapter "Recapitulation"—"for your consideration, so that you can determine whether my translation can possibly be published."

Before mailing his letter, Count von Moltke happened to see Fanny's letter of November 1905 in the *Herold*, in which she had told Eddy, ". . . and I am waiting silently and patiently, knowing that the right time [for a translation] will be revealed to you."[204] The Count felt that now, two years later, "the right time" had come and, undaunted, took up his pen again the very next day. "Dear Mrs. Eddy," he wrote from Kreisau on May 24 (again in German):

> Just after I finished writing my letter to you I found in Der Herold der Christian Science Vol. 4, No. 2, the letter of Countess Fanny von Moltke, the answer to your refusal in regard to the translation of Science and Health. However, since I am thoroughly convinced that the time has come that a translation into German is necessary, I shall send you my letter anyway.

On behalf of the German people, he urged her approval on the basis of the universality of her divine revelation.

> Furthermore, my conception of the love of God is too great to think He would give His revelation to *one* nation and *not* wish that any other nation share in it. Christ did not come for the Jews alone. Rather, he commanded that the Gospels be preached to all the world, in all tongues. . . .

Trustingly, he closed with a quotation from the Gospels.

> "Ask and it shall be given you." With these words I come to you and know that God, Who is Love, will lead your heart aright. With perfect confidence in you, I close my letter.
>
> Sincerely yours,
>
> Count Moltke[205]

The Count sent both letters off to Boston.

Evidently, Moltke's letters had their desired effect, for Eddy's secretary, H. Cornell Wilson, replied on June 11 that "Mrs. Eddy would like very much to have a correct German translation, if it could be had, and wishes that you might be the means of overcoming the difficulties which have heretofore been encountered."[206] She had read (in translation) the Count's letter of May 23 "with great interest" and asked Wilson to tell him that "to have the Christian Science text-book translated

263

into German would afford her the keenest satisfaction and joy." Wilson added, "It would gratify a long wished for hope of our Leader's. Our Leader fully appreciates much that you say in favor of a German translation."

Wilson's letter concludes with Mary Baker Eddy's enthusiastic acceptance of the Count's proposal to send her his translation of "Recapitulation."

> The results you attain with this very important chapter will serve to indicate whether or not it is practicable to bring out the results our Leader wishes to arrive at.

Over a year later, in September 1908, Moltke, who was at that time in London, wrote to Eddy again, this time in English, asking "if you would give the chance to me, to talk with you about the translation of 'Science and Health.'"[207] Eddy, however, was too much occupied with other matters at that time to grant his request.

As late as December 1909, Eddy was still averse to a German translation. After reading Theodor Stanger's report on conditions in Germany, William Rathvon noted the intense demand for a German translation of *Science and Health*. He also noted, however, that Eddy firmly let it be known that she did not wish to consider the matter of a translation, and her secretary, Adam Dickey, did not bring the subject up. As The Christian Science Board of Directors was unable to make any decisions without her approval, it did not look as though there would be any action on a translation of the Christian Science textbook. [208] It seemed that a German translation was dead in the water.

"God-inspired to act"

Three months later, during a visit to London in March 1910, the thought suddenly came to Count von Moltke that he should immediately set sail for Boston. According to Frances Bagnell, a worker in the translation department at The Mother Church who knew him well, he felt impelled to "see once more if Mrs. Eddy would not approve a German translation of the textbook, for which he felt there was great need among German-speaking Scientists who then had only the German Herold and German Bible Lessons."[209]

Within days, he was on a ship headed for Boston and the headquarters of the Christian Science movement. The right time for a German translation, he was convinced, had come.

From their flat in Berlin, Dorothy related to her parents the news of Helmuth's sudden departure. With her husband's mission needing to be clothed in the utmost secrecy, she wrote cryptically on March 15:

> You are used to us doing things suddenly, but nevertheless you will probably be very astonished to hear that Helmuth left today for Boston via Liverpool! We had talked of it for some weeks and this really seemed the right moment, so—voilà! I expect him back towards the end of April. [Berlin, 15.3.1910]

Upon his arrival in Boston in late March, the Count met with officials at The Christian Science Publishing Society, presumably to discuss plans for the German translation. Frances Bagnell recalled the Count's visit.

> He had lunch with [William] McKenzie, already a good friend. They had previously discussed the matter of Science and Health in German, but Mr. McKenzie had hitherto agreed with Mrs. Eddy that a translation from the inspired English would not be feasible. This time Mr. McKenzie saw the need, however; asked the Count if he would not see our Leader, but the Count asked Mr. McKenzie to do so.

Frances Bagnell viewed the Count's visit as providential—and indispensable.

> The whole affair must have been in accordance with God's will; for Mrs. Eddy consented at once, and asked that a committee of three German Scientists be appointed without delay. That was in August 1910[210]; and since Mrs. Eddy passed on in December of that year, the Count always felt that he had been God-inspired to act when he did. Otherwise there might not have been

translations at all, without our Leader's express approval.[211]

Writing to Eddy on March 30 from his hotel in Boston, Moltke expressed his deep gratitude for the work being done there on behalf of the German Christian Scientists.

> I am so thankful, that I have seen the loving and faithful work the men in the Publishing House are doing for our work in Germany. God's blessings rest on such a work. . . . My thankfulness to you is expressed in my work for the Cause of Christian Science.[212]

On the very next day, March 31, 1910, Mary Baker Eddy finally granted permission to have *Science and Health with Key to the Scriptures* translated into German.[213] In her crisp, decisive style, she gave the order to her publisher, Allison V. Stewart.

> Please take immediate steps to have SCIENCE AND HEALTH translated into the German language. This new edition shall be printed with alternate pages of English and German, one side to contain the divinely inspired English version which shall be the standard, the other to contain the German text which shall be a translation.
>
> This work must be done by a committee of not less than three persons who are thorough English and German scholars, and good Christian Scientists.[214]

The reasons for Eddy's decision are explained in the preface to the German translation that came out two years later.

> . . . observing the spread of Christian Science among German-speaking people, also noting the difficulties under which many of them labored in their desire to gain an understanding of her teachings, Mrs. Eddy finally concluded that it would be wiser to authorize a translation which could be generally adopted, than to permit the confusion inevitable from many partial renditions of an unofficial nature.

The following day, on April 1, 1910, the Count sent her a letter of thanks (written in English), with another request for

266

an interview.

> Dear Mrs. Eddy
>
> I thank you so much for your kind and loving letter.
>
> And now I want to ask you, if I could see you. I asked Mr. McLellan, if he thought it right to ask you, and he said he did so; but if you would see me or not, he thought probably not. Nevertheless I ask you, and I will not be disappointed, if you say "no." I thought only, I would ask you in regard to the people in Berlin, that I could tell them something about yourself, and I know, that would be a great joy to them.
>
> I leave Monday morning, after having had nine lovely and helpful days in Boston.
>
> > Yours—
> >
> > in Truth and Love
> >
> > and thankfulness
> >
> > Helmuth Graf von Moltke.[215]

Again, however, Mrs. Eddy reluctantly declined his request.

> Beloved Student:
>
> I cannot make an exception in your behalf much as I would like to. So many wish to see me, and if I give the time to one, why not to all? This would be impossible and to make an exception would give me pain.[216]

The Count returned to Germany without having met Mary Baker Eddy. Yet she had granted permission for a German translation, and so he could rejoice that he had fulfilled his mission.

A committee is formed

The Christian Science Board of Directors, per Eddy's instructions, soon appointed three native speakers of German to translate *Science and Health* into German separately, after which they would convene in Boston to compare their versions and compose the final translation. The three German translators were Helmuth von Moltke, Renate Hermes (later King), and the Moltkes' close friend, Ulla Schultz (Oldenbourg). A year and a half later, they would be joined by three other committee members: Theodor Stanger,[217] editor of the German *Herold*; Dorothy von Moltke; and Adam H. Dickey, Mary Baker Eddy's secretary (February 1908–December 1910) and a Director of The Mother Church (November 1910–March 1925).[218]

Because this was a work of such momentous significance, those involved adhered to a policy of the strictest confidentiality and secrecy, with a view to protecting the work until its completion. The elaborate process by which Ulla was selected to be one of the translators illustrates the assiduousness with which the Directors and others followed this rule.

Ulla Schultz had already proven her linguistic abilities in her translations of numerous articles for the German *Herold*,[219] but before she was chosen for this translation job, she was put to a final test. In May 1910, she received a letter from the *Herold's* editor, Theodor Stanger, asking her to translate two articles into German, which were to be included, he explained, in a pamphlet that would comprise twenty-five German translations of the best articles in the *Monitor*. No mention was made of the real purpose of his request, nor of any plans to translate the textbook.[220] Enclosing the two articles, he asked her to translate them within four to five weeks.[221]

Ulla evidently passed the test, for she soon received a confidential letter from the publisher of *Science and Health*, Allison V. Stewart, inviting her to come to Boston to discuss "some matters pertaining to the work." Stewart added, "For reasons which I will explain to you when you arrive here, I think you should not say to anyone that you are coming to Boston at my request."[222]

"Mr. Stewart fetched Mrs. Eddy's letter . . . from the safe"

That summer, Ulla Schultz boarded a ship and trustingly

crossed the Atlantic, arriving in Boston in August 1910. There she met with Stewart; Archibald McLellan, Chairman of The Christian Science Board of Directors;[223] and William P. McKenzie, a Trustee of The Christian Science Publishing Society.[224] Years later, in her 1926 report to the Board of Directors, Ulla related the events of August 1910.

> After a general talk about Christian Science Mr. Stewart fetched Mrs. Eddy's letter of March 31, 1910 . . . from the safe and read it to me. I was informed, that a committee of three should do the work, each making a translation separately—the chapter "Fruitage" to be omitted—without communicating with each other. When finished, the committee was to meet in Boston and complete the work there; the book was to be published with alternate pages of the original and of the translation, in a cloth and leather edition.[225]

In actual fact, it was Ulla Schultz who had originally proposed the "alternate pages" format for the translation. From the moment she was first introduced to the healing power of Christian Science—in 1899, long before she knew that she would be serving on the translation committee—she had been pondering the need for a German translation and how it should be done. "Ever since," she wrote, "the deep longing for our Leader's works, above all for the textbook in German has been in my heart 'trusting God with' my desire, that He might mould it (Science and Health 1:12), never getting discouraged by the severe objections from almost all Christian Scientists."[226]

Ulla's father, a former theologian, had suggested that the Greek-German New Testament, with alternate pages in Greek and German, might serve as a model for the Christian Science textbook, and Ulla forwarded this idea to Boston with a copy of the Greek-German Testament. During her visit to Boston in 1910, Ulla learned from McLellan that after Mary Baker Eddy had been presented with a copy of the Greek-German New Testament, she had said, "That is the way."[227]

The Leader of The Church of Christ, Scientist, had spoken,

and the alternate-page format was adopted for the entire textbook, except for the last chapter, entitled "Fruitage," which would appear in German only.[228] Although some Germans objected to this format, Eddy, according to Theodor Stanger's daughter, Irene Bremner, "was adamant on this point and insisted that no translation ever be separated from the original text."[229]

Ulla Schultz mmediately embarked on her return voyage to Germany and diligently set to work on her new assignment. "Presented with a copy of 'Science and Health,'" she wrote, "I left the next day and began to work right away on shipboard." By April 1911—eight months later—Ulla had completed her translation, and she continued to work on it through the spring and summer.

Breaking the news

In none of her letters to her parents did Countess von Moltke mention that her husband was one of the three Germans chosen to prepare individual translations of *Science and Health* prior to the meeting with the rest of the committee in Boston. In a letter written that spring, she stated only that "at present Helmuth has the work he is doing for the C.S. Directors in Boston and is therefore fully occupied, . . ." [Kreisau, 21.3.1911].

Helmuth had originally planned on going to Boston alone. But "as the time for our departure drew nearer the thought of being separated so long weighed on us dreadfully and I felt that Helmuth needed me greatly," Dorothy explained to her parents, who were anxiously awaiting her visit to them in South Africa [Kreisau, 25.7.1911]. The Count cabled headquarters to ask if his wife could participate in the work there, and the church officials agreed [Kreisau, 25.7.1911]. And so, although it meant postponing the visit with her parents—and thus prolonging a separation from them that was emotionally painful for parents and daughter alike—the Countess decided to make her first trip to the United States and travel with her husband to Boston, where she, too, would play an important role on the German translation committee.

Chapter Six

Trip to Boston:

Translating *Science and Health* into German

At last, in early August 1911, leaving their three young children[230] in the care of family and nannies, Helmuth and Dorothy sailed with their friend Ulla Schultz on the S.S. *George Washington* to Boston, where the three of them would devote themselves for the next seven months to the work of bringing *Science and Health* to the German people in their mother tongue. Quartered at the Hotel Beaconsfield in Brookline, a suburb of Boston, the six-member committee promptly set to work, on August 15, and, throughout the fall and winter months, labored diligently at their appointed task.

According to an historical sketch of Adam Dickey, Archibald McLellan informed the committee on the very first day that Mary Baker Eddy had told Dickey to make sure that the metaphysics given in the translation were true to the original. The translation work was so carefully done under Dickey's supervison that, once completed, no corrections were ever needed.[231]

But in order for Dickey to perform this vital function, someone was needed to translate the German translation back into English.

The only member of the committee who was both fluent in German and a native English-speaker was Dorothy von Moltke, and so it was she who provided this necessary link in the translation work. This she did paragraph by paragraph, thus enabling Dickey to judge whether "the Committee had given the metaphysics right."[232]

The wisdom of Eddy's decision to assign to Dickey the unique role of overseeing the translation work is seen in the unremitting watchfulness and diligence with which he carried it out. In her 1926 report to the Board of Directors, Ulla Schultz Oldenbourg praised Dickey's "stupendous work" over the long months of the translation work. "Only his great love for our Leader, for her textbook and his dutiful care to carry out her wish," she wrote, "could have enabled him to self-sacrificingly 'watch' in never ceasing patience and encouraging love. Indeed, his works do follow him."[233]

Each day began with silent prayer, followed by the audible repetition of the Lord's Prayer. Their sessions, which lasted six hours, adhered to a systematic procedure. "After having selected the copy which was the most practically written for corrections," Ulla Schultz Oldenbourg recalled, "we read from each other's manuscripts in turn, so that each manuscript was read every third day and not by the one who had written it." Ulla described the process as meticulous and painstaking.

> When the sentence read had the unanimous approval, it was accepted; when not, it was read from each copy, discussed—in English—, re-formed and accepted. When thus a paragraph was finished it was literarely [sic.] translated back into English to Mr. Dickey, and often only after careful discussion with Mr. Dickey re-changed and re-read to him, and then finally accepted.[234]

The work progressed slowly at first, requiring patience and persistence as they sought the best ways to convey the central ideas. "The first weeks," Ulla recorded, "often only twenty to thirty lines were accomplished during the day, from August 15th till September 1st we got only to p. 31:24, because we had to come to satisfactory decisions, on the main concepts." For the most important decisions, the committee resorted to the Board of Directors.

"Unto whomsoever much is given, of him shall be much required." [Luke 12:48]

While the work of translating *Science and Health* was an inspiring opportunity, it was also in many ways very demanding. For Dorothy, and especially for her husband, living in the United States was a major adjustment, and they longed for their three young children, from whom they were separated for seven months.[235] The postponement of Dorothy's visit to her parents in South Africa added to their stress. In fact, in none of Dorothy's other letters is the tension between her devotion to Christian Science and her obligations to her family—children in Germany and parents in South Africa—so evident as it is in the letters written during her time in Boston.

What shines forth from these pages with equal intensity, however, is the Moltkes' profound belief in the transcendent importance of their mission—their conviction that a German translation of *Science and Health* would benefit thousands of Germans. With her heart aching, Dorothy wrote in early September, "My darling old Mother, . . . I love you both so, and it is such a sorrow to me to feel I have hurt you so. And yet I still think I did right, and feel sure that, when we are once together, you too will be quite happy and content that the visit was delayed until the summer" [Boston. 4.9.1911].[236]

By now, her mother and father were bursting with curiosity to know why their daughter and son-in-law were spending such a long time in Boston, and they were pressing her for an explanation. Finally, Dorothy revealed their secret mission.

"I was astonished at your asking what our work here was, as I thought you knew," she told them in mid-September. "Begs pardons. Well, we are translating Science and Health into German. This is extremely difficult and it has to be most thoroughly done because about 5000 people will study it daily, more than any other book except the Bible, and the number is increasing rapidly." She asked her parents to keep their work confidential, "as it is better that it should be as little know [*sic*.] as possible till the book appears" [Boston, 10.9.1911].

The Moltkes had originally expected that the translation work would require a two-month stay in Boston [Boston, 11.11.1911]. When it turned out that it would take considerably more time to complete the assignment, Dorothy had to explain to her parents the necessity of postponing her visit even longer than originally planned [Boston, 19.9.1911]. "It is not easy to be separated from [the children] for so long," she wrote, "and to have had my visit to you postponed, but at the same time Helmuth could not have stood the life here without me, and so I know that I am in my right place, and that is always consoling" [Boston, 22.9.1911]. She confessed that "if it were not for the comfort C.S. [Christian Science] gives me, I should be hopelessly unhappy," but felt that "if I do my part God will look after the rest" [Boston, 30.9.1911]. She explained to her parents the importance of the translation work and the necessity for personal sacrifice.

> We consider the translating of the book a very important and big work, because hundreds of thousands have become better and healthier because of it and we hope that through the translation thousands more will find the happiness we have. So you see we look upon it as a great privilege to partake in the work, which is vastly interesting, and regard the translation as a matter of great importance. . . . We know that very many are hungering for the book in Russia, Germany, Switzerland, and so we feel that our personal wishes and plans are nothing compared to the necessity of doing the work thoroughly and well. You understand our point of view I am sure. [Boston, 30.9.1911]

"German style and construction . . . are fearfully difficult"

The actual work of translating the Christian Science textbook into German proved extremely challenging, partly because of the complexity of the German language. It proceeded slowly at first because, as Dorothy explained, "It is a work that cannot be rushed and that needs much consideration and thought" [Boston, 4.9.1911]. While the Moltkes found the work "extremely interesting," teaching one "to be thorough and to consider the meaning of each word one uses," Dorothy found German style and construction "fearfully difficult and involved," and "as thorough, specialized, and personal as the nation itself" [Boston, 4.9.1911].

Using several editions of *Science and Health*, including the

274

first, second, third, seventh, and twenty-eighth,[237] and many English and German dictionaries,[238] the committee delved deeply into the research, "for we have to get to the bottom of words and terms and study constantly Webster, philosophical dictionaries, *Grimms Woerterbuch,* (which is the "standard" of the German language, in 47 volumes!), as well as looking up points in various books in the Library here. Several are doing the work together, as no one of us combines enough knowledge of English, German and metaphysics to tackle it alone" [Boston, 10.9.1911].[239]

According to the preface, the committee strove for "the best German without sacrificing any of the scientific sense." However, when this led to an obscuring of the original metaphysical meaning, "style and beauty of diction" were subordinated to substance in favor of "a clear presentation of the spiritual sense." [240]

Overcoming linguistic stumbling blocks

Dorothy von Moltke observed that the difficulty of translating *Science and Health* lay in its being "full of new metaphysical ideas for which Mrs Eddy had to almost coin words and we have to do the same. This needs great discrimination, and we have to go to the root of all the words we use"[Boston, 30.9.1911].

As Countess Fanny von Moltke had found, the use of the word Mind for God had proven a stumbling block in previous attempts to translate the textbook into German, but the translation committee tackled it head-on.

> We have some difficulty with the word as in the German of today there is only "Geist" for both Mind and Spirit, and we must have two expressions. So the question arises, shall we coin a word or resuscitate [*sic*.] an old one. And if Mrs. Eddy really coined Mind as used in connection with God, we may as well too. Only none of us know if God was ever spoken of as Mind in other philosophies.[241]

Looking for a precedent, she asked her parents to find out

whether the word Mind had ever been used in English for God before *Science and Health* was written. Whatever their reply, the committee finally resolved this issue by using *Geist* to translate Spirit, and *Gemüt* for Mind.[242] And so, the phrase from the first *Herold* cited earlier—"the only sufferer is mortal mind, for the divine Mind cannot suffer"—translated in 1903 as *das sterbliche Gemüt* [mortal mind] *das einzig Leidende ist, denn der göttliche Geist* [divine Mind] *kann nicht leiden* became, in the 1912 translation, *allein das sterbliche Gemüt* [mortal mind] *leidet, denn das göttliche Gemüt* [divine Mind] *kann nicht leiden.*"

Visits to libraries, a prison, and the State House

As they pursued their research, Count and Countess von Moltke took full advantage of Boston's splendid libraries, spending every Friday—their free day—looking up points concerning their work at the library of Harvard University and at the Boston Public Library. One Friday, they planned to spend several hours studying the works of Immanuel Kant, "looking up his philosophical terms for sense pleasures (among others)." They also intended to look up Darwin's works on evolution, to learn how the word evolve and other technical and physiological terms had been translated into German [Boston, 19.9.1911].

That Friday morning turned out to be very profitable indeed for Dorothy, as she became deeply engrossed in a biography of Kant by Houston Stewart Chamberlain,[243] an English author "who writes in German and writes splendidly." The biography proved to be a boon for the translation work.

> Not only is the book a feast in itself but the very technique, the handling of words, points of style are of the greatest interest and help in our work. I am constantly running to the Y. T.[Helmuth] or Schultzchen [Ulla Schultz] to show them some way of using a word or phrase which we might profitably follow. [Boston, 1.12.1911]

Another German philosopher whose works she studied while

in Boston was Friedrich Nietzsche, of whom Dorothy wrote, "I enjoy dipping into his books occasionally and admire the fire works he lets off when speaking of mortal man" [Boston, 3.2.1912]. She also wrote enthusiastically, "A whole new world has opened to me through the work we are doing, and the growth, use, peculiarities etc of language are quite an engrossing study" [Boston, 1.12.1911].

Meeting Christian Scientists

During their stay in the United States, Count and Countess von Moltke met several prominent Christian Scientists, including fellow committee member Adam Dickey and his wife, Lillian; the Clifford Smiths;[244] the well-known New York-based practitioner and teacher Laura Lathrop, who had taught their teacher, Bertha Günther-Peterson; Irving Tomlinson, Mrs. Eddy's secretary from 1907 to 1910 and author of *Twelve Years with Mary Baker Eddy*; Alexander Dodds, managing editor of *The Christian Science Monitor* from 1908 to 1914; and successful businessman John Munro Longyear and his wife, Mary Beecher Longyear, who later founded Longyear Museum in Chestnut Hill, Massachusetts.

Seeing the sights

During this period of intense labor, the Moltkes occasionally took time out to enjoy some of the local sights, with trips to the North Shore, paddling on the Charles River amidst the spectacular New England foliage, and some pleasant excursions along the country roads in the Count's rented Cadillac [Boston, 30.9.1911].

Most of the time, however, the Moltkes and the rest of the translation committee kept their noses to the grindstone, doing "nothing but work, eat, sleep and take the air" [Boston, 11.11.1911].

By January 1912, the committee was engaged in proofreading the translation. "Indeed we are working *very* hard in our efforts to finish as soon as possible, 8 or 9 hours a day of concentrated mental work is what we are doing, and even on

Saturdays and Sundays we do 4 or 5 hours work. . . . Our one wish is to get the work done, and done well, and then be off [to South Africa] the very next moment," Dorothy assured her parents. "The work is getting on well, but it *does* take a lot of time," she explained, adding, "Another day of work is gone, but it has [was] a day of great inward happiness and contentment" [Boston, 4.1.1912].

At last, on Valentine's Day, 1912, the translation was finished. The second reading was completed on March 9, and soon the galleys were proofed.

Count and Contess von Moltke boarded the R.M.S. *Mauretania* and headed for Southampton, England, where they were reunited with their three young children, nannies, and other members of the family entourage. The family immediately set sail for South Africa and Dorothy's waiting parents. They would remain there for several months, before returning to Germany and the next chapter of their life at Kreisau.

In April, *Der Herold* announced that *Science and Health with Key to the Scriptures* had been translated into German and was now in the hands of the printers.[245] The June issue stated that orders for copies would be accepted from the first of July.[246]

While not claiming the translation to be "equal in value to the original text," the preface expresses the hope that "German readers will avail themselves of the opportunity to absorb the spiritual meaning it is designed to impart,"[247] concluding reverently:

> The more thoroughly SCIENCE AND HEALTH is studied, both in English and in German, the better the student will apprehend and appreciate the profound depths of wisdom and understanding displayed by the author, the Discoverer and Founder of Christian Science, Mary Baker Eddy.

When the news reached Germany through announcements in *Der Herold*, the Germans were jubilant, expressing their gratitude in *Danksagungen* (expressions of thanks) in subsequent issues of *Der Herold*. Fanny von Moltke exclaimed, "How glorious is the certainty that in a short time we shall have a translation of 'Science and Health,' the work of our revered Leader." She expected that the translation, while never a substitute for the original, would be a steppingstone for Germans to reading the textbook in English. "The original text must, of course, remain the norm for all time," she acknowledged, "but it is and always has been my hope that it should become known through a translation to the millions of people who cannot read it because it is in a foreign language. Through the translation, they will learn to better understand the meaning of the original and then more and more turn to it."[248]

Helmuth and Dorothy's teacher, Bertha Günther-Peterson, added her note of gratitude. "The entire German nation will not cease to thank God as well as Mrs. Eddy for this blessing," she wrote. "I am certain that the work of translating the textbook has been conducted in the most conscientious manner. The Board of our church [in Hannover], as well as my fellow workers here, joins me in sending our most heartfelt greetings and wishes."[249]

On Sunday, August 4, 1912, Germans at *Erste Kirche Christi, Wissenschafter, Berlin* (First Church of Christ, Scientist, Berlin), were able to hear for the first time the Lesson-Sermon read from the authorized German translation of *Science and Health with Key to the Scriptures*.[250] Interestingly, the subject of the Lesson-Sermon that Sunday was "Mind" (*Gemüt*)—the very word that had previously proven to be such a stumbling block to a German translation.

Chapter Seven

Bringing up "five young ideas": The Moltke children

By the time the Moltkes had finished the German translation and gone off to visit the Rose Inneses in South Africa, they had three sons: Helmuth James, Jowo, and Willo. The following year, 1913, another son, Carl Bernd (C.B.), joined the family. Their only daughter, Asta Maria, arrived in 1915.

The parents' love for their children glows from the pages of Dorothy's letters, which are filled with warmth and tenderness for each one of them, as well as appreciation for their unique individualities. There are countless references to their progress in school, their character development, their sports events and other activities, and their careers and ideas. Many touching episodes in the children's lives as they grow up on the estate at Kreisau are related. Above all, the letters show Dorothy's deep dedication to her role as mother and nurturer of the young "chicks."

From Dorothy's letters, it is also evident that she and her husband lovingly gave their children the basic teachings of Christian Science. She describes the children reciting Christian Science prayers; reading the Christian Science Lesson-Sermon (composed of excerpts from the Bible and *Science and Health*); and singing Christian Science hymns, including some by Mary Baker Eddy.

Asta regularly went to the Christian Science Sunday School and church,[251] and the letters mention that the sons, too, sometimes attended their parents' church in Schweidnitz, as in this excerpt from a letter written in April 1928, when Dorothy was in charge of the Sunday School:

Asta, C.B. & I caught the 9:30 a.m. train to Schw.[eidnitz] to Sunday school (I am acting as head of the Sunday School for a year) then the Y.T. motored in to the English service. . . . [Kreisau, 6.4.1928]

In 1918, Dorothy noted that "the Boy"—Hemuth James—then aged eleven, was reading "his C. S. [Christian Science]'Lesson' every evening to me [in] English." [Kreisau, 19.5.1918]. Asta, too, then aged three, was taught to pray in English. "JoWo understands [English] quite well now," Dorothy continued, "& even Asta says her Eng. prayer!" [Kreisau, 26.8.1918]. In a letter written in the fall of 1919, Dorothy mentions singing hymns from the *Christian Science*

Hymnal with her children, including a hymn by Mrs. Eddy: "I sang with the 3 boys this afternoon Lead Kindly Light, Abide With me & Shepherd Show me how to go" [Kreisau, 16.11.1919].[252]

Helmuth James

Countess von Moltke felt particularly close to her eldest son, Helmuth James. Because of his posthoumous celebrity for the courageous stand he took against Nazism before and during World War II, his upbringing is of particular interest.

While Dorothy recognized the spirituality of her first child, she was, at first, apprehensive about introducing prayer to him at too young an age.

> I have often wondered whether Little Helmuth were old enough to learn to pray, but he seemed up till now to have so little understanding for anything of that sort that I left it alone as it is such a pity when children learn things like parrots, for the inner meaning is then quite lost and often never returns, so that saying ones prayers means little more than cleaning ones teeth—a necessary part of getting up. [Berlin, 6.12.1909]

From his earliest childhood, however, Dorothy delighted in the signs of his emerging spirituality. She was surprised and touched by the child's natural desire to pray, as in the instance when, without any promptings by Dorothy or the nanny, he was found trying to recite a prayer written by Mary Baker Eddy for little children. The letters reveal that she was reading Bible stories to him and contain many references to Helmuth James's awakening to spiritual phenomena, even at a very young age. The letters also reveal that, as he grew up, Helmuth James occasionally attended Christian Science services with his parents, as mentioned in this letter from 1920, when he was thirteen:

Two days ago the Boy & Madi [Madi Leonardi, cousin of Helmuth von Moltke] went for a 12 hours excursion to Silberberg, walking 7½ hours in all, & in the evening he changed & came with his Father & me to the C. S. meeting in

Schweidnitz. [Kreisau, 24.7.1920]

Memories of Mami

Many years later, Helmuth James would reflect on his happy childhood with Mami (his mother, Dorothy), of whom one of his fondest memories was being taught by her to pray. In a long letter written from prison in 1944 to his young sons, he tenderly remembers the room in the *Schloss* where he slept as a child.

> In this room I also slept when I was little, and in this room I learned from Mami to pray. I still remember exactly how she would come in the evening, tuck me in, and then, as the last thing of the day, pray with me.[253]

This was obviously a sacred time for him, and with deep affection, he recalls the atmosphere his mother created in the family home as one of all-embracing love—a love that never left him.

> All who came to the house felt at home there, not because it was nice and jolly there, but because such a deep, human warmth prevailed in the home, which embraced everyone. In this warmth, my two dear little ones, we grew up, and whoever has experienced this warmth will never again feel any coldness in his heart.[254]

When it was time for the lad to leave home for boarding school, separation from his mother proved to be a soul-wrenching experience.

> How warm and safe I felt in the first period with Mami, I didn't know at all at the time; rather, I first noticed it when I was no longer there, and my love for my mother and my homeland were merged together into one. All this became clear much later only when I went to boarding school in Schondorf, where I wept from homesickness virtually every night for many months. It was, however, not only homesickness, but longing for my mother.[255]

Helmuth James was able to live at Kreisau once more with his mother when he was in his twenties, from 1928 to 1931, the year he married Freya Deichmann.[256] He especially cherished this time spent with his mother. The family had very little money during these years, and Dorothy had to make many sacrifices in order to help bring the family out of debt. But she always maintained an atmosphere of peace and love in the home. "We could have been much, much poorer," Helmuth James later told his sons, "and, thanks to Mami this would in no way have changed the peaceful, contented, happy atmosphere of the house."[257]

Influence of Christian Science on the children

In spite of the many indications that Count and Countess von Moltke took their children to the Christian Science church services and to Sunday school, and taught them Christian Science prayers and hymns, when the children grew to adulthood, none of them formally adopted their parents' religion. There are a number of explanations for this.

First of all, according to their daughter-in-law, Freya, Count and Countess von Moltke took a very liberal approach to raising their children, choosing to let them decide for themselves whether or not to follow Christian Science. It was Freya's understanding that Helmuth and Dorothy did not wish to "push" their own beliefs on their children as they grew to adulthood but wanted them to feel free to make their own choices in life.[258]

Another factor was the consideration that Lutheranism was the traditional faith of the Moltke family and of the society around them, and it was the family's inherited duty to continue this tradition by raising their children in the state denomination. For this reason, all four of the Moltke sons were baptized in the Lutheran faith.[259] Their daughter, Asta, proudly maintained that she was the only one who had not been baptized a Lutheran. The result was that, while the children were never opposed to Christian Science, none of them adopted it for themselves.

Yet given the parents' devotion to Christian Science, and their closeness to the children, it would be hard to believe that Christian Science did not have some influence on the children—on their thinking and spiritual development.

In the case of Helmuth James, about whom so much has been written and who left a legacy of writings that reveal his inner life, there is considerable evidence of this influence. His long letter to his young sons quoted above, as well as his many letters to his wife written during the last year of his life and published in the well-known *Letters to Freya,*[260] indicate that the seeds of a deep spirituality had been planted.

Chapter Eight

Committee on Publication: Trials and tribulations

The effects of World War I (1914–1918) on the German population, including the aristocracy, were devastating. The ensuing political and economic conditions were such that running the large estate and farm at Kreisau presented overwhelming challenges: inflation was rampant, farm workers' wages were constantly rising, and resources, even for the Moltkes, were scarce. Sometimes there would be disastrous weather—too much rain, which spoiled the seeds, or too little rain, causing devastating droughts. And it could be extremely cold in the winter months.

The country was in a deep depression, with unemployment eventually reaching over fifty percent. Dorothy refers to "that tragic army of unemployed" [Berlin, 14.11.1930]. Hitler's promises and eventual success in reversing this situation by bringing full employment to Germany after he became Chancellor, in 1933, account to a large extent for his tremendous popularity.

The Count struggled heroically for the next ten years with the management of the farm, but he had meanwhile become increasingly absorbed in his work in Berlin for the Christian

Science Church. He eventually turned the estate over to a manager, and from then on, he was centered in the capital, where he continued his Christian Science healing practice.

In August of 1928, Count von Moltke received an important appointment by The Church of Christ, Scientist: Committee on Publication for Germany.[261] The *Manual of The Mother Church* defines the duties of this one-man Committee:

> It shall be the duty of the Committee on Publication to correct in a Christian manner impositions on the public in regard to Christian Science, injustices done Mrs. Eddy or members of this Church by the daily press, by periodicals or circulated literature of any sort.[262]

As the senior representative of the Christian Science Church in Germany, the Committee on Publication was, in effect, the director of public and governmental relations for the Christian Science Church in Germany; consequently, all matters at issue between the Christian Science Church and the German Government came to him.

Taking on this position meant that the Count would spend almost all of his time in Berlin, far from his family in Kreisau, making only occasional visits home. He would be well paid, however, and it was work that was deeply interesting to him. With a competent manager in place to look after the estate, it seemed a perfect opportunity for the Count, and he accepted the appointment [Kreisau, 15.8.1928].[263]

Summoned to Boston by the Directors, Moltke immediately boarded the S.S. *George Washington* and steamed across the Atlantic Ocean to the United States once again for a visit of only a few days. Although in her letters to her parents Dorothy refrained from giving any specific indication of the work involved, writing vaguely, "Headquarters at Boston wanted to see him about some matters, so he went off at a moments notice," the purpose of his trip was, presumably, to receive instructions for his major new responsibility of protecting Christian Science in Germany legally and from misinformation in the media [Kreisau, 5.10.1928].

Moltke's new position would prove to be nearly a full-time job, requiring extensive traveling, but it would bring the Count great satisfaction as well as needed remuneration. "The Y.T. likes his Berlin work very much, finds it most interesting," Dorothy exults one month later. She explains, "He has to keep in touch with newspapers, men (or women!) framing laws which might affect Christian Science (quackery, laws dealing with religious organisations & so on,) & has to travel about the country a good deal" [Kreisau, 17.11.1928]. For this gregarious man with a large family, his new lifestyle was often lonely, but the Moltkes were glad he had this work and were willing to put up with whatever inconveniences it involved.

Meeting the Nazi challenge

As the National Socialist German Workers' (Nazi) Party gained in power and became more and more suspicious of and aggressive toward the Christian Science Church in Germany, the challenges for German Christian Scientists—and especially for the Committee on Publication for Germany— became increasingly acute.

During the first two decades of the twentieth century, the Christian Science movement had enjoyed a rapid expansion in Germany. From 1920 to 1933, the number of Christian Science churches in the Fatherland had risen from eight to sixty-six, with nine of them in Berlin alone. Church services were so crowded that many people had to be turned away, and the circulation of the German *Herold* was growing by leaps and bounds along with the new churches.[264]

The Nazis observed this development warily and sought accordingly to reign in the flourishing new religion. Once Hitler had assumed control of the Government, in January 1933, and, on February 28, passed the "*Reichstag* Fire Decree," which did away with most of the freedoms and human rights that had been guaranteed by the now-defunct Weimar Republic, the Third Reich began to revive the religious persecution of Christian Scientists that had attended the earliest days of Christian Science in Germany half a century before.

With his religion now in jeopardy, the Count, as Committee on Publication for Germany, found himself caught between two diametrically opposed forces: the Church he served and the Nazi Regime. Given the fundamental antagonism between Christian Science and Nazism—between the worship of Spirit and the worship of matter—being an intermediary between the Church of Christ, Scientist, and the Third Reich was anything but easy for Moltke.

As devoted to Chrisitian Science as he was antagonistic toward Nazism, Moltke refused to participate in Nazism at any level, remaining permanently aloof. He never joined the Nazi Party, and in defiance of Nazi law, the family refused to fly the hated swastika at Kreisau.[265] It is reported that during a Christian Science church service, the Count asked a Nazi to remove his Nazi badge. Another instance of his overt contempt for Nazism was when he received an invitation to give a speech at an *Erntedankfest*—a harvest festival of thanksgiving—sponsored by the Nazis. His response was blunt and to the point: "The farmers," he told them, "have no reason to be grateful to the government of the Third Reich," and he declined the invitation.[266]

Moltke's strong sense of principle made it difficult for him to deal with the Nazi Government. In a letter to her parents at the end of April 1933, three months after Hitler's accession to power, Dorothy describes her husband's situation:

> His work too at the moment is very difficult & very responsible, for the authorities view anything so "foreign & un-deutsch" [un-German] as C.S. [Christian Science] with much suspicion & as they are about to ban the old testament & some of the epistles (it is said) from the Schools as exuding the Jewish spirit, there's no knowing what will come next, & that of course is precisely the Y.T's job, i.e. to be an intermediary between the Government & the C.S. organization. [Berlin, 30.4.1933]

287

When the American Christian Science lecturer, Richard J. Davis, was on tour in Germany in March 1933, his lectures were well attended and unimpeded by the Nazi authorities. After the tour, however, in a letter Davis wrote on April 12 to The Christian Science Board of Directors, he reported that Christian Scientists were experiencing considerable fear and anxiety in the Nazi world. Davis advised the Directors of the need to pray for the protection of the German churches and the activities of The Christian Science Publishing Society. "Those living outside of Germany," he explained, "can work [pray] with greater freedom and less personal mesmerism than citizens of this country, who have so much fear of the police. . . ."[267]

In spite of the atmosphere of fear generated by the Nazi secret police—the Gestapo—the Moltkes continued to steadfastly attend Christian Science services and faithfully support the movement. While his wife and his sister, Margarethe von Trotha, spent three days in May at their Christian Science students' association meeting in Hannover, the Count was making trips around Germany to cities like Danzig and Königsberg, where he was undoubtedly conducting church business.[268]

Dorothy wrote her parents in early July that Helmuth had suddenly set off on another official visit to the Christian Science Church headquarters in Boston, most likely to discuss the difficulties facing the branch churches in Germany [Friedenau (Berlin), 2.7.1933]. In September, Moltke made a short trip to London "to talk things over with his colleague there"—his British counterpart, Charles Tennant, the Committee on Publication for the United Kingdom—"& to be able to cable freely," Dorothy wrote, something he could not do from inside Germany [Friedenau (Berlin), 25.9.1933]. As with many of her other communications, the letter does not disclose the subject of these talks, but it is obvious from the tone of her letters that the threat of Nazism to the Christian Science Church in Germany was heating up, and her husband was feeling it.

Soon after his return from England, Helmuth was back in Berlin, where he had a very heavy workload that included daily interviews and conferences. His wife joined him there, explaining to her parents that "things are rather precarious in that quarter, & it is a very great responsibility for him to carry, so that I am really very necessary for him at present" [Friedenau (Berlin), 25.9.1933].

Ribbentrop and the Christian Science churches

Christian Science was one of several religious groups that were considered inimical to the philosophy and interests of the Third Reich. The Third Reich made an exception, however, for the Christian Science churches in Germany. Apparently, this was primarily because of one man, Joachim von Ribbentrop.

Having lived in Canada and in New York and Boston, Ribbentrop was familiar with American and English culture and spoke excellent English. In the 1930s, when he was Hitler's chief advisor on foreign affairs, he hobnobbed with the British aristocracy, including some noblemen who were also Christian Scientists, notably the Marquis of Lothian; Viscount Astor, owner of *The Observer;* and Astor's equally influential wife, Nancy.[269] He also got to know Lord Halifax, who was mistakenly thought to be an adherent of Christian Science.

Because of these associations with Christian Scientists in positions of power and influence, Ribbentrop concluded that, if Hitler did not want to offend Britain and America—and at this time he did not—it would be a good idea not to offend the Christian Science Church, which was considered to have significant influence in British and American political circles. *The Christian Science Monitor* was also perceived as a powerful influence on American politics, especially on the members of the United States Congress, many of whom read the *Monitor*—one more reason to steer clear of offending the Christian Scientists.

Although not everyone agreed with him—Heinrich Himmler, in particular— Ribbentrop succeeded in persuading Hitler to allow the Christian Science churches in Germany to remain open. And so an exception was made: the Third Reich did not include the Christian Science Church in its ban on churches.[270]

Waldorf Astor meets with Hitler

In spite of the Third Reich's policy regarding the Christian Science churches in Germany, however, some of the German states, such as Thuringia and Bavaria, exerted their local authority to suppress Christian Science. They began shutting down the churches in their areas and outlawing Christian Science lectures. On September 11, 1933, the Ministry of the Interior for the State of Thuringia banned several churches considered inimical to Nazi ideology, including the Shepherd and Flock Societies, the Berlin Baptist Tent Mission, the Pentecostals and Holy Rollers, and Christian Science churches.[271]

In reponse to these events, The Christian Science Board of Directors called upon Lord Astor to meet with Hitler, to protest the dissolving of Christian Science organizations in southern Germany and the ruthless treatment of a Christian Science church in Weimar, the capital of Thuringia.[272] It is well known that Astor was one of a group of supporters of a conciliatory approach to Hitler; perhaps it was thought that he might succeed in influencing the *Führer* where Count von Molkte, who kept his distance from Nazism, could not.

And so, in September 1933, Lord Astor came to Berlin to assist the Count in dealing with the plight of the German Christian Scientists.

Prior to his meeting with Hitler, Lord Astor spoke with the American Ambassador to Germany, William Dodd, who assured him that he (Dodd) "thought the matter had been corrected by the German authorities . . . and that he might perhaps rest easy." Dodd had seen it all before. "It is the same troublesome story: inexperienced Nazi local authorities acting hastily, and evil results with difficulty corrected," the Ambassador noted in his diary.[273]

As a consequence of Astor's meeting with Hitler, the persecution of the Christian Science churches in Weimar ceased. Astor's international prominence and prestige proved to be a great asset to the Christian Science Church in Germany.

Lord Astor's purpose in meeting with Hitler included another mission: to discuss world peace, which, according to Dodd, "his Lordship came here to promote if possible, after his Christian Science fellows are relieved." The Ambassador suggested that Lord Astor "impress upon [Hitler] the importance of improving his British and American relationships, and the need for Germany of an agreement as to disarmament at Geneva, . . ." But Lord Astor was not optimistic and "went away, not very hopeful." [274]

In mid-October, Dorothy wrote, . . . "we are in for a very serious crisis between C. S. & the Government, which he, as Committee on Publication has to deal with [Berlin, 16.10.1933]. Because of the looming crisis, Dorothy had to cut short her letter-writing at that very moment to help her husband translate and prepare a memorandum for the Government. "We are living in a state, it seems, of perpetual crises [sic.], not only political," she wrote the next day, "but in the Y.T's sphere there are problems & difficulties galore, which need very careful handling [Berlin, 17.10.1933]."

Her letter written one week later clearly reveals the intention of the Nazis to eliminate the work of the Christian Science Committee on Publication altogether. "These are very exciting days too for the Y.T's work," Dorothy wrote, "for the Government, as is its wont, would like to put a stop to it" [Berlin, 21.10/1933].

"A horrid shock"

On October 17, 1933, the Count received a telephone call, informing him that his position as Committee on Publication

291

for Germany had been terminated. "About 10 days ago the Y. T. had a horrid shock, from which he has not yet completely recovered," Dorothy told her parents in late October. "He was suddenly, & quite unexpectedly, relieved of his post as Committee on Publication for Germany. The whole business is quite incomprehensible, for he has been most successful in his office, . . ." The shock was all the greater because, during her husband's recent trip to Boston, he had been asked by the Board of Directors to remain permanently in his post as Committee on Publication for Germany. The Count, wishing to wait for the results of the current church election in Hamburg, declined their offer to step in on his behalf. "The Hamburg Church (which is *very* Nazi) didn't want to nominate him," his wife explained, "but Boston intervened, saying at the present critical time a change was undesirable, so on 9th October at the express wish of the Directors in Boston, the Y T. was reelected" [Berlin, 30.10.1933].[275]

All of this was overturned, however, when the Hamburg church telephoned the Count to tell him that "'at the Directors' wish' another man had been appointed from that very day." The Moltkes were utterly perplexed. Why this sudden reversal by the Directors? "We are now awaiting a letter of explanation from Boston which ought to arrive this week," Dorothy wrote, "for the matter is quite unintelligible to us all at present" [Berlin, 30.10.1933].

Dorothy suspected that the real explanation lay in some behind-the-scenes maneuvering by a Christian Science lecturer from the United States. He had apparently listened to two or three German Christian Scientists who were unhappy about the appointment of Moltke—primarily, it seems, because he refused to align himself with the Nazi Regime.

"There must have been a lot of intrigue," Dorothy confided, "principally on the part of one of the lecturers who was over here from America & two or three other men (all Nazis) who evidently think a man with Nazi sympathies in that position a safeguard. A point of view which is quite intelligible,"

Dorothy acknowledged; but while she understood the logic of this position, she was dismayed by the lack of forthrightness on the part of their fellow Christian Scientists. "What is however incomprehensible is that not one of these men spoke to the Y. T. first before cabling so strongly to Boston" [Berlin, 30.10.1933].

Yet Moltke took it well. "The Y. T. has behaved splendidly about the whole matter," Dorothy reported, "for of course it really was a great rebuff, but he felt it horribly, & . . . he was suddenly faced with unemployment." Of their economic predicament she wrote, "If we had foreseen all this we probably wouldn't have leased another flat, but as we have it for a year, we will remain here for the winter at least, & the Y. T. will start taking patients again." She continued optimistically, "The financial loss is very serious too, but we can manage quite well. Luckily the Y.T. now earns something annually from his teaching" [Berlin, 30.10.1933]. Freed from his Committee on Publication responsibilities, he would rebuild his healing practice, too, which Dorothy was confident would "grow in time, for his is a very spiritual nature" [Kreisau, 22.12.1933].

In the view of Countess von Moltke, the decision to dismiss her husband from his post as Committee on Publication was not the fault of the Directors. She believed, rather, that the American lecturer in question had come under the influence of some pro-Nazi church members, who evidently felt that the Count's anti-Nazi stand disqualified him.

> Boston is not to blame. They evidently got strong recommendations from their trusted co-worker (the lecturer) to remove the Y. T. for the sake of the cause. And the lecturer again got into the hands of 2 or 3 Nazi fanatics who disapproved of the Y.T's aloofness [from the Nazis].[Berlin, 30.10.1933]

The relatively clumsy medium of communication by cablegram, too, may have contributed to the misunderstanding. When the Count cabled the Board of Directors immediately after the call, asking for an explanation, he received the ambiguous answer, "Our action designed to be considerate & protective to you." The Board's cable also promised, "Letter of explanation following." And so the Moltkes waited.

Letter from Boston

When the letter from the Directors finally arrived, the Moltkes felt "much relieved," but their suspicions about the role of politics in the decision were confirmed. The Board, Dorothy said, had "thought a man 'more in touch with the government' would be more suitable, & the suddenness & seeming injustice arose from misunderstandings between the Hamburg Church (which had to make the nomination) & Boston, misunderstandings that occur easily enough when everything has to be done by cable" [Berlin, 5.11.1933].

Writing in December, Dorothy once again defended The Christian Science Board of Directors, which, she felt, had "behaved quite correctly in the matter." The real source of the trouble, in the Moltkes' view, was "the man they sent from England probably the American lecturer Richard J. Davis who did everything behind the Y. T's back for lack of moral courage, plus the wish of some of the [German Christian Science] Churches to have a man with more Nazi sympathies in that position" [Kreisau, 22.12.1933].

The Davis letters [276]

The American lecturer, to whom Dorothy refers in her letter of October 30 as having been influenced by "2 or 3 Nazi fanatics who disapproved of the Y.T's aloofness," was the same lecturer, Richard J. Davis, who, in April 1933, had written letters to The Christian Science Board of Directors about the situation for Christian Science in Germany under the Nazis. These letters, dated April 12, 14, and 15, 1933, now held in the National Archives of the United States, were probably intercepted by a U.S. intelligence agency (unidentified) and may never have reached their destination.

Regarding the Committee on Publication for Germany, Davis's letter of April 12, 1933, presents a diametrically opposite view of this episode. Davis was strongly critical of Moltke's handling of his job as Committee on Publication, particularly in relation to the Nazi Regime. He accused the Count of "blundering" in his dealing with the authorities, and putting his own safety ahead of the interests of the Church. "I do not feel sure of von Moltke," Davis wrote.

> He seems like a very gentle, kindly man but does not appeal to me as a man with courage, stamina and force. He may have blundered by going to the authorities. . . . He is probably as troubled as the other workers are.

Writing two days later from Dresden, where he had delivered a lecture, Davis continued his report on his talks with Moltke.

> Count von Moltke and Mr. Bode [Alfred Bode, advertising representative for *The Christian Science Monitor* in Berlin] came down later for the lecture and to have a conference with me. The Count had heard yesterday from the Munich Church that the government had refused to let me lecture next Thursday and the officials had said that from now on there would be no lectures permitted in Germany and that they intended to close the churches, reading rooms and our work generally. This, of course, coincides with what the Count had been told in Berlin, day before yesterday. The Scientists in Munich had gone with their text books, Bible and Manual to the police but were unable to secure any concessions or dissolution of the government order. We have not heard from other places where I am scheduled to lecture but von Moltke thinks it is a general order from the Nazi headquarters in Berlin.

Davis then asked Moltke if he had written to the Board about these developments.

> To my amazement he said he had not. I then recommended that he get in touch with you [the Board of Directors] at once. He replied that he could do nothing—that all telegrams, wires, and cables were under observation and that if he did anything he

would be thrown into prison.

Davis was shocked, vouchsafing the opinion that "the man is plainly terrified, and utterly incompetent and incapable of handling such a vital situation." He added:

> One statement he made was very revealing. He asked me when I would be leaving Germany. I replied in May, for Switzerland. Well, he said, "at that time I will give you a letter to the Board of Directors which you can mail in Switzerland." In other words he proposed to wait a month before even writing to you!

The letter draws the particularly damning conclusion that "just now [Moltke] is not so concerned about a German movement, as his personal safety."

These criticisms, obviously intended to convince the Board of Directors of the necessity of ousting Moltke from his position as Committee on Publication for Germany, were patently unjust. It is clear from Dorothy's letters that the Count was deeply distressed over the conditions in Germany at this time and felt the pressure of the Third Reich intensely as it bore down on the Christian Science Church and on himself as the Church's representative in Germany. The accusation that Count von Moltke was "utterly incompetent and incapable of handling such a vital situation" is grossly unfair, given the appalling conditions in Germany under the Nazi Regime at that time.

In her book, *Christian Science im Lande Luthers,* German scholar Dr. Britta Waldschmidt-Nelson explains:

> Open opposition to the Nazi Régime—at least before the war— hardly existed. The majority of Christian Scientists tried from the start to behave as unpolitically as possible, in order to avoid any potential conflict of loyalties between The Mother Church and the Fatherland. Even those who early on recognized the danger of National Socialism as well as its inherent opposition to their own religious convictions, who refused to be swayed by pressure or promises of the Party, were careful about publicly making critical remarks about the new Régime.[277]

Helmuth von Moltke, she states, was a rare exception to this political "reserve."

> Helmuth von Moltke and his wife, Dorothy, both important leaders of the Church in Germany, were strong opponents of the Hitler Régime. In contrast to many others, the Count, who, since 1928, had been in charge of the public relations of the Church in Germany, was not always prepared to conceal his aversion to National Socialism.[278]

Professor Waldschmidt-Nelson then relates the Count's attitude toward Nazism to his dismissal.

> But this critical position of Moltke's led him into conflict with other leading Christian Scientists in Germany, and was probably the main reason for which, in the middle of October 1933, he was dismissed from the Department of the Committees on Publication. . . . The Hamburgers were apparently supported by two members of the Christian Science Board of Lectureship, who were traveling through Germany in 1933. Both of them, Richard J. Davis and Hermann Hering, informed Boston that it was urgently necessary to appoint someone as CoP [Committee on Publication] in Germany who was "more in touch with the government."[279]

Waldschmidt-Nelson points out that, in his letter, Davis "bases his argument not only on [the Count's] aversion to the Nazis, but also on his alleged fear of them."[280] Judging from the evidence that Moltke was one of the few Christian Scientists in positions of authority at that time who stood up to the Nazi Government, Davis's argument is clearly without foundation.

Waldschmidt-Nelson concludes that the decision to let Moltke go was, as Dorothy and her husband suspected, based not on the Count's performance as Committee on Publication for Germany but on politics.

> Since the Church leadership in Boston was really of the opinion that one should try in the best possible way to work together with the new National Socialist government, they decided, on the basis of this information, to recall their earlier promise to

Moltke and replace him with someone who seemed to them more suitable to support the interests of the Church through diplomatic negotiations and cooperation with the Nazis.[281]

That man was General August Kündinger, who, "in contrast to his predecessor, was neither a practitioner nor a teacher of Christian Science, but who contributed a high military rank and political neutrality."[282] Waldschmidt-Nelson adds that "although Kündinger was not a Nazi, he strove with considerably more commitment than Moltke for a constructive cooperation with the Nazi Régime."[283] Obviously, it was this kind of "constructive cooperation with the Nazi Regime" that Davis and others were seeking and did not find in Count von Moltke.

There is another argument to be made here in refutation of Davis's assertion that the Count was "paralyzed by fear." On April 15, after leaving Germany for Vienna, Davis wrote:

> Von Moltke told me of four or five specific instances of torture, cruelty and murder of which he personally knew.

The Nazis were highly suspicious of the Count's activities as Committee on Publication, evidently watching his every move and keeping track of his communications—telephone calls, cables, letters. In view of his awareness of "several cases of torture, cruelty and murder of which he personally knew," is it any wonder he would try to find a way to get word to the Board without compromising his safety—and that of his wife and five children and others for whom he was responsible? Was it not reasonable for him to ask Davis to take his letter for the Board to Switzerland and deliver it to Boston from there, even if it meant a few weeks' delay? It was a terrifying time in Nazi Germany for those who opposed the Third Reich, and the Count was obviously trying to find a reasonable way to walk the tightrope between serving his church and dealing with one of the most oppressive regimes in history. It was easy for Davis, an American visiting in Germany, to criticize Moltke's concern for his safety: all Davis had to do was get on a ship and sail away. Moltke faced certain imprisonment and the possibility of torture, cruelty, and murder.

Other statements in Davis's letter undermine his credibility as a judge of character. For example, of Alfred Bode, the advertising representative for the *Monitor* in Berlin, Davis wrote in complimentary terms, describing him as "a courageous little fellow." He relied on Bode for much of his information about Moltke.

> Mr. Bode has just told me confidentially that Count von Moltke called him this morning and said he had been in touch with the authorities about the attutide of the present government toward our church and had been informed that it was the intention of the government to dissolve by law our church and prohibit any services or lectures, that they had kept a file of the Monitor articles and regard our organization as hostile to their aims and ideals.

Yet Bode turned out to be a man of profoundly weak character and eventually betrayed his loyalty to the Christian Science Church. In order to comply with a Nazi rule passed in 1935, that fifty-one percent of a church's membership had to be Nazi Party members in order for the church to be recognized by the Third Reich, it was Bode who urged compliance with this unchristian requirement. Finally, Bode defected from the Christian Science Church established by Mary Baker Eddy to the "German Christian Science Church," an independent organization not recognized by The Mother Church that was accommodating Nazi requirements by excluding Jews and using only the New Testament, because the Old Testament was considered so much *Judentum* (Jewishness) by the Nazis. It was Bode who, in an article in an anti-Semitic newspaper called *Der Judenkenner* (*The One Who Knows the Jews*), claimed that members of The Christian Science Board of Directors and senior leaders of the Christian Science Church were high-ranking Freemasons, further damaging the Church's standing among the Nazis, who were deeply suspicious of the Freemasons and had outlawed them in Germany. And when Charles Gratke, the *Monitor*'s Berlin correspondent [later the

Monitor's foreign editor) was beaten up by Nazis, it was Bode who had claimed that Gratke was a Jew.

Judging from his comments on the treatment of Jews in Germany, one wonders if Davis himself was anti-Semitic. In his letter he observed complacently, "While [the Nazis'] attitude toward Judiaism [*sic*.] shocks our free sense and their methods are crude, and even cruel, a careful investigation will show that there is some basis for the anti-Semitic movement, and that there is something to be done or corrected about Judiaism [*sic*.]in every country."

In Davis's attitude toward Count von Moltke, there is an element of hypocrisy as well. Davis criticized Moltke for his reluctance to send communications directly from Germany, lest he be thrown into prison. He did suggest to Moltke, however, that he "go to London at once, confer with Tennant and let Tennant cable for him to you [the Board of Directors]." Later in the letter, Davis writes:

> Being the object of immediate scrutiny and attack, I am not in a position to cable you from Germany or assume any responsibility in advising the Scientists here, except in a very general way. For that reason I again at 6 A.M. this morning talked long distance with Tennant and he is cabling my recommendation to you that he or some one be given authority from you to confer with von Moltke, Bode and myself in the interests of the movement and keep you reliably and officially informed.

Finally, after Moltke had told him of the "four or five specific instances of torture, cruelty and murder of which he personally knew," Davis acknowledged that "of course I *do* think it unwise for any cabling to be done to him at present directly—that is why I believe an outside representative of the Mother Church can watch and advise you better than can some German citizen." Ironically, it seems that, by the time he got to the end of his letter, Davis had come around to Moltke's view, that wisdom was necessary in communicating to the outside world, including Boston, the horrendous conditions in

300

Germany and the difficulties that the German Christian Scientists were having under Nazi repression.

Count von Moltke was deeply pained by this blow, which not only was humiliating and unfair but also involved the loss of much needed income in difficult times. Yet, in spite of the injustice with which he was treated by his fellow Christian Scientists, Count von Moltke rose above this painful experience with admirable fortitude and grace. "He has behaved splendidly throughout," Dorothy wrote. "The Moltkes," she added, "are a family you can always depend upon to take the big view & never to be petty, that is a great thing" [Berlin, 30.10.1933].

Difficult as the situation was for the Count, he was now free to devote thought and prayer to another important responsibility he had taken on—teaching Christian Science.

Sidebar

Christian Science is banned in Germany

In 1939, the Nazis outlawed simultaneous membership in the NSDAP (Nazi) Party and the Christian Science Church. On June 9, 1941, the Church came under much more severe persecution when the notorious Reinhard Heydrich, known as the "Nazi butcher," ordered the immediate purging of secret and religious societies—a category that included "Followers of Christian Science."[284] This meant the arrest and internment in concentration camps of all active members of these societies, the raiding of their organizations, and the confiscation of their literature and records. Other groups included on the list were "Astrologers," "Occultists," "Spiritualists," "Followers of the Occult Theories of Rays," "Fortune Tellers, fake or otherwise," "Faith Healers," "Followers of Anthroposophy," "Followers of Theosophy," and "Followers of Ariosophy." The order stated that "the German people can no longer be exposed to occultist teachings which pretend that the actions and missions of the human being are subject to mysterious magic forces."[285]

One month later, on July 14, the Third Reich issued a decree specifically banning Christian Science. The decree, consisting of two short paragraphs, read simply:

General Duties of the Police

Prohibition of Christian Science (dated) 14.7.1941.

(1) On the basis of § 1 of the BD. of the President of the Reich for the protection of the people and the state of 28.2.1933 . . . the sect "Christian Science" shall be dissolved and forbidden with immediate effect for the entire land. The assets will be confiscated.

(2) With regard to the penalties ordered by § 4 caD. all activity is forbidden which attempts to continue this organization, or its reestablishment in another form with the same or similar aims.

The Third Reich issued a statement explaining the reasons for the decree, with a summary at the end, titled *Gesamturteil* (Final Judgment), which states:

The teachings of Christian Science are in contrast to the reality of life and therefore of the National Socialist philosophy of life. The teachings are likely to seduce people to lead unrealistic, mystic, occult lives that are lost in the spiritual world and thus making them useless for a healthy national life. The teachings are in contrast to the National Socialist race doctrine and entail the utmost dangers to the national health.

In circulars 51/1039—dated March 6th, 1939—and 122/39—dated June 3rd, 1939—dual membership in Christian Science and any groups in the NSDAP area has already been prohibited.

In the total action against the secret teachings and secret sciences on June 9th, 1941, all branch churches of Christian Science in Germany have been disbanded and all members

302

of Christian Science have been banned from any further activity.

According to the Gestapo decree of 14-07-1941-IV B 2—580/41 S the cult "Christian Science" has been disbanded and prohibited in the entire area of the realm and its property confiscated. To ensure the safety of the people and the state in accordance with the strict order in §4—from February 28th, 1933 [the infamous "*Reichstag* Fire Act," which suspended many key civil rights of German citizens]—every activity according to Christian Science was prohibited. At the same time, it was proclaimed that the aims of Christian Science are hostile to the nation and the state.

Following the enactment of this decree, Christian Science Reading Room attendants were harassed; church literature was confiscated from the homes of Christian Scientists; churches and Reading Rooms, together with church records, were destroyed; and many practicing Christian Scientists were sent to jails and concentration camps, where a number of them perished.

Count von Moltke's sister, Margarethe von Trotha, who was a Christian Science practitioner in Schweidnitz, personally experienced the consequences of this decree. In 2008, Margarethe von Trotha's granddaughter, Vera Pindter, told me the story she had heard from her father, Claus von Trotha:

What I know from my father is that, in fact, Margarethe was put [in] prison, because [the Nazis] found Christian Science books in her house. My father, who was an officer in the army at that time, got her out again.[286]

When my father went to the prison, he said to the warden, "How do you expect me to fight for Hitler, when you are keeping my mother in prison?"

With that, Trotha obtained his mother's release.[287]

Chapter Nine

Die reine Wahrheit: Teacher of Christian Science

Two years prior to being dismissed from his post as Committee on Publication for Germany, Count von Moltke took on another important role in the Church—teacher of Christian Science. In November 1931, while his wife was involved in some translation work for The Mother Church, the Count once again sailed to Boston, this time for further instruction in Christian Science. The Normal class, as this further instruction is called, would be taught by a man well known in the Christian Science movement, Duncan Sinclair, CSB [Kreisau, 22.11.1931]. The Normal class would prepare Moltke to teach Christian Science Primary classes.

After concluding the Normal class, Moltke returned to Berlin, where, in addition to continuing his work as a practitioner, he would establish himself as a prominent Christian Science teacher.[288] Every October, beginning in 1932, he would teach a course—a Primary class—on Christian Science, and every October, Dorothy would go to Berlin to be at his side as his enthusiastic and devoted helpmeet in this important enterprise.

But the Nazi activities that were so disruptive of Moltke's work as Committee on Publication for Germany also threatened to interfere with his work as a Christian Science teacher. The disturbances in the summer of 1932 were such that, in July, he fled from Berlin to Kreisau to prepare to teach his first Primary class [Kreisau, 14.7.1932].

Translating the Powell biography

Another circumstance made teaching his first Primary class especially difficult: Moltke was asked to translate a new biography of Mary Baker Eddy by Lyman P. Powell, with an imminent deadline. As usual, Dorothy assisted her husband with the translation work, which necessitated her going to Berlin earlier than originally planned. "On Thursday morning the Y.T. telephoned to tell me that the translation work which we are to do together had arrived," she told her parents, "&

that I had better come as soon as possible, as the book is to be published before Christmas" [Berlin, 19.9.1932].

Hard as it was for her to leave their beautiful country estate at Kreisau, the Countess was "delighted to be able to help the Y.T. & earn some money" [Kreisau, 6.8.1932], and she happily adapted to her more constricted circumstances in the city. "The little flat here is small & quite unpretentious, but warm, sunny & comfortable," she wrote in early October [Berlin, 7.10.1932].

Despite living two hundred miles (322 kilometers) away in Berlin, the Moltkes continued to enjoy the fruits of their estate's farm, from which they received "butter … & potatoes & a pig, & Mamsell [the cook] sends us up some poultry every week while it lasts. All this is a great help" [Berlin, 23.10.1932].

In their apartment, away from the *Berghaus* and Mamsell, Countess von Moltke performed domestic duties by herself, which, to her surprise, gave her considerable satisfaction and a sense of independence. "I've been cooking all the morning, as this is wash day," she wrote. "I really rather enjoy it, for it is the first time in my life that I have ever done any cooking entirely alone & I find it very exciting & unexpected" [Berlin, 12.12.1932].

Helmuth was working harder than ever but enjoying it, too. "The Y. T. never seems to have a moment & generally works in the evening too," Dorothy told her parents, adding, "such a contrast to his former life; but he's happy & interested & of course its a great blessing that he's got work" [Berlin, 26.11.1932].

Much as they enjoyed translating the Powell biography of Mary Baker Eddy, the Moltkes looked forward to the completion of this work, which had proven extremely taxing. When the family hosted a lunch party, Dorothy reported that "the poor Y. T. had to spend all his time at his writing table, reading proof sheets. I *will* be glad when the book (a life of Mrs. Eddy) is off our hands." She concluded, "It has been a

305

great work, but in about a weeks time it ought to be finished, & in a fortnight on the market, just in time for Christmas" [Berlin, 5.12.1932].

A superhuman task

With the intensification of difficulties that the Count was facing in his position as Committee on Publication for Germany, teaching his Primary class in the fall of 1933 was particularly challenging. "Poor dear, if only these events had come singly it would have implied much work, but it would have been more or less normal, whereas, as it is, it is really a superhuman task which he has to perform," Dorothy noted in mid-October, after the first week of her husband's two-week course. "First he has his class (it lasts a fortnight, 4 hours every morning) which in itself is enough, for one needs much consecration & aloofness during those two weeks," and then, as Committee on Publication, he had to deal with the "very serious crisis between C.S. & the Government" [Berlin, 16.10.1933].

The day after writing this letter, Dorothy and Helmuth received the news that he had been dismissed from his position as Committee on Publication for Germany. Yet, in spite of this "horrid shock," Moltke was able to summon the strength and courage to continue teaching the two-week Primary class in a manner that proved both fruitful and harmonious. "The Y.T's class ended yesterday," Dorothy wrote at the end of October. "It was *such* a nice class. He had students from Switzerland & North Italy as well as Germany, & it was all most interesting & happy. But we both feel the need of a few days of quiet & rest now that it is over" [Berlin, 21.10.1933].

A student's recollections

One of the last surviving students of Count von Moltke was Elfriede Fleischhut of Cuxhaven, Germany. She was in her late nineties when she shared with the author her recollections of her teacher.

306

According to Elfriede Fleischhut, the Count was a much respected and beloved teacher, who taught *die reine Wahrheit* [the pure truth].[289] She had been forcibly impressed by Moltke as "an imposing and good person" who had great presence.[290] Although not a tall man—neither "big nor grand"—Elfriede Fleischhut recalled that he was "a very grand man in the things he said about Christian Science." He had "a very strong personality and had great charisma, above all, in the way he demonstrated Christian Science and in the way he expressed himself."

In the eyes of Elfriede Fleischhut, the Count was a truly "noble" person in both senses of that word. While he enjoyed a high status as a member of the nobility and, as she put it, "knew what a *Graf* [Count] was," he was very unassuming, never arrogant, for he "wasn't proud to be a *Graf*. A *Graf* had to be of sound character, of a certain nature, and he was well aware of that."

Elfriede and her husband, who was also a Moltke student, felt the uplifting influence of the Count's spirituality. Referring to her teacher, she observed, "When you spend time with a noble person, you are lifted up automatically—in the spirit, in your consciousness, the one consciousness that elevates." The Fleischhuts had nothing but respect, gratitude, and affection for their teacher. Elfriede stated that he was "*eine Seele von einem Menschen*" (literally "a soul of a man" or "a man with real *soul*") and that "he was an extremely loving, supportive man, generous of spirit."

Elfriede recalled Moltke as being very intelligent and an excellent teacher, whose way of thinking was *sinnvoll* (logical), that is, he was able to explain things well, in a way that made sense. A calm person who was not given to loquaciousness, he was "in perfect equilibrium, with no need to talk about things unnecessarily." She added, "And then when we were with him, we didn't discuss things so much, but we knew each other in our souls." Her daughter, Christel Fleischhut, explained, "I think she meant to say that he lived very clearly in the Christ-consciousness and expressed that outwardly, and this could be felt without his needing to talk much about it."

Elfriede Fleischhut remembered Count von Moltke as being a thoughtful listener and speaker. "He generally listened more to what was going on in the other person," she recollected. "When he had thought a lot about something, he talked about it, but not otherwise." Her daughter explained, "He paid attention to what others said, and then he responded to that with just a few words and corrected things so that they would be clear and true." Christel recalled also that her father had been impressed by "the *Graf*'s ability to explain Science, to demonstrate Truth," and "to express entire statements with a few words."

According to Elfriede Fleischhut, who, with her husband, was in a class of thirty students, Count von Moltke's pupils not only held him in high esteem but also felt a "natural affection" for this man whom she described as being "very warmhearted." A happy atmosphere pervaded his classes and association meetings, in which, she recalled, there was "always lots of joy." Christel observed this in her parents when they came home from meetings with their teacher.

> The association meetings were very important experiences for my parents because of the Graf's abilities to explain Science, to demonstrate Truth, to put it into words. My parents always understood so much and took so much home, and then it was an inner joy that was expressed during those meetings with him.[291]

Handling Nazism

Elfriede Fleischhut's recollections of having Christian Science Primary class instruction in the 1930s, at the time the Nazis were gathering momentum and becoming increasingly antagonistic toward Christian Science, shed light on the way her teacher dealt metaphysically with Nazism. Asked what advice the Count gave his students for dealing with the Nazi menace, Elfriede replied that, although he generally did not discuss Nazism openly with his students, he did tell them to "focus on only the absolute, unadulterated Truth, and on nothing else."

According to Elfriede, the Count believed that there was only so much that one could do to educate others and that it was fruitless to press an issue before the hearer was prepared for it. Christel recalled her father's repeating an illustration used by the Count in his teaching: "If someone stands on his head and wants to keep it that way, we should not try to force him to stand on his feet. He has to find the way himself and discover for himself what the correct picture is, the correct being."[292]

This was a lesson in metaphysics—reversing error with the truth of being—but perhaps the Count was also hinting at something that he could not state openly: that the way to deal with the Nazi madness was to view the Nazis correctly, i.e., as sane and upright, as God had made them, even though, with their insane ideas and cruel actions, they appeared to be upside down, standing on their heads.

Count von Moltke on Church work

Elfriede Fleischhut's memories of the Count's method of explaining Christian Science are corroborated by an address he gave in 1935. In this address, titled "Church Work," Moltke discusses a metaphysical approach to problems that come up in branch churches. He writes (in German), "The question arises, how do we arrive at Truth in a church meeting?" The answer: "This is possible if each one turns off his personal ego as much as possible and turns on God. In other words, if each individual strives to know that the only lawgiver is Principle, God. It is not important that what we *think* is Truth is made manifest, but that *God's* directives are implemented and not *our own*."[293] He writes, "The laws everything rests on are laws of love, of honesty, of loyalty, of truthfulness, of complete obedience towards the good, the real."

In conclusion, Count von Moltke refers his audience to the *Church Manual*:

The Church Manual is the final law we have at this time; the completion of all of Mrs. Eddy's work; the complete giving up of any personal ego and the absolute consecration to the law of Love.[294]

Chapter Ten

Holding fast in dark times

In many ways, Dorothy and Helmuth von Moltke's life together as Christian Scientists was a balancing act that required all their strength and devotion. Count von Moltke had to balance his role as head of Kreisau with his love for Christian Science and his work in the Christian Science Church. Living in a society—the conservative German landed aristocracy—that had little tolerance for whatever did not conform to its own traditions, especially anything as radical as Christian Science, it took a measure of courage to identify himself with this religion in a country where one was, by and large, either a Lutheran or a Roman Catholic. His stand for a more liberal political philosophy also set him apart from the prevalent thinking of his social class.

Dorothy, too, had her own balancing act in this pas de deux: between her adopted country, Germany, and her beloved homeland of South Africa, nearly eight thousand miles away; between her love for and desire to be near her parents, and her love for and need to take care of her own family; and between her love for her parents and her devotion to her religion, about which her father was openly skeptical. The letters of Dorothy von Moltke show a woman struggling to balance these opposing elements, and succeeding with marvelous grace.

Yet, in spite of tensions in her life, Dorothy's letters are unmistakably those of a deeply contented woman who loved her husband—despite her parents' disapproval of him—and who cherished and nurtured their five children with complete devotion.[295] Her family brought her great joy and fulfillment, and she enjoyed her role as the *Gutsherrin* (Lady of the

Manor) at Kreisau, a part she played to perfection, engaging the loyalty and affection of all those around her: her family, the many relations who either lived on the estate or visited there, their many friends and visitors, the workers on the estate, and the people in the village and in the neighboring town of Schweidnitz.[296]

Sense of destiny

When they married at the dawn of the twentieth century, Dorothy and Helmuth von Moltke did not know about the cataclysmic events that lay ahead. Through all the twists and turns of their lives, however, both Moltkes were sustained by a strong sense of God's direction and support, which enabled them to carry out their mission together, in their family life and in their work for the Christian Science Church, which, one of the sons observed, formed "the ethical basis of [their] marriage."[297]

Dorothy always had the firm conviction—even a slightly mystical sense of destiny—that she was in her "right place." In 1910, after five years in her new life in Germany, she wrote her parents that she still felt that "this is my place, that I have a work to do that none other could do (this sounds conceited but it is not for I know too well that each has a work which is *his* to accomplish) and therefore is it any wonder that I am happy? But it certainly was a strange business that the Fates should have chosen me to fill this place!" [Kreisau, 17.7.1910].

The Count, too, had a sense of being guided by God in his decisions and actions. Of his marriage he said, *Das war Destiny* (It was destiny) that had brought Dorothy and him together. In March 1910, a mere nine months before Mary Baker Eddy died, he felt a divine impulsion to make the trip to Boston that resulted in her approving the first official translation of her textbook, *Science and Health*—without which it is possible that no translations of *Science and Health* into any foreign language would ever have been authorized by the founder of Christian Science. His last living student, Elfriede Fleischhut, spoke of being uplifted by his spirituality, his "nobility of character," and the "Christ consciousness" he expressed.

Overcoming obstacles during the Nazi era

Helmuth von Moltke faced formidable obstacles in his work, especially during the Nazi era. He was at odds with the Nazi Regime and paid a price—the loss of his position as Committee on Publication for Germany. Yet he remained true to his ideals both as a Christian Scientist and as one who opposed the Nazi Regime, which was terrorizing his country. Living in the capital, Berlin—the headquarters of Hitler's evil machine—he continued his teaching and practice of Christian Science healing, despite the danger and chaos swirling around him.

As the mother of four sons of military age, Dorothy, too, faced seemingly overwhelming odds. Yet she, too, took her stand against the Nazis at her home in Kreisau, refusing to fly the hated swastika. During this turbulent period, when Christian Science was under siege, she faithfully supported her husband's work as a Christian Science practitioner and teacher, and as Committee on Publication for Germany.

Soon after returning from a five-month visit to her parents in South Africa, Countess von Moltke died suddenly in June 1935. Her daughter-in-law, Freya von Moltke, linked this tragic event to the shock of returning from a free country to a Nazi-dominated Germany that threatened the lives of her children.

Dorothy's remains were interred at Kreisau, in Kapellenberg, the family graveyard, by the great Field Marshal's tomb. There were two memorial services for her: one at Kreisau; the other, a few days later, in Cape Town, South Africa. The Kreisau service, conducted in German, included many passages from the Bible and from the German translation of *Science and Health* that she and Helmuth had helped translate twenty-three years earlier.

The next two years were lonely ones for the Count, and in

1937, he married one of his students, Anne Marie Altenberg.

Count Helmuth von Moltke died in 1939. Countess Anne Marie von Moltke died in 1951.

Epilogue

The Moltke children: "A blessing to the world"

In 1911, Dorothy wrote prophetically, "My three little sons—I dream that some day they may prove a blessing to the world" [Kreisau, 30.5.1911]. In a letter to her mother and father written two years later, she linked the influence of her parents' liberal ideals to the part she believed her children would play in the future of Germany.

> It is strange to think that, through the sons, you may have a large part to play in the making of a more liberal Germany, which again will be a great factor in the history of the growth [of] peaceable understanding among nations, a new concept of the word "patriotism". And so it is, wheels within wheels, how small man is & yet how infinitely great. [Kreisau, 22.12.1933]

Because she died so young—at age fifty-one—Dorothy did not live to see how her children's lives would turn out. Her daughter-in-law Freya felt that it was perhaps for the best, as it would have "broken her heart" to learn of Helmuth James's early and violent death, in January 1945. Her fourth son, C.B. (Carl Bernd), was also killed in the war, when his plane was shot down over North Africa in 1941. The other three children—Jowo, Willo, and Asta—all survived the war and went on to lead happy, successful lives.

At the end of the war, the family had lost Kreisau, and all of Germany was in utter chaos. Jowo and his family were already living in western Germany, but Silesia had been ceded by the Allies to Poland, and Freya and her two young sons, as well as her sister-in-law, Asta, were refugees. Fortunately, thanks to their connection with South Africa through Countess von Moltke, the families of Jowo, Freya, and Asta were offered asylum by the South African Government, and they all went to Cape Town in 1947 and 1948.[298]

Jowo (Joachim Wolfgang)

During the war, Jowo served as a junior officer in the German Army. He married Inge von Dippe, by whom he had two children. He achieved distinction in his chosen field of art history, on which he published several books and articles, and taught at the University of Cape Town. Later, he was invited to serve as the first director of the new *Kunsthalle* Bielefeld, an art museum in Bielefeld, Germany, where he remained from 1962 to 1974. Jowo died in 2002.[299]

Willo (Wilhelm Viggo)

In 1937, Willo emigrated from Germany to the United States via England and Scandinavia. Although he was a German with a famous military name, he served as an officer in the American Army—first, in the Philippines, then, after the war, in Japan. Later, he worked for United States Intelligence in Germany. From 1953 to 1961, he was chief designer for the Philadephia City Planning Commission and headed a major project to redevelop the city's downtown slums. Subsequently, under the auspices of the Joint Center for Urban Studies at Harvard University and the Massachusetts Institute of Technology, he designed a new city—Puerto Ordaz, which merged with San Felix to form Ciudàd Guyana—for the first national steel plants in Venezuela. In 1964, he became Professor of Urban Design at Harvard University's Graduate School of Design, from which he retired in 1977. Married in 1961 to concert pianist Veronica Jochum (daughter of conductor Eugen Jochum), he lived with his wife in Cambridge, Massachusetts, until his death, in 1987.

Asta Maria

Asta spent most of the war years in Kreisau, where, with the men away in the army, she worked extensively on the farm. She married Wend Wendland, who served as a soldier and survived the war. Two years after the war, Asta, her husband,

and their young son moved to South Africa. There Wend worked as a librarian, and they had one more son. But the marriage ended in divorce, and Asta and her two sons moved back to Germany. She later married publisher Karl Heinz, with whom she lived in Berlin until her death, in 1993.[300]

Helmuth James

Countess von Moltke always had the sense that her eldest son would accomplish great things in the world. "There's no doubt the Boy has ideas," she wrote in 1929, when he was twenty-two, "& I feel sure has a great future before him" [Kreisau, 21.4.1929].

One who met Helmuth James and was deeply impressed by his moral stature was the eminent diplomat and historian, George F. Kennan.[301] In his *Memoirs*, Kennan describes Helmuth James von Moltke as "the greatest person, morally, and the largest and most enlightened in his concepts that I met on either side of the battle lines in the Second World War. . . ."[302]

Life story

From 1927 to 1929, Helmuth James studied law and political science in Breslau (now in Poland and renamed "Wrocław"), Vienna, Heidelberg, and Berlin. He later qualified for the bar in London. After completing his legal studies, he went on to become an international lawyer, serving in a law firm in Berlin. From there, he would undoubtedly have risen to a judgeship, like his revered grandfather, or to a position of power and influence in the government. Indeed, young Moltke seemed destined for an important career in his chosen fields of law and politics.

The rise of Hitler and Nazism, however, abruptly changed the course of Helmuth James's life. Any career as a justice was ruled out for him, as it required membership in the Nazi Party, which was anathema to him. After the Second World War broke out in 1939, he was drafted into the *Abwehr,* the German military intelligence organization, where he served as legal adviser to the German High Command. The Nazis believed that they could put to use his knowledge of English, as well as his American and British connections (many of them through *The Christian Science Monitor*), for German intelligence-gathering activities. What they did not know, however, was that, like his parents, Helmuth James was vehemently opposed to Hitler and Nazism—as was also, he soon discovered, the head of the *Abwehr,* Admiral Wilhelm Canaris.[303] In the *Abwehr,* Helmuth James used his influence and legal acumen to hold the Germans to agreed international laws. He succeeded, for instance, in having hundreds of captured Polish soldiers recognized as combatants, as opposed to rebels, and thus saved their lives. In his position within German Intelligence, Moltke was also able to help hundreds of people, including many Jews, escape from Germany—an activity that eventually cost him his life.

In 1943, Helmuth James and Dietrich Bonhoeffer were sent by the *Abwehr* to Denmark and Norway, ostensibly for the purpose of pacifying the Norwegian clergy, who were protesting against Nazi interference. The real mission of Moltke and Bonhoeffer, however, was to spread the news of resistance activities in Germany and to encourage the Norwegian resistance.

The Kreisau Circle and Helmuth James's arrest

Moltke opposed the Nazi Regime in another way as well—a way that was as constructive, imaginative, idealistic, and farsighted as it was dangerous. During the war, in 1940, Helmuth James, together with his friend and cousin Peter Yorck von Wartenburg, began bringing together a group of individuals of various persuasions and backgrounds— Socialist, Capitalist, Protestant, Roman Catholic—all serious opponents of the Nazi Regime. They laid out plans for the reconstruction of a new Germany—a Germany that would be democratic and that could be made part of a more unified Europe—after Nazi Germany's expected defeat. The group did its work over a period of three years, mostly in Berlin.

Because of three special meetings that were held at Kreisau, the group was later named the *Kreisauer Kreis* (Kreisau Circle). But in January 1944, Moltke was apprehended by the Nazi security services for having warned an acquaintance of his imminent arrest, and Moltke was thrown into prison.

On July 20 of that year, Colonel Claus von Stauffenberg attempted, unsuccessfully, to assassinate Hitler. Using his position as an officer in close proximity to the Military High Command, he put a bomb in a briefcase and entered Hitler's briefing hut at *Wolfsschanze* (Wolf's Lair) near Rastenburg, East Prussia (now Poland). After placing the briefcase on the table near the *Führer*, Stauffenberg left the room, then took a plane to Berlin to lead the planned coup d'état. But an officer at *Wolfsschanze* picked up the briefcase and put it under the table. The bomb detonated, killing four people. But Hitler, protected by the large oak table, received only minor injuries from the explosion. With Hitler still alive, the coup failed, and the Nazis executed Stauffenberg that night. The threads of the Stauffenberg plot led the Nazis to most of the members of the German Resistance, including the Kreisau Circle, and ultimately to Moltke himself, already in prison. Like many others, he was tried by the infamous *Volksgerichtshof* (People's Court). The trial began on January 9, 1945; two days later, on January 11, he was sentenced to death. On January 23, four months before the end of World War II in Europe, he was executed by hanging.

On a November afternoon in 2004, nearly sixty years later, I had the privilege of interviewing Helmuth James's widow, Freya, in her cozy Vermont living room.[304] "Helmuth said to me I should arrange an interview for him with Müller,"[305] she told me. She was referring to SS (*Schutzstaffel*) *Obergruppen-Führer* (General) Heinrich Müller, head of the Gestapo.[306] To her surprise, she was able to get an appointment with him. She was astounded that Müller treated her as well as he did:

> I went in there, and up there, there were young, black-uniformed SS people. I waited, and then I was let in to Mueller. I had a

317

conversation with Mueller, and you know, Mueller did either not want to know that I knew something, or he believed I knew nothing about anything. At least, he treated me as if I knew nothing, and in the end he said to me—he ran after me after I had finished, and he said, Yes, he would give him an interview. But it didn't help: from their point of view he [Helmuth James] was an arch-enemy.[307]

I asked her how it was that, during all those years before her husband's arrest, when he was helping Jews and prisoners of war, and holding meetings of the Kreisau Circle, the Nazis hadn't interfered with their lives and activities. Freya explained:

Ja, but then we were very young and inconspicuous in our way of life, we didn't show off very much. Actually, in these higher bourgeois classes in the privileged people's sphere, the Nazis did not interfere very much. The Nazis were terrible to socialists and communists, to workmen, and destroyed everything and killed them all. But in that group [of privileged people] they had a sort of a respect. They'd let us be much more than their awful methods towards other people seemed to show. They were not awful, they let us be. And did not interfere very much. In a way, they admired that group.

I commented to her that, nevertheless, she showed great courage and daring in going to see the chief of the Gestapo.

I must tell you, I always sort of did things without thinking whether they were difficult or not difficult. Looking back, it was quite enterprising. I wasn't thinking on those lines at all at the time.

Freya then told me about Müller's surprising offer:

In any case, I was in the corridor—after all, Müller was the top man of the Nazi SD—and he came running after me and he said to me, "And you know, when it's all over"—which of course means Helmuth's dead—"you come to us and we will help you." Oh! As if I would ever have come to *them*!

318

"After killing your husband!" I interjected. Freya continued:

> And then I come running and want their money? No. But I mean, there you see this extraordinary thing, why we could do so much for so long without being found out.

Asked whether, at the time of his arrest and imprisonment, her husband became more interested in spiritual matters and started reading the Bible at that time, Freya replied, "*Ja, absolutely, much more.*" She described the spiritual struggles her husband went through during his incarceration and how he would, time and again, rise out of the depression that seemed to engulf him.

> Then he'd rise—several times, not only once. It was a very hard year. But he also says it was a quite extraordinary year—he would be nobody without it. He's very much impressed with what he lived through, but it was hard.[308]

Letters to Freya and the Farewell Letters

During his time in prison and before, Helmuth James wrote hundreds of letters to his wife, which she was able to preserve during the war by hiding them in the beehives at Kreisau. They have since been published in two books, *Briefe an Freya 1939-1945 (Letters to Freya 1939-1945)* and *Abschiedsbriefe Gefängnis Tegel September 1941-Januar 1945 (Farewell Letters Tegel Prison September 1941-January 1945)*—now classics of World War II literature.[309]

These letters document Helmuth James's spiritual struggle during the last year of his life. They reveal that he possessed an unusual degree of spiritual sensitivity and a religious conviction that became the focal point of his stand against Nazism. In his extremity, Moltke discovered his own deep spirituality and a clarification of his identity as a Christian. In his final letter, written on January 11, 1945, following his trial by Nazi judge Roland Freisler,[310] he defined himself not as a landowner, nobleman, Prussian, or German, but "as a Christian and nothing else."[311]

Helmuth James was ultimately executed, not for the stated charge of treason against the Fatherland (he never committed an unpatriotic act and was never involved in an attempt to assassinate Hitler) but, as he stated, for "the practical, ethical demands of Christianity. Nothing else; for that alone we are condemned." That Moltke and Freisler represented diametrically opposite and mutually exclusive views is brought out not only in Freisler's recognition that both Christianity and Nazism demanded "the whole man" but also in Moltke's recognition that Freisler was the only one in the "whole gang" who, for that reason, understood why he had to kill Moltke.

Helmuth James and Christian Science

Helmuth James took his stand as a Christian but never adopted the religion of his mother and father. Yet, given his parents' deep dedication to Christian Science, and given his closeness to them, particularly his mother, it would be hard to imagine that their religion did not have an influence on him.

Freya explained to me that, although her husband did not adopt Christian Science for himself, he was not opposed to it. In fact, in his hour of need, when he was in Tegel Prison and fighting for his life, Helmuth James wrote several letters to Freya, urging her to get in touch with Ulla Schultz Oldenbourg, the family's great friend and a Christian Science practitioner. Freya explained that he was reaching out to whatever might help him find freedom.

> He wanted to open all possibilities that might help him, because he would have liked to survive. There were years when he was thinking life wasn't worth living. But he — well, that was not so easy within himself, but later on, the older he got, the more he enjoyed living, and he would have liked to go on living, and he had this background of Christian Science, of course he had, so why not try everything?[312]

Although the letters indicate that Helmuth James's concept of God and salvation differed from the teachings of Christian

Science, in that he seemed to accept the possibility that God's will could be death as well as life, they also make it clear that the spiritual support of this Christian Science practitioner was extremely important to him. Several times he instructed Freya to "ask Ulla to work diligently for me, and thank her for her support." In late November, he wrote:

> That Ulla is working for me makes me very happy. Every strengthening thought of every person is for me a joy, and Ulla is especially strong. In spite of my momentary return of good spirits, I feel the need for every bit of strengthening, and accept it gladly.[313]

Through his letters to his wife, Helmuth James kept Ulla apprised of the progress of his case at the *Volksgerichtshof* (People's Court). Feeling quite hopeless, he wrote on December 10:

> Please tell Ulla that [the case] has apparently gone to the last and therefore decisive stage. Please thank her very much for her help thus far, but it is still very necessary, for nothing has changed and there is still no land in sight, rather, only a completely mechanical run from the departure at Tegel [Prison] to the oven in Plötzensee, where the V.G.H. [Volksgerichtshof] is in reality only a traffic stop in the bureaucracy, a stop where the conductor must ring the bell to "Get out of the way," but nobody can get on or get off the trolley.[314]

On December 17, a few weeks before his death, he wrote:

> Speak also, please, very carefully [sorgfältig] with Ulla; tell her how much I need her help, that I thank her and beg her to continue working for me.[315]

In late December, Helmuth James asked Freya specifically to take a letter from him to Ulla, so that she would continue praying for him. This, too, is an indication of Ulla's importance to him, because every letter to and from the prison had to be transmitted by a prison pastor named Harald Pölchau, who was a friend of the Moltkes' and who risked his life every time he carried letters to and from Moltke. Helmuth

James would, therefore, send letters that were only of the utmost consequence. In fact, in this instance, he asked his wife not to let his sister, Asta, know about his letter to Ulla, because he did not want to hurt Asta's feelings by not sending one to her. He did not feel justified in risking Pölchau's life when he had nothing special to tell her.[316]

From these heartfelt pleas in Helmuth James's last letters, it is clear that Ulla—this close friend of his mother and father and of the whole family, this dedicated Christian Scientist who had bonded so deeply with the Moltkes over the years—was someone who meant a great deal to him and to whom he now, in his extremity, looked for prayerful support.

Spiritual overtones

Helmuth James's last letters from prison are imbued with spiritual overtones, which suggest that Christian Science did indeed have an influence on his thinking. Writing on the second day of his trial—January 10, 1945—he spoke of the tremendous demonstration of the presence and all-power of God.[317] Anticipating a difficult path ahead, he prayed that God would continue to be gracious to him, and he found comfort and consolation in the words of St. Paul:

> But we have this treasure in earthen vessels, that the excellency of the power may be of God, and not of us. [II Cor. 4:7]

Although he acknowledged the possibility of gaining his freedom—however unlikely that might have been at this point—he expressed the overwhelming certainty of God's presence and omnipotence, which is manifested in His doing "precisely what doesn't suit us."

To his beloved wife, Helmuth James affirmed God's omnipotence even in the most everyday situations, such as cooking for their two young sons. Making pancakes for them and cleaning up, for example, were, in Helmuth James's eyes, not too trivial an activity for God to use to show His all-power. Selflessly, he writes, "May God be as gracious to you as to me."[318] His mind was on the grace of God, not on his impending death.

Helmuth James also spoke of a sense of complete protection during his ordeal. He considered this protection a treasure that could not be taken away and was more important than life itself—an idea, he comments, that was incomprehensible to the "miserable creatures" such as Freisler and the rest of the "whole pack" who were about to kill him.

In his final days, Helmuth James wrote of listening to his inner voice, which he was disposed to obey, whether it led him back to Kreisau or whether it was God calling him to Himself.[319]

As he thought back to his family at Kreisau and of his early years growing up there—of Mami and Papi and his brothers and sister; of his own little sons, Helmuth Caspar and Konrad; of Kreisau and its challenges; of the work camp at Löwenberg; of the family's refusal to fly the swastika or to join the Nazi Party; of his English friend Lionel Curtis and his German Resistance comrades, Adam von Trott zu Solz, Peter Graf Yorck von Wartenburg, and Carlo Mierendorff—he saw these experiences in a spiritual light for the first time. All these experiences had at last become "comprehensible in a single hour."[320]

Helmuth James felt that he had been chosen by God for "a mighty task" and that, for the first time, all the "zigzag curves" and "infinite detours" of his life journey suddenly made perfect sense to him. At last, everything in his life finally "acquired its meaning," which, up until this moment, had been hidden. In a flash, at the end of his earthly life, Moltke could see the logic of events that had made up his life, and he understood clearly that God had led him to this moment of vision, however terrible it might seem to the human view.

In his last letter to Freya, Helmuth James asked her to remember that, in telling the story of the trial of himself and other members of the German Resistance, he must be the main character. This was not an egotistical claim, but a recognition that he was God's vessel and that without him the story would have no center.

Moltke concluded his letter with the serene certainty that "the task for which God made me is done"—a declaration that indicates an exalted spiritual state and is reminiscent of Jesus' words on the cross: "It is finished" [John 19:30]. Although Moltke was not averse to the efforts of others to save his life, it would only be so that he could accomplish another task, if God had another one for him to do. Meanwhile, he closed his last letter with a blessing: "The grace of the Lord Jesus Christ, and the love of God, and the communion of the Holy Ghost, be with you all. Amen " [II Cor.13:14].

Dorothy and Helmuth James's sense of mission

Helmuth James's sense of mission and his statement that he had been chosen, bear a striking resemblance to his mother's glowing conviction that "after nearly 5 years in this new circle [her life in Germany] I still feel that this is my place, that I have a work to do that none other could do (this sounds conceited but it is not for I know too well that each has a work which is *his* to accomplish) and therefore is it any wonder that I am happy?" Dorothy, too, had felt chosen, adding, "But it certainly was a strange business that the Fates[321] should have chosen me to fill this place!" [Kriesau, 17.7.1910].

In the introduction to her translation of Dorothy's letters into German, which was published under the title *Ein Leben in Deutschland* (*A Life in Germany*), Beate Ruhm von Oppen, who also translated *Letters to Freya* into English, noted this parallel sense of mission between mother and son. She wrote that they "both had the feeling of a work, of a mission that had been given to them." In Helmuth James's case, it was a conviction of his identity as a Christian, regardless of national or denominational or class interests; in Dorothy's case, it was a sense of being in her right place, with a work that was hers alone to accomplish.[322]

The letters that Helmuth James wrote in the last year of his life reveal that spiritual existence had become for him a vivid reality, outweighing and transcending the material world, and enabling him to triumph morally over the injustice he experienced at the hands of the Nazi Regime.

But was Helmuth James a Christian Scientist? He certainly did not identify himself as one. Baptized in the Evangelical Lutheran Church, he died, as he said in his letter of January 11, 1945, "a Christian and nothing else." Not a Christian Scientist, not a Lutheran; simply a Christian.

Yet it is clear from Dorothy's letters that Helmuth James's natural receptivity to the Christ was protected and nurtured by his Christian Scientist parents during his formative years. And while his interpretation of Christianity differed from Christian Science once he became an adult, the profound spirituality of his thinking, as evidenced in his last letters, would suggest that the gentle upbringing he had received from his mother and father, their abiding faith in the all-power of God, their dedication and courageous stand for their religion likely influenced his own deep commitment to Christianity, which led to his martyrdom, in January 1945.

POSTLUDE

Since the death of Helmuth James von Moltke, in 1945, there has been a crescendo of interest in this courageous hero of the German Resistance, culminating in a nationwide celebration in Germany of the 100th anniversary of his birth, in 1907. In addition to *Letters to Freya*, several biographies—one in 2007, another in 2008—and articles about this extraordinary man have been published. Commemorative stamps bearing his image were issued by the German Government in 1964 and 2007. Also in 2007, events to honor his memory took place in Germany, including a memorial service held on his 100th birthday, March 11, at the *Französische Friedrichstadtkirche* (French Friedrichstadt Church) in Berlin, followed by a performance of Mahler's Second Symphony.

The New Kreisau

With the redrawing of the boundaries between Germany and Poland after World War II, Silesia became part of Poland. After the family was forced to leave Kreisau in 1945, their estate was turned into a state farm, owned by the Polish Government. But Kreisau soon fell into disrepair. In early 1989, the Governments of both Germany and Poland held their Mass of Reconciliation at Kreisau and agreed to restore the buildings. Kreisau, now called Krzyżowa, has been beautifully restored by Poles and Germans working together. Thus was born the Kreisau Foundation for European Understanding, based on the ideals of Helmuth James von Moltke and the Kreisau Circle. Here thousands of young Europeans come together every year, to get to know each other and to learn about ways to bring greater understanding and peace between the nations of the world. A fund has been created in Germany to support Kreisau and its activities. Named the Freya von Moltke Foundation for the New Kreisau, it is a fitting tribute to her and her husband, and to their work for the cause of truth and justice.

CODA

"Important foundational work"

The German translation of *Science and Health* that was published in 1912 remained the authorized translation for the next eighty-five years. In 1997, The Christian Science Publishing Society issued a new German translation, followed by yet another revision in 2012, as well as a new Spanish translation.

In the May 7, 2012, issue of the *Christian Science Sentinel*, The Office of the Publisher's Agent for Mary Baker Eddy's Writings issued a statement explaining the reasons for the new translations.

> Modern languages evolve as their speakers encounter new ideas. When conveying the ideas of Christian Science, they may need new vocabulary or flexibility to clearly and precisely communicate its radical statements regarding God, man, and the universe. Thus, translating *Science and Health* . . . requires a remarkable amount of ingenuity and inspiration when conveying the ideas in a language for the first time. Over time, subsequent revisions then draw on the previous translation and the growth and inspiration it impelled to deliver a more precise rendering of the original English text.

> These revisions are a natural step in the evolution not only of the language, but also in the ability of Christian Scientists who speak that language to contribute substantially to the translation work. As with any translation of *Science and Health,* the goal of the translation is to represent Mary Baker Eddy's original English text as clearly and accurately as possible.

The paragraph ends with a note of appreciation for the work of the early translators of *Science and Health*.

> We are immensely grateful for the quality and care that previous translations show in this regard and the important foundational work they provided.

ACKNOWLEDGEMENTS

I wish to thank the Moltke family—in particular, Helmuth Caspar von Moltke, Veronica Jochum von Moltke, and the late Freya von Moltke—for sharing Dorothy von Moltke's letters with me and patiently answering my many questions about their family history. I thank them for their warmth, generosity, and trust.

I am also very grateful to Stephen R. Howard, Director Curator of Longyear Museum, for encouraging me to pursue this research. Sincere thanks are due to Senior Research Archivist Judy Huenneke of The Mary Baker Eddy Library in Boston for her diligent research on my behalf. The late Rosemarie Francis helped me with the translation of many documents from the German, as did Jürgen Kurt Stark, CS. Cynthia Sunderland, Allen and Lenore Parker, and David R. Francis, former economic columnist for *The Christian Science Monitor,* read the manuscript and made many helpful suggestions.

The following scholars gave me encouragment and a deeper understanding of German history: Dr. Richard M. Hunt, former University Marshal and Senior Lecturer at Harvard University; Dr. Robert Spaethling, Professor of German Language and Literature at the University of Massachusetts, Boston (emeritus); Dr. Joachim W. Stieber, Professor of History at Smith College (emeritus); and the late Dr. Klemens von Klemperer, former Professor of History at Smith College. I am indebted to Baron Manfred and Karla von Malapert-Neufville for sharing information about Christian Science in the Hamburg area; to Wolfgang Bluhm for putting me in touch with the *Bundesarchiv* (German Federal Archives) in Berlin; to Annemarie Franke, former Director of the Kreisau Foundation for Mutual Understanding, for assistance with my research at Kreisau; and to William E. Stillman for sharing his knowledge of Christian Science in Germany under the Third Reich.

331

My thanks also to Vera Pindter for the account of her grandmother, Margarethe von Trotha; to the late Elfriede Fleischhut and her daughter, Christel Fleischhut, for their recollections of Count von Moltke; and to Christa Koenig for the letters from Irene Bremner and Frances Bagnell.

Finally, I wish to express my sincere gratitude to publisher and editor George Spitzer, and editor and copyeditor Jane Spitzer, of Nebbadoon Press, for their expertise and hard work, without which such a beautiful presentation of these extraordinary letters would not have been possible.

Ich danke Ihnen allen! (Thank you all!)

Catherine K. Hammond

BIBLIOGRAPHY

Balfour, Michael, and Julian Frisby. *Helmuth von Moltke: A Leader Against Hitler*. London: MacMillan & Co., Ltd., 1972.

Brakelmann, Günter. Helmuth James von Moltke 1907-1945: Eine Biographie. Munich: C. H. Beck, 2007.

Dodd, William E. *Ambassador Dodd's Diary 1933–1938*. Edited by William E. Dodd, Jr., and Martha Dodd. New York: Harcourt, Brace and Company, 1941.

Eddy, Mary Baker. *Manual of The Mother Church The First Church of Christ Scientist in Boston, Massachusetts*. Boston: The First Church of Christ, Scientist.

Eddy, Mary Baker. *Miscellaneous Writings 1883-1896*. Boston: The First Church of Christ, Scientist, 1895.

Eddy, Mary Baker. *Poems*. Boston: The First Church of Christ, Scientist, 1910.

Eddy, Mary Baker. *Wissenschaft und Gesundheit mit Schlüssel zur Heiligen Schrift*. Boston: The Christian Science Publishing Society, 1912.

Friedrich, Otto. *Blood and Iron: From Bismarck to Hitler the von Moltke Family's Impact on German History*. New York: HarperCollins, 1995.

Gandhi, Mahatma. *The Selected Works of Mahatma Gandhi*, Vol. 3. Edited by Shriman Narayan. Ahmedabad, India: Navajivan Publishing House, 1928.

Kennan, George F. *Memoirs 1925-1950*. Boston: Little, Brown & Co., 1967.

Köhler, Jochen. Helmuth James von Moltke: Geschichte einer Kindheit und Jugend. Reinbek, Germany: Rowohlt, 2008.

Moltke, Dorothy von. *Ein Leben in Deutschland: Briefe aus Kreisau und Berlin 1907-1934*. Translated by Beate Ruhm von Oppen. Munich: C. H. Beck, 1999.

Moltke, Freya von. *Memories of Kreisau and the German Resistance*. Translated by Julie M. Winter. Lincoln: University of Nebraska Press, 2003.

Moltke, Hemuth James von. *Abschiedsbriefe Gefängnis Tegel September 1944–Januar 1945*. Munich: C. H. Beck, 2011.

Moltke, Helmuth James von. *Briefe an Freya 1939-1945*. Munich: C. H. Beck, 1988.

Moltke, Helmuth James von. *Letters to Freya 1939-1945*. Edited and translated by Beate Ruhm von Oppen. New York: Alfred A. Knopf, 1990.

Peel, Robert. *Mary Baker Eddy: The Years of Authority*. New York: Holt, Rinehart and Winston, 1977.

Rose Innes, James. *James Rose Innes: Chief Justice of South Africa, 1914-27: Autobiography*. Edited by B. A. Tindall. London: Geoffrey Cumberlege, Oxford University Press, 1949.

Seal, Frances Thurber. *Christian Science in Germany*. Philadelphia: John C. Winston, 1931. Reprint, Chestnut Hill, Massachusetts: Longyear Museum, 1977.

Stillman, William E. "Christian Science under the Nazi Regime." Elsah, Illinois: private printing, 1977. Revised in 2012.

Waldschmidt-Nelson, Britta. *Christian Science im Lande Luthers: Eine amerikanische Religionsgemeinschaft in Deutschland 1894-2009*. Stuttgart: Franz Steiner Verlag, 2009.

OTHER SOURCES

The Mary Baker Eddy Collection, The Mary Baker Eddy Library, Boston, Massachusetts.

Longyear Museum, Chestnut Hill, Massachusetts.

Publications of The Christian Science Publishing Society:

Christian Science Hymnal

Christian Science Sentinel

Der Herold der Christian Science

The Christian Science Journal

NAMES INDEX

Elbe, Lili von, 30
Ete, see Trotha, Margarethe von
Eugen, *Onkel* see Moltke, Eugen von
Eulig (gardener), 93

Farlow, Alfred, 256, 357
Feder, Gottfried, 167, 354
Fleischhut, Christel, 307, 308, 332, 364
Fleischhut, Elfriede, 306-309, 311, 332, 355
Flinck, Govaert, 355
Flower, Catherine M., 72, 251, 253
Frau *Doktor*, see Schwarzwald, Eugenie
Freisler, Roland, 319, 320, 323
Friedrich II, King of Prussia (the Great), 352
Friedrich, Kaiser III, 353
Friedrich Heinrich Albrecht, Prince of Prussia, 352
Friedrich Wilhelm, Crown Prince (eldest son of Kaiser
    Wilhelm II), 352
Frisby, Julian, 212, 333
Fritz, see Eitel Friedrich, Prince of Prussia
Fritz, *Onkel*, see Moltke, Fritz von
Furtwängler, Wilhelm, 152, 353

Gaffron, Tilla, 100
Gandhi, Mohandas Karamchand (Mahatma), 5
Garnier, Frau von, 242
Garvin, James Louis, 138
Genia, see Schwarzwald, Eugenie
George V, King of the United Kingdom, 64, 73
Gert, 69
Gilchrist, 104, 105
Goethe, Johann Wolfgang von, 42, 88, 89
Göring, Hermann, 191
Gravina, Countess, 152
Gregory, Lady (née Isabella Augusta Persse), 80, 351
Günther-Peterson, Bertha, 28, 241, 242, 244, 252, 255, 277,
    279

Rhodes, Cecil, 5, 222
Ribbentrop, Joachim von, 289-290
Richthofen, Herbert von, 143
Rittbach, Monika von (née von Moltke), 22, 38, 58, 59, 84, 99, 100, 169, 216, 225
Röhm, Ernst, 203, 356
Rose Innes, Dorothy, see Moltke, Dorothy von
Rose Innes, Jessie, vii, 3-6, 223, 224, 355
Rose Innes, James, 3-5, 21, 222, 228, 231, 232
Rosenstock-Hüssy, Eugen, 151

Sachsen-Meiningen, Princess of, 242
Saint-Saëns, Camille, 80, 81
Sauer, Jacobus Wilhelmus, 63, 351
Schiller, Friedrich von, 42
Schleicher, Kurt von, 183, 187-188
Schnitzler, Liselotte von (Lilo), 175, 201, 204, 356
Schnitzlers (Freya von Moltke's grandparents), 201
Scholander, 33
Scholtz (South African airman), 105
Scholtz, Mrs., 103
Scholz, Herbert, 204, 356
Schönberg, Arnold, 141
Schönberg, Manon (Schönchen), 69, 97, 98, 103, 148, 244
Schönchen, see Schönberg, Manon
Schorcht, Fräulein, 40
Schreiner, William Philip, 5, 108, 135, 349,
Schultz, Ulla, see Oldenbourg, Ulla
Schultzchen, see Oldenbourg, Ulla
Schumann, Robert, 352, 354
Schumann-Heink, Ernestine, 81, 352
Schwarzwald, Eugenie, 141, 142, 161, 172, 186, 236
Schwarzwald, Hermann, 212
Schwester Ida, see Hübner, Ida
Schwester Marie, 23, 73, 114, 212, 250, 251
Schwester Oberin, 82
Seal, Frances Thurber, 255-256, 356, 357
Seidlitz, Frau von, 20

NOTES

[1] Michael Balfour and Julian Frisby, *Helmuth von Moltke: A Leader Against Hitler* (London: MacMillan & Co., Ltd., 1972), p. 15.

[2] Jochen Köhler, *Helmuth James von Moltke: Geschichte einer Kindheit und Jugend* (Reinbek, Germany: Rowohlt, 2008), p. 130.

[3] Leonore (née Moltke) von Hülsen. Köhler, *Helmuth James von Moltke*, p. 130.

[4] Conversation with Freya von Moltke, November 16, 2004. Freya told me that, although the Count's singing was of professional caliber, his status and responsibilities as a Count ruled out a concert career. "No," she said, "he never had a concert career, because, you see, in that generation that wasn't done. Graf Moltke would not sing."

[5] Conversation with Freya von Moltke, November 16, 2004.

[6] 13,000 kilometers.

[7] James Rose Innes, *Autobiography*, B. A. Tindall, ed. (London: Oxford University Press, 1949), p. 80.

[8] Ibid., p. viii. Lord Alfred Milner (1854–1925) was High Commissioner in South Africa and Governor of the Cape Colony in 1897.

[9] *The Selected Works of Mahatma Ghandi*, Vol. 3, Shriman Narayan, ed. (Ahmedabad, India: Navajivan, 1928), p. 438. William P. Schreiner (1857–1919), formerly Prime Minister of the Cape Colony, later High Commissioner of the Union of South Africa.

[10] Rose Innes, *Autobiography*, p. 49.

[11] Balfour and Frisby, *Helmuth von Moltke*, p 57.

[12] Helmuth James von Moltke to Caspar and Konrad von Moltke, January 19, 1944 (original in German).

[13] Balfour and Frisby, *Helmuth von Moltke*, p. 14.

[14] DvM (Dorothy von Moltke) letter, Bresa, April 2, 1924.

[15] Ibid.

[16] Conversation with Helmuth Caspar von Moltke, Nov. 7, 2006.

[17] This involved a degree of artistic license, as the Field Marshal was not actually present at the march into Paris.

[18] After the Moltkes left Kreisau at the end of World War II, the Schloss fell into disrepair. Many years later, it was totally renovated and is now a center for peace studies known as the Kreisau Foundation for European Understanding. For more on present-day Kreisau, see Epilogue.

[19] Balfour and Frisby, *Helmuth von Moltke*, p. 10.

[20] Balfour and Frisby, *Helmuth von Moltke*, p. 10.

[21] Conversation with Freya von Moltke, November 16, 2004.

[22] A ferry.

[23] The cannons had been given to the great Field Marshal by the Government in Berlin.

[24] One of the Moltkes' properties.

[25] Hans Adolf von Moltke (1884-1943), a cousin and neighbor. Hans Adolf was German Ambassador to Poland from 1934 to 1939, when Hitler invaded Poland.

[26] Rose Innes, *Autobiography,* p. 54.

[27] Conversation with Freya von Moltke, November 16, 2004.

[28] For more on class instruction with Bertha Günther-Peterson, see Part II.

[29] Hermann Sudermann (1857–1928), German dramatist and novelist.

[30] Eugen Francis Charles d'Albert (1864-1932), Scottish-born German pianist and composer.

[31] Eugène Ysaÿe (1858-1931), Belgian violinist, composer, and conductor.

[32] Lilli Lehmann (1848-1929), German soprano.

[33] One of Helmuth's aunts who lived on the estate.

[34] James Keir Hardie (1856-1915), Scottish socialist, who rose from poverty to become an influential leader of the Labour Party.

[35] Ellen Key (1849-1926), Swedish feminist and writer.

[36] Henrik Ibsen (1828-1906), Norwegian playwright.

[37] Diana (the horse) nearly drowned after falling off a small bridge.

[38] Marie Wilhelmine Burt von Moltke, wife of the great Field Marshal, was of English descent.

[39] Initials of a term of endearment (unknown) for Dorothy's father.

[40] *History of Friedrich II of Prussia, Called Frederick the Great* by Thomas Carlyle, 6 vol. (1858-1865).

[41] One £ in 1908 corresponds to approximately £73 in 2013.

[42] Dorothy's grandson, Helmuth Caspar von Moltke, remembers swimming in the Smuts' pool at their home in South Africa.

[43] Monthly journal founded in 1890 by British reform journalist William Thomas Stead (1849-1912).

[44] Rigid airship designed by Ferdinand Graf von Zeppelin (1838-1917).

[45] A beachside suburb of Cape Town, South Africa.

[46] Stephanus Johannes Paulus Kruger (1825-1904), better known as Paul Kruger, Prominent Boer resistance leader against British rule and president of the South African Republic (Transvaal).

[47] Gabriel Sénac de Meilhan (1736-1803), French playright.

[48] Ulla Schultz (later Oldenbourg), close family friend and Christian Science practitioner and teacher.

[49] Köhler, *Helmuth James von Moltke*, p. 56. Presumably, they were singing hymns of gratitude and praise from the German *Christian Science Hymnal*.

[50] Selma Kurz (1874-1933), born into a poor Jewish family in Polish Silesia, became a prima donna at the Vienna Opera House and a world-renowned coloratura.

[51] "Mother's New Year Gift to the Little Children" by Mary Baker Eddy.

[52] Dorothy is probably referring to the statue of Field Marshal Helmuth von Moltke that is located in Berlin in the *Grosser Sterne* (Great Star), the central square of the *Tiergarten*.

[53] The Field Marshal's military decorations.

[54] Informal gatherings for conversation.

[55] Lower chamber of the German parliament.

[56] Jacobus Wilhelmus Sauer (1850-1913), prominent Afrikaans liberal politician of the Cape Colony, who advocated equal rights for black South Africans.

[57] Chapel Hill: the graveyard and site of the great Field Marshal's tomb on the Moltke estate.

[58] Matthew Arnold (1822-1888), British poet and cultural critic.

[59] Johanna von Bismarck (1824-1894), wife of Otto von Bismarck (1815–1898). Bismarck, under whom Helmuth von Moltke's great-uncle served as Field Marshal, was the architect of German unification and first Chancellor of the German Empire.

[60] Joan Manén (1883-1971), Catalonian violinist and composer.

[61] Nickname for Margarethe von Trotha.

[62] The quote is from James 3:16.

[63] Carl Dietrich von Trotha, son of Margarethe von Trotha (née Moltke), and Helmuth James's first cousin.

[64] "Flen," the origin or exact meaning of which is unknown, was a pet name used by Dorothy both for her father and for herself.

[65] Since Dorothy was in Boston at this time and the children remained in Germany, she must have learned this from a letter, probably sent by Schönchen.

[66] I John 3:1 (King James Version).

[67] From "The Cloud" by Percy Bysshe Shelley.

[68] Dispute between Germany and France over Morocco and the Congo, which was settled in November 1911.

[69] John Hays Hammond (1855-1936), American mining engineer, diplomat, and philanthropist.

[70] Rose Innes, *Autobiography*, pp. 123-137.

[71] William Butler Yeats (1865-1939), Irish poet.

[72] Isabella August, Lady Gregory, née Isabella Augusta Persse (1852-1932), Irish dramatist and folklorist.

[73] John Millington Synge (1871-1909), Irish playwright.

[74] Vladimir de Pachmann (1848-1933), Russian pianist.

351

[75] Wealthy entrepreneur from the Middle West who, with his wife, Mary Beecher Longyear, moved to Brookline, Massachusetts, where Mrs. Longyear established the Longyear Museum in 1927.

[76] Camille Saint-Saëns (1835-1921).

[77] Austrian-Czech tenor (1873-1946), father of soprano Margarethe Slezak and actor Walter Slezak.

[78] Ernestine Schumann-Heink (1861-1936).

[79] First Balkan War, October 1912 to May 1913, between the Balkan League (Serbia, Montenegro, Greece, and Bulgaria) and the Ottoman Empire. The Balkan allies were victorious.

[80] Daniel-Francois-Esprit Auber (1782-1871), French composer of light opera.

[81] Toto Leonhardi, a cousin of Helmuth von Moltke.

[82] Hugo von Hofmannsthal (1874-1929), Austrian poet, dramatist, librettist, and essayist.

[83] Rose Innes, *Autobiography*, pp. 224-225.

[84] Crown Prince Wilhelm (1882-1951), eldest son of Kaiser Wilhelm II, married to Duchess Cecilie of Mecklenburg-Schwerin (1886-1954).

[85] Prince Friedrich Heinrich Albrecht of Prussia (1874-1940), great-grandson of Friedrich Wilhelm III, King of Prussia.

[86] Ferruccio Busoni (1866-1924), Italian pianist and composer.

[87] August Strindberg (1849-1912), Swedish playwright and novelist.

[88] A decade earlier, the British had defeated the Dutch Afrikaner settlers in the Boer War (1899-1902).

[89] Helmuth James von Moltke to his sons, January 19, 1944.

[90] Ibid.

[91] Ibid.

[92] Ibid.

[93] This is the last letter of 1914 in the collection; other letters from 1914 may have been lost during the war.

[94] Helmuth James von Moltke to his sons, January 19, 1944.

[95] Jowo did, in fact, have a long life: he died in 2002 at the age of ninety-three.

[96] The Battles of Verdun and the Somme, in which huge casualties were incurred on both sides.

[97] In addition to her war work, Lady Rose Innes was well known in South Africa as a prominent advocate for women's rights.

[98] Rose Innes, *Autobiography*, p. 267.

[99] Ibid., pp. 266-267.

[100] The people living at the Bethusy-Hucs' estate in Bankau.

[101] Woodrow Wilson (1856-1924), President of the United States, 1913-1921, and one of the founders of the League of Nations.

[102] Willo grew up to become a prominent city planner and professor at Harvard University (see Epilogue).

[103] Gustav Stresemann (1878 – 1929), Chancellor of Germany (1923) and Foreign Secretary (1923–1929).

[104] Gustav Ritter von Kahr (1862-1934), German right-wing conservative politician; Prime Minister of Bavaria (1920-1921).

[105] Erich Ludendorff (1865-1937), German Chief of Staff during World War I. He supported Hitler in the Munich Putsch (November, 1923), and became one of the first Nazi Party members of the *Reichstag*.

[106] Hitler was sentenced for treason to five years in *Festungshaft* (literally, "fortress confinement"), where he was kept in comfortable quarters (and where he wrote *Mein Kampf*). As it turned out, Hitler only served a little over eight months. Due to his war service and connections, Ludendorff was acquitted.

[107] Max Baldner (1887-1946), prominent German cellist.

[108] Christian Science churches hold regular services on Wednesday nights.

[109] Richard Strauss (1864-1949), German composer and conductor.

[110] William P. Schreiner had been High Commissioner of the Union of South Africa and was the friend of the Rose Inneses who had helped the family in 1919.

[111] This turned out to be the case (see Epilogue).

[112] August Strindberg (1849-1912), Swedish playwright and novelist.

[113] Hugo von Hofmannsthal (1874-1929), Austrian poet, dramatist, librettist, and essayist.

[114] Kaiser Friedrich III (1831-1888), son of Kaiser Wilhelm I, was married to Princess Victoria, daughter of Queen Victoria; he died only three months into his reign. Their son was Kaiser Wilhelm II.

[115] Ernst von Wildenbruch (1845–1909), German poet and dramatist.

[116] Edward Mandell House (1858-1938), author of *The Intimate Papers of Colonel House*.

[117] Aristide Briand (1862–1932), Prime Minister of France. He was an active participant in the Locarno Pact and a strong advocate of the League of Nations.

[118] Paul von Hindenburg (1847-1934), German Field Marshal and statesman; President of Germany from 1925 to 1934.

[119] Paintings by Franz von Lenbach (1836-1904), German artist.

[120] One of Dorothy's South African relatives, possibly her father's sister.

[121] As Wierischau is still part of Kreisau, perhaps this deal was never completed (or perhaps it was later bought back from Hildebrand or the next owner). Conversation with Helmuth Caspar von Moltke, August, 2009.

[122] Wilhelm Furtwängler (1886-1954), German conductor and composer.

353

[123] Lauritz Melchior (1890–1973), Danish opera singer.

[124] Madi Leonardi, cousin of Helmuth von Moltke.

[125] *Abitur*: the final examinations that young adults (aged 18, 19 or 20) take at the end of their secondary education, usually after twelve or thirteen years of schooling.

[126] Heinrich Brüning (1885-1970), Chancellor of Germany, 1930-1932.

[127] Hermann Dietrich (1879-1954), Vice-Chancellor of Germany and Finance Minister, 1930-1932.

[128] Dorothy Thompson (1893-1961), American journalist. The "Hans" to whom she addressed her wartime broadcasts, published under the title "Listen, Hans," was a pseudonym for Helmuth James von Moltke.

[129] Hans Adolf von Moltke would remain Ambassador to Poland until Germany invaded Poland in 1939. Although a senior civil servant in the German Government, he was not a Nazi, but an intelligent conservative with links to the German Resistance, particularly the Kreisau Circle, which was headed by his young cousin Helmuth James von Moltke, and of which his wife's brother, Peter York von Wartenburg, was a prominent member. He also helped Helmuth James save Kreisau by purchasing the Wernersdorf part of the estate. The younger Moltke shared many of his thoughts with Hans Adolf, who evidently became concerned about his young cousin and warned him, "I don't want a von Moltke to die on the gallows." In 1943, Hitler strong-armed Hans Adolf von Moltke into accepting an ambassadorship to Spain (he could either consent to the appointment or go to a concentration camp), but soon after Hans Adolf arrived in Madrid, he became ill and died on the operating table. Conversation with Helmuth Caspar von Moltke, August 15, 2009.

[130] Helmuth James von Moltke to his sons, January 19, 1944.

[131] Gregor Strasser (1892-1934), Nazi politician and Party organizer. Strasser opposed Hitler on issues of social reform and anti-Semitism, and was murdered in the Röhm Putsch in 1934.

[132] Gottfried Feder (1883-1941), economic theoretician and an early member of the Nazi Party.

[133] The Deichmanns were patrons of the arts, and one summer day, a musician came to the door of their summer home in Mehlem. The unexpected guest was Johannes Brahms. Frau Deichmann welcomed the young man into her home, where she showed him some music of Robert Schumann. Although Brahms knew of Schumann, he knew only a little of his music. He promptly sat down at the Deichmanns' piano, and as he played some of Schumann's compositions, he was astonished at their beauty. His hostess suggested that he go to Düsseldorf, where Schumann was then living, and meet the great

354

composer. This the younger composer did, and thus began one of the most important musical associations in history. Conversation with Freya von Moltke, November 16, 2004.

[134] Sir James and Lady Jessie Rose Innes, Dorothy and Helmuth, and Helmuth James and Freya, who were all married on the same date, October 18.

[135] Leno, Ete, and Peter: sisters (Leonore and Margarethe) and brother of Count von Moltke.

[136] Claus von Trotha, a military officer and the son of Helmuth's sister, Margarethe von Trotha.

[137] The *Sturmabteilung* (SA) was the Nazi militia created by Hitler in 1921. Functioning as a paramilitary organization of the Nazi Party, it helped him to power in the 1930s, but by 1939 its role had been reduced to training men for Home Guard units.

[138] The *Reichsbanner* was a militia organization of the center-left Social Democratic Party, the purpose of which was to defend the Weimar Republic against Nazism and Communism.

[139] Dorothy wrote the name "Flank," but perhaps meant the Dutch artist Govaert Flinck (1615-1660), who was a pupil of Rembrandt.

[140] Iron Front for Resistance Against Fascism, created by the leaders of the Social Democratic Party (SPD) in December 1931, in opposition to Nazism, Communism, and Monarchism.

[141] Franz von Papen (1879-1969), Chancellor of Germany, June–November, 1932.

[142] Lyman P. Powell, *Mary Baker Eddy* (Boston: The Christian Science Publishing Society, 1930).

[143] Hans Carl von Hülsen was the son of Helmuth's older sister, Leonore von Hülsen.

[144] Kurt von Schleicher (1882–1934), the last Chancellor of Germany during the Weimar Republic, December 1932–January 1933.

[145] Alfred Hugenberg (1865–1951), German industrialist and leader of the conservative German National People's Party (*Deutschnationale Volkspartei*).

[146] Hermann Göring (1893-1946), a leader of the Nazi Party and commander of the Storm Troopers (SA). Two months later, Göring established the *Gestapo* (*Geheime Staatspolizei*)—the Secret Police.

[147] It is generally believed that the fire was set by the Nazis, then blamed on the Communists. The next day, a decree was signed, suspending the civil rights that had been guaranteed by the Weimar constitution, including freedom of speech.

[148] Assessor exam is the final examination to qualify as a lawyer.

[149] Founded in 1902 as International Woman Suffrage Alliance. In the late 1920s, changed its name to International Alliance of Women for

Suffrage and Equal Citizenship. In 1946, it changed its name to International Alliance of Women.

[150] Waldorf Astor (1879-1952), a Christian Scientist, was heir to the Astor fortune and a Member of Parliament, representing Plymouth. In 1919, he became a member of the House of Lords.

[151] Bendlerstrasse: street where the Bendlerblock—Nazi military headquarters—was located, directly south of the *Tiergarten* in Central Berlin. Helmuth James and Freya had a small apartment nearby, also on Bendlerstrasse.

[152] Jan de Bray (1627-1697), Dutch artist, contemporary of Rembrandt (1606-1669).

[153] Ernst Röhm (1887-1934), one of the founders of the Nazi Party, the leader of the SA (*Sturmabteilung*—"Brownshirts") and a former supporter of Hitler. Röhm was assassinated later that year in the massacre ordered by Hitler, known as the "Night of the Long Knives."

[154] Scholz was killed during the war, leaving Lilo with two young children. Lilo died in 2009. Conversation with Helmuth Caspar von Moltke, August 15, 2009.

[155] *Schutzstaffel*—Protection Squadron—the armed wing of the Nazi Party. The SS increased from 300 to 50,000 members by the end of the war.

[156] Austria was annexed by Germany in 1938.

[157] Julian Frisby, a young English friend of the Molktes and co-author of *Helmuth James von Moltke: A Leader against Hitler*.

[158] The Rose Inneses' home in South Africa.

[159] *Memories of Kreisau & the German Resistance* by Freya von Moltke, English translation by Julie M. Winter (Lincoln: University of Nebraska Press, 2003), p. 16.

[160] Köhler, *Helmuth James von Moltke*.

[161] Rose Innes, *Autobiography*, p. 309.

[162] IC #84, Helmuth von Moltke to Mary Baker Eddy, May 23, 1907, The Mary Baker Eddy Collection, Boston, Massachusetts.

[163] Frances Thurber Seal, American Christian Science practitioner, who helped establish Christian Science in Germany in the 1890s; author of *Christian Science in Germany*, Longyear Museum.

[164] According to one biography, the Count was a baritone, not a tenor (see Balfour and Frisby, *Helmuth von Moltke*, p. 15).

[165] Margarethe von Trotha (née Moltke), who later became a Christian Science practitioner, listed in *The Christian Science Journal*.

[166] This article was reprinted in the *Christian Science Sentinel,* vol. 2 (Mar 15, 1900).

[167] Datelist on Count Helmuth von Moltke, The Mary Baker Eddy Collection.

[168] Theodor Stanger to Mary Baker Eddy, November 26, 1909, IC713(b), The Mary Baker Eddy Collection.

[169] DvM, October 15, 1907, and November 17, 1907.

[170] DvM, Hannover, November 26, 1907.

[171] Although he had begun his healing work by 1908, Count von Moltke was not listed in the *Journal* until 1929, probably because of his obligations to the estate at Kreisau.

[172] "Disharmonie ist unwirklich," by Helmuth von Moltke, *Der Herold der Christian* Science, March 1910, reprinted in English as "Discord Unreal," *Christian Science Sentinel,* #15 (Sep 14, 1912), p. 24; "The Works of God Made Manifest," by Dorothy von Moltke, *Sentinel,* 1911, issue #13, p. 803; and "Our Garden," by Dorothy von Moltke, *Sentinel,* 1913, #15, p. 604.

[173] On Wednesday evenings, oral testimonies of healing are given in Christian Science churches.

[174] Reinhard Heydrich, Secret Report (*Darstellung*) on Christian Science, August 11, 1941. Courtesy of the Bundesarvhiv, Berlin.

[175] DvM, Kreisau, June 15, 1909.

[176] Report to Christian Science Board of Directors, July 26, 1926, pp. 29-31, The Mary Baker Eddy Collection.

[177] *Sentinel*, vol. 2 (Jan 4, 1900), p. 283.

[178] Mary Beecher Longyear (1851-1931), wife of prominent entrepreneur John Munro Longyear. Mrs. Longyear also loaned the money for the enterprise to Mrs. Seal, who later repaid it with interest. Longyear Museum Collection.

[179] Frances Thurber Seal, *Christian Science in Germany* (Reprint, Chestnut Hill, Massachusetts, Longyear Museum, 1977), pp. 7-8.

[180] Ibid., p. 8.

[181] Ibid.

[182] Mary Baker Eddy to Carol Norton, September 26, 1896, L02377, The Mary Baker Eddy Collection. Quoted in Robert Peel, *Mary Baker Eddy: The Years of Authority* (New York: Holt, Rinehart and Winston, 1977), p. 119.

[183] Mary Baker Eddy to Laura Lathrop, April 29, 1897, L04371, The Mary Baker Eddy Collection. Quoted in Peel, *Authority,* p. 119.

[184] Mary Baker Eddy to Alfred Farlow, June 28, 1902, L01637, The Mary Baker Eddy Collection. Alfred Farlow was the first Committee on Publication for The First Church of Christ, Scientist.

[185] Peel, *Authority*, p. 119.

[186] Lewis C. Strang to Babette Riessner, April 11, 1906, L14069, The Mary Baker Eddy Collection.

[187] Peel, *Authority,* p. 119. Septimus J. Hanna served the Church of Christ, Scientist, in many positions of responsibility, including Editor of the Christian Science periodicals (1892-1902).

357

[188] Mary Baker Eddy to Alice Tournier, July 22, 1897, L05582, The Mary Baker Eddy Collection. Quoted in Peel, *Authority,* pp. 120, 121.

[189] Preface to German translation of *Science and Health,* 1912, p. i.

[190] See *Journal,* vol. 9 (Dec 15, 1906): "Countess Fanny von Moltke is unmarried; also . . . her father was a cousin of the great field marshal." As Helmuth was the Field Marshal's grandnephew, he and Fanny would have been cousins.

[191] Calvin Frye diaries, #81, June 17, 1908, The Mary Baker Eddy Collection.

[192] Countess Fanny von Moltke was listed in the *Journal* from 1910 to 1915.

[193] Fanny von Moltke to Mary Baker Eddy, January 14, 1904, IC #196, The Mary Baker Eddy Collection.

[194] Mary Baker Eddy to Fanny von Moltke, undated, but presumed to be 1904, L09568, The Mary Baker Eddy Collection.

[195] In addition to being a Trustee, William P. McKenzie was also, at various times, a member of the Christian Science Board of Lectureship, President of The Mother Church, Editor of the Christian Science periodicals, and a Director of The Mother Church.

[196] Mary Baker Eddy to William P. McKenzie, April 29, 1904, L14679, The Mary Baker Eddy Collection.

[197] Unless she is referring to a later one, the letter she wrote asking for a German translation was actually almost two years earlier (January 14, 1904).

[198] Fanny von Moltke to Mary Baker Eddy, November 24, 1905, and Eddy's reply, printed in *Sentinel,* vol. 8 (Dec 23, 1905), p. 264; *Journal,* vol. 23 (Jan 1906), pp. 648, 649; and in *Der Herold der Christian Science,* vol. 4 (May 1906), p. 83.

[199] Mary Baker Eddy to Sarah Conger, March 2, 1906, L02621, The Mary Baker Eddy Collection. Printed in *Journal,* vol. 24 (Apr 1906), "Christian Science and China," p. 49. (Excerpt reprinted in *The First Church of Christ, Scientist and Miscellany,* by Mary Baker Eddy, p. 234.) Conger, the wife of the United States Minister (Ambassador) to China, was a Christian Scientist and had expressed an interest in introducing Christian Science to China.

[200] Louise Kollmorgen to Mary Baker Eddy, October 6, 1907, in *Sentinel,* vol. 10 (Nov 3, 1907), p. 231.

[201] Fanny von Moltke to Mary Baker Eddy, July 22, 1908, IC #196, The Mary Baker Eddy Collection.

[202] According to the *Journal* listings for churches and societies in Germany in 1907, there were three churches—in Berlin, Dresden, and Hannover—and two societies, in Frankfurt and Stuttgart.

[203] IC #84, Helmuth von Moltke to Mary Baker Eddy, Kreisau, May 23, 1907, The Mary Baker Eddy Collection. See Appendix for facsimile of original letter.

[204] Fanny von Moltke to Mary Baker Eddy, November 24, 1905, and Eddy's reply, printed in *Sentinel,* vol. 8 (Dec 23, 1905); *Journal,* vol. 23 (Jan 1906), pp. 648, 649; and in *Der Herold der Christian Science,* vol. 4 (May 1906), p. 83.

[205] IC #84, Helmuth von Moltke to Mary Baker Eddy, Kreisau, May 24, 1907. The Mary Baker Eddy Collection.

[206] Cornell Wilson to Helmuth Graf von Moltke, June 11, 1907, L14083, The Mary Baker Eddy Collection.

[207] IC #84, Helmuth von Moltke to Mary Baker Eddy, from London, September 20, 1908, The Mary Baker Eddy Collection. Although the Count did not succeed in meeting Eddy, Fanny von Moltke had the good fortune of having a brief interview with her on June 17, 1908 (Diaries of Calvin Frye, MBEL).

[208] William Rathvon reminiscence, pp. 251-253. The Mary Baker Eddy Collection.

[209] Frances Bagnell to Christa König, November 4, 1971, Longyear Museum Collection. Ms. Bagnell "had the honor of being appointed" to assist Count von Moltke in Boston whenever he came for biennial COP meetings and needed someone with excellent English and some German to help him prepare his reports for the Board of Directors. She said she "very much enjoyed working with the Count at that time and in subsequent years at similar visits." In 1935 (the year Dorothy von Moltke died) he invited her to come to Germany to serve as his secretary; however, the tense political relations between Germany and the United States at that time prevented her from accepting.

[210] Correction: it was in March 1910.

[211] Bagnell, p. 2.

[212] IC #84, Helmuth von Moltke to Mary Baker Eddy, Boston, March 30, 1910, The Mary Baker Eddy Collection.

[213] Peel, *Authority,* p. 415, fn. 121.

[214] Mary Baker Eddy to Allison Stewart, March 31, 1910, quoted in Preface to German translation of *Science and Health,* 1912, p. ii.

[215] IC #84, Helmuth von Moltke to Mary Baker Eddy, April 1, 1910, The Mary Baker Eddy Collection.

[216] Mary Baker Eddy to Helmuth von Moltke, April 2, 1910, V03386, The Mary Baker Eddy Collection.

[217] According to his daughter, Irene Bremner, Theodor Stanger was born in Africa to German Lutheran missionaries, who then emigrated to Michigan, where Theodor grew up. He eventually moved to Chicago, where, using his command of both English and German, he taught German in the public schools, until his health failed. When he

was quickly healed through the prayers of a Christian Science practitioner, he joined the Christian Science Church and soon entered the practice. While serving as First Reader in Third Church, Chicago, he was appointed editor of *Der Herold der Christian Science* (Irene S. Bremner to Christa König, September 7, 1971). Longyear Museum Collection.

[218] The Preface to the 1912 German translation describes the formation and procedures of the new committee: "A committee of three Germans (two in Germany and one in the United States) was appointed, and each member of the committee, without conferring in any way with the others, made a full translation of the text of *Science and Health*. This committee met in Boston, August 15, 1911, and, augmented by three more members, began the consideration and revision of the translations. Word by word and sentence by sentence, these were gone over, and a new and complete translation evolved therefrom. Twelve months had been devoted to the first undertaking, and seven more months of conscientious labor by the whole committee were necessary before the book was ready for the printer."

[219] Oldenbourg Report, p. 2, The Mary Baker Eddy Collection.

[220] Ibid.

[221] Theodor Stanger to Ulla Oldenbourg, Boston, May 2, 1910, Oldenbourg Report, The Mary Baker Eddy Collection. One of these was an article titled "Man's Unity with God."

[222] Allison V. Stewart to Ulla Oldenbourg, Boston, May 15, 1910, Oldenbourg Report, The Mary Baker Eddy Collection. Stewart was also a member of the Christian Science Board of Directors (1908-1917).

[223] McLellan served as a Director from 1903 to 1917.

[224] William P. McKenzie, served as Trustee of the Christian Science Publishing Society from1898 to 1917, and again from 1922 to 1932. McKenzie also served as Lecturer on Christian Science, President of The Mother Church (1899, 1909, and 1906), Editor of the Christian Science periodicals (1917-1920), and Director (1933-1943).

[225] Oldenbourg Report, The Mary Baker Eddy Collection, p. 2. In her cover letter to the report, Ulla Shultz Oldenbourg wrote that "it was a wonderful uplift to go through the whole experience of the translation during the preparation of the account, and I am very grateful to you for this work."

[226] Ibid., p. 1.

[227] Oldenbourg Report, p. 2, The Mary Baker Eddy Collection.

[228] In her report (pp. 2-3), Ulla explains why the committee omitted the original English version of "Fruitage": "Speaking about the size of the volume, Mr. McLellan took the pages of the chapter 'Fruitage', doubled them, showing in that way the size of the book without said

chapter. Being under the impression that our Leader had ordered this chapter to be omitted, it did not occur to me to even ask about it, nor did the question arise amongst the committtee during the mutual work in Boston, surely because it took it for granted too that our Leader had ordered it like that." In 1937, a German translation of "Fruitage" was added to the German translation of *Science and Health*.

[229] Irene S. Bremner to Christa König, September 7, 1971, Longyear Museum Collection.

[230] Helmuth James, Jowo, and Willo. The Moltkes eventually had five children.

[231] Historical sketch of Adam H. Dickey, prepared by the Association of Pupils of Adam H. Dickey, CSD, 1948, The Mary Baker Eddy Collection.

[232] Oldenbourg Report, November 30, 1925, p. 3, The Mary Baker Eddy Collection.

[233] Ibid., p. 5.

[234] Ibid., pp. 3-4.

[235] In September 1911, the Moltke children were ages four, two, and four months.

[236] She is referring to the South African summer, which is during the European and North American winter.

[237] The seventh edition would corresond to the sixth edition, a major revision, while the twenty-eighth would correspond to the sixteenth (also a major revision). Why the seventh and twenty-eighth were selected, we do not know, but most likely they were the editions at hand, and the sixth and sixteenth, being collectors' items, may have been difficult to come by.

[238] According to Ulla Schultz Oldenbourg, the dictionaries used by the committee were: "Webster; A New English Dictionary by Murray, Oxford; an old dictionary of like contents, which Mr. Dickey procured...; Grimm's *Wörterbuch*. Eisler, *Philosophisches Handwörterbuch*; Schmidt, *Philosophisches Wörterbuch*; Krug, *Allgemeines Handwörterbuch der philosophischen Wissenschaften*; Heyse, *Fremdwörterbuch*. Muret-Sanders; Flügel; John Ebers, from 1796." Oldenbourg Report, The Mary Baker Eddy Collection, p. 4.

[239] The Preface to the 1912 translation, p. iii, notes: "The best lexicons available were consulted, and Grimm's Dictionary was adopted as authority for the German language."

[240] Ibid.

[241] DvM, Boston, September 10, 1911.

[242] The Preface has: "After much study and consideration, the word *Gemüt* was adopted as a translation of the word 'Mind' as used by Mrs. Eddy, and it was clearly shown, as the work progressed, that it best served the purpose."

[243] *Immanuel Kant,* by Houston Stewart Chamberlain., English/German author, pub. 1905.

[244] Clifford P. Smith, originally a district court judge in Iowa, later served in many important positions at The First Church of Christ, Scientist, in Boston, Massachusetts. He is the author of *Historical Sketches from the Life of Mary Baker Eddy and the History of Christian Science* (Boston: The Christian Science Publishing Society, 1941).

[245] *Der Herold,* 10, 1 (April 1912): 32.

[246] *Der Herold,* 10, 3 (June 1912): 128.

[247] Preface, p. vi.

[248] *Der Herold,* 4 (July 1912): 175.

[249] Ibid.

[250] Oldenbourg Report, The Mary Baker Eddy Collection, p. 5.

[251] Freya von Moltke to Catherine Hammond, April 15, 2007: "Asta attended Sunday School and church for quite a while."

[252] *Christian Science Hymnal,* Hymns 169, 7 and 8; "Shepherd Show me how to go" refers to Mary Baker Eddy's hymn, " 'Feed My Sheep' "— Hymns 304–309 in the *Christian Science Hymnal.*

[253] Helmuth James von Moltke to his sons, January 19, 1944.

[254] Ibid.

[255] Ibid.

[256] Freya von Moltke, born in 1911, was a young law student from a prominent banking family, the Deichmanns, in Cologne. In 1931, during the Great Depression, the Deichmann fortune was lost, just before she married Helmuth James.

[257] Helmuth James von Moltke to his sons, January 19, 1944.

[258] Conversation with Freya von Moltke, November 16, 2004.

[259] Conversation with Helmuth Caspar von Moltke, November 7, 2006.

[260] *Letters to Freya 1939-1945,* Edited and translated by Beate Ruhm von Oppen (New York: Alfred A. Knopf, 1990).

[261] Committees on Publication are appointed by the Readers in the three largest Christian Science branch churches in any given state or country (*Manual of The Mother Church*, pp. 98-99). In the Germany of that time, those churches were the branch churches in Hamburg, Hannover, and Berlin.

[262] *Manual,* p. 97.

[263] As it turned out, the man he had put in charge turned out to be far from competent, and in 1929, the estate fell on the verge of bankruptcy. At that point, Count von Moltke turned over the administration of the estate to his eldest son, who, through hard work and astute management, succeeded in saving Kreisau.

[264] In 1920, there were five churches and three societies in Germany. Five years later, there were twelve churches and eleven societies. By

1930, there were nineteen churches and twenty-two societies, including five churches and one society in Berlin alone. By 1933, the figures had risen to thirty-three churches and thirty-three societies in Germany, with eight churches and one society in Berlin. By 1940, the total number of churches and societies in Germany was eighty-eight.
[265] The Moltkes' manager, Zeumer, was a Nazi but remained loyal to the Moltkes. His flying of the swastika served as a protection for the Moltkes during the Nazi era. (See *Memories of Kreisau and the German Resistance* by Freya von Moltke, p. 13.)
[266] Britta Waldschmidt-Nelson, *Christian Science im Lande Luthers: Eine amerikanische Religionsgemeinschaft in Deutschland 1894-2009* (Stuttgart: Franz Steiner Verlag, 2009), p. 157.
[267] Richard J. Davis, Letters of April 12, 14, and 15, 1933, to The Christian Science Board of Directors. Courtesy of the National Archives and Records Administration, Washington, D.C.
[268] During the mid-1930s, there were a number of reports that Nazi "Brownshirts" (SA) stood outside the doors of Christian Science churches, taking down the names of churchgoers, or attended Christian Science lectures, listening for potentially subversive statements. Other accounts from this period indicate that Nazis were harassing attendants in Christian Science Reading Rooms and destroying church literature. It is quite possible that it was in response to actions such as these that Moltke was visiting the various churches around the country in his role as Committee on Publication. See William Stillman, "Christian Science under the Nazi Regime" (Elsah, Illinois: private printing, 1977. Revised 2012), pp. 8-9.
[269] Waldorf Astor (1879-1952), heir to the Astor fortune, was elected to the House of Commons in 1910, representing Plymouth until 1919. His wife, Nancy Astor (1879-1964), was an American from a prominent Virginia family, the Langhornes. After her husband received the title Viscount and entered the House of Lords, in 1919, she was elected to the House of Commons, representing Plymouth.
[270] See Stillman, "Christian Science under the Nazi Regime," pp. 7–8.
[271] Ibid., pp. 9–11.
[272] *Ambassador Dodd's Diary 1933-1938*, Edited by William E. Dodd, Jr., and Martha Dodd (New York: Harcourt, Brace and Company, 1941), p. 40. Entry for September 27, 1933.
[273] Ibid., pp. 40-41.
[274] Ibid., p. 41. Entry for September 29, 1933.
[275] Although the *Manual* stipulates on page 70 that "The Mother Church of Christ, Scientist, shall assume no general official control of other churches," it also clearly allows the Board of Directors to "notify any Church of Christ, Scientist, to remove its Committee on Publication and to appoint another Committee to fill the vacancy; and

it shall be the duty of that church to comply with this request. In such cases it shall be the privilege of this Board to name the Committee if it so desires, and any Committee so named by the Board shall be elected by the branch church" (p. 100).

[276] Richard J. Davis, Letters of April 12, 14, and 15, 1933, to The Christian Science Board of Directors. Courtesy of the National Archives and Records Administration, Washington, D.C.

[277] Waldschmidt-Nelson, *Christian Science im Lande Luthers*, pp. 155-156.

[278] Ibid., pp.156-157.

[279] Ibid., p. 157.

[280] Ibid., p. 157, n. 119.

[281] Ibid., p157.

[282] Ibid., pp.157-158, n.120.

[283] Ibid., p. 160.

[284] Reinhard Heydrich (1904-1942), organizer of the *Sicherheitsdienst* (SD—Security Service); later head of the *Reichssicherheitshautptamt* (Reich Main Security Office); author of the "Final Solution"— extermination of the Jews.

[285] Document D-59, Record Group 238, Entry NM66-1, Office of the U.S. Chief Counsel for the Prosecution of Axis Criminality, Evidence Files, 1945-1946, Series D. Courtesy of The National Archives and Records Administration.

[286] E-mail from Vera Pindter, May 23, 2008.

[287] Conversation with Vera Pindter, May 29, 2008.

[288] Count von Moltke was first listed as a teacher in the *Journal* in 1932 and remained so until his death, in 1939.

[289] Conversation with Elfriede Fleischhut of Cuxhaven, Germany, January 2007. Frau Fleischhut died on July 2, 2007.

[290] Conversation with Christel Fleischhut, on behalf of her mother, Elfriede Fleischhut, December 19, 2005, in Cuxhaven, Germany: *Er war nicht so groß. Er war trotzdem eine sehr starke Persönlichkeit, hatte eine sehr starke Ausstrahlung, und vor allen Dingen wie er [die Christliche Wissenschaft] demonstrierte und wie er sich ausdrückte. Und da hat die . . . obwohl so im kleineren Wuchs, aber doch diese Persönlichkeit sehr stark auf sie gewirkt.* For her, he was a very grand man in things he said about Christian Science.

[291] Ibid.

[292] Converation with Christel Fleischhut, January 2007. Oral Histories, Longyear Museum, Chestnut Hill, Massachusetts.

[293] Graf von Moltke, Address on Church Work to the Association Meeting, 1935, p. 2. Longyear Museum Collection.

[294] Ibid. p. 8.

[295] Recently, it has been rumored that the Count was unfaithful to his wife. So far as this writer knows, however, such assertions have not been substantiated by any specific instances of infidelity. His daughter-in-law, Freya, vaguely mentioned to me that he was considered "wobbly," but did not elaborate. Dorothy's letters clearly indicate how deeply she loved her husband and that this love was reciprocated by him. In any case, it is the author's opinion that such suggestions, even if true, would not negate Count von Moltke's significant contributions to the Christian Science Church.

[296] Schweidnitz is about 4 1/3 miles (7 kilometers) from Kreisau.

[297] Köhler, p. 57.

[298] Helmuth Caspar von Moltke to Catherine Hammond, Montreal, August 16, 2009.

[299] Ibid.

[300] Ibid.

[301] George Frost Kennan (1904–2005), American advisor, diplomat, political scientist, and historian.

[302] *Memoirs 1925-1950* by George F. Kennan (Boston: Little, Brown, & Co., 1967), pp. 121-122.

[303] Admiral Wilhelm Canaris (1887-1945), German admiral who became head of the Nazi *Abwehr* (military intelligence). While secretly a member of the German Resistance, he enlisted other opponents of Hitler into the *Abwehr,* where he protected their activities. A participant in the Stauffenberg plot to assassinate the *Führer*, he was executed by the Nazis, in April 1945.

[304] In 1960 Freya von Moltke emigrated to the United States with her two sons, Helmuth Caspar (b. 1938) and Konrad (1941-2005). She settled in Vermont, where she remained until her death, in January 2010.

[305] Heinrich Müller (1901–1945?) chief of the infamous Nazi Gestapo, or *Geheime Staatspolizei* (Secret State Police), from 1936 to 1945. After the attempt by Stauffenberg to assassinate Hitler on July 20, 1944, Müller was placed in charge of the arrest and interrogation of all those suspected of involvement in the Resistance. Over 5,000 people were arrested and about 200 executed. Müller disappeared in May 1945.

[306] The SS, which stands for *Schutzstaffel* (Protective Squadron), was an elite military force of the Nazi Party, known as the Black Shirts. The SS also ran the SD, or *Sicherheitsdienst* (Security and Intelligence Service), and the Gestapo (Secret Police).

[307] Conversation with Freya von Moltke, November 16, 2004.

[308] Ibid.

[309] *Briefe an Freya 1939-1945* (Munich: C. H. Beck, 1988) was translated into English by Beate von Oppen as *Letters to Freya 1939-*

1945 (New York: Alfred Knopf, 1990). An important and moving correspondence, it has since found a wide audience of readers and become an historical document. A second volume of letters from Helmuth James to Freya, which were considered too personal to publish during Freya's lifetime, was published one year after her death, in January 2010, under the title *Abschiedsbriefe Gefängnis Tegel September 1944 – Januar 1945* (Munich: C. H. Beck, 2011). The letters that mention Ulla Schultz Oldenbourg in relation to Christian Science are from the latter collection.

[310] Roland Freisler (1892-1945), President of the notorious *Volksgerichtshof* (People's Court of Justice) from 1942 and the Nazi judge at Helmuth James's trial. Less than a month later, Freisler was killed, during an Allied air raid on February 3, 1945.

[311] *Letters to Freya*, pp. 408-410.

[312] Conversation with Freya von Moltke, November 16, 2004.

[313] *Abschiedsbriefe*, p. 225.

[314] Ibid., p. 307.

[315] Ibid., p. 346. "Working" for a patient in Christian Science means praying for that person.

[316] December 20, 1944, *Abschiedsbriefe*, p. 367. Pölchau was a member of the Kreisau Circle. The love and esteem the Moltke family have for him may be measured by the dedication of *Abschiedsbriefe Gefängnis Tegel* to Pölchau and his wife, Dorothee.

[317] Ibid., pp. 406-407.

[318] *Letters to Freya*, p. 407.

[319] Ibid., p. 407.

[320] Ibid., pp. 410-411.

[321] As a Christian Scientist, Dorothy could not have believed that it was the "Fates" who had chosen her. She was writing informally to her father, and perhaps it was out of modesty that she wrote "Fates" rather than "God."

[322] *Ein Leben in Deutschland: Briefe aus Kreisau und Berlin 1907-1934*, Translated by Beate Ruhm von Oppen (Munich: C.H. Beck, 1999), p. viii.

All sources from The Mary Baker Eddy Collection and The First Church of Christ, Scientist, Boston, are used courtesy of The Mary Baker Eddy Collection and The Mary Baker Eddy Library.